KT

CL|FF

RICHARD

The
Dreamer

An autobiography

with
Ian Gittins

EBURY
PRESS

1

Ebury Press, an imprint of Ebury Publishing
20 Vauxhall Bridge Road
London SW1V 2SA

Ebury Press is part of the Penguin Random House group of companies
whose addresses can be found at global.penguinrandomhouse.com

Penguin
Random House
UK

First published by Ebury Press in 2020
This paperback edition published in 2021

www.penguin.co.uk

A CIP catalogue record for this book is available from the British Library

ISBN 9780957490789

Typeset in 9.78/16.18 pt SabonNext LT Regular by Jouve UK, Milton Keynes
Printed and bound in Great Britain by Clays Ltd, Elcograf S.p.A.

The authorized representative in the EEA is Penguin Random House Ireland,
Morrison Chambers, 32 Nassau Street, Dublin D02 YH68

Penguin Random House is committed to a sustainable future for our
business, our readers and our planet. This book is made from
Forest Stewardship Council® certified paper.

FSC
www.fsc.org

MIX
Paper from
responsible sources
FSC® C018179

*This book is about my wildest dreams
and how they all came true.
Fans have played a major role in those dreams.
I dedicate this book to all of you.*

CONTENTS

INTRODUCTION

'SOME MIGHT SAY A LUCKY ONE . . .'

All my life I've been a dreamer, some might say a lucky one,
For every dream come true, many come undone . . .

— 'Rise Up', 2018

As well as playing lead guitar in my band for years, Terry Britten has written and produced some of my biggest hits. Terry has penned tunes for me that are known all over the world, such as 'Carrie' and, of course, 'Devil Woman'. Yet I think *this* may be the most important song he ever co-wrote for me.

All my life I've been a dreamer, some might say a lucky one . . .

In many ways, my life *has* been a dream. It was a dream that began one sunny spring day in 1956 when, aged fifteen, I heard Elvis Presley's 'Heartbreak Hotel' blaring from a car window in Hertfordshire. It ignited in me a love of rock and roll, and of singing, that has never died.

1

My life changed that day and ever since I have pursued my dream avidly and doggedly. I have been lucky enough that it has come true. I've enjoyed success beyond my wildest imaginings in Britain and around the world. Yes, I've been a dreamer – and I *would* say a lucky one!

Yet there was a time, not so long ago, when I certainly didn't feel lucky. In fact, Terry wrote this song – the title track from my 2018 album, *Rise Up* – when I was just emerging from the worst, darkest period of my life. A time that was not a dream, but a living nightmare.

A time that I thought might kill me.

In August 2014, the police began an investigation into me, triggered by allegations that I had molested a teenage boy nearly thirty years earlier. The allegations were nonsense, but they travelled around the world at the speed of light. And they travelled around a world where many people are inclined to think, *No smoke without fire*. They became known so quickly because, when the police raided my British home, the BBC, an institution that I love, saw fit to broadcast the raid live on TV. It was the first that I knew about it – and it was the opening scene of a nightmare that was to last for four years.

For every dream come true, many come undone . . .

My world collapsed. I didn't feel like a dreamer the day after that raid, when my legs went from under me and I fell to the kitchen floor at my home in Portugal. I was in the deepest and darkest hole of my life and I could see no way out.

I felt as if, overnight, everything I had achieved in nearly sixty years had been taken away from me – *had it all been a dream?* – and I had become a disgrace. A pariah. I knelt on that kitchen floor and I cried, uncontrollably, like a child.

I heard footsteps behind me. My good friend, John McElynn, had walked into the kitchen. We had house guests at the time and John was horrified to see me kneeling there.

'What are you *doing?*' he asked me, *sotto voce*. He knelt down on the hard floor beside me. 'Look, did you do this thing they are accusing you of?' he asked me, gently.

'Of course not!'

'No! And have you ever done anything like that?'

'Of course not!'

John used to work as a priest in New York. He knows how to console people.

'Well, *I* know you haven't!' he said. 'And *you* know you haven't! The truth is on your side. So, what are you doing down there? Get up! Get up – and hold your head up! You have nothing to feel guilty about or to cry about!'

John was right – but it took me two years of heartache and pain to clear my name and to show people that, sometimes, there *is* smoke without any fire at all. It took me a long time to escape my nightmare and get back in touch with my dream.

But I did it.

The things that mean the most to me in my life are what saved me in my darkest hours. My faith, because I prayed long and hard to God every day during my ordeal. I would not have got through it without Him. My family, friends and fans, who were right behind me all the way.

And music. I would not have survived it without *music*.

Ever since the day I heard Elvis, music has been my life. It has lifted me up and it has made me what I am. I have often had to be strong to make my dream come true and that strength was what helped me to survive when I thought I might not.

At my lowest point, I thought back to all that has happened to me. My teenage days in a skiffle band; pioneering British rock and roll at the 2i's club and on the *Oh Boy!* TV show; my years with The Shadows; my movies; my Number 1 albums and singles; my many nights headlining the London Palladium, the Royal Albert Hall and Wembley Stadium. *My life*.

I had worked so hard, for so many years, to make all of these things happen: why should I let a tissue of lies take them away?

Terry Britten has known me for more than forty years and he knows I'm a lot stronger, as a person, than my public image may suggest. And I think it was that knowledge that led him to pen another, equally insightful, lyric in 'Rise Up':

> *Yesterday the clouds were darkest, I could not see the end of it*
> *But something inside of me never learnt to quit . . .*

And that's it: *I never learnt to quit*. And, just as importantly, I learned to count my blessings again.

Because, with the exception of that horrendous nightmare, my life *has* been a dream. I *have* been a dreamer – *and* a lucky one!

I have had an utterly wonderful time singing, performing, making music . . . and it's not over yet.

As I write this, I am nearing eighty years of age. *Eighty!* Yet, in some ways, I still feel eighteen, and just as in love with music. The world has changed a lot, for better *and* worse, but the joy of getting up in front of a crowd and singing a song is as real as ever.

As soon as I can, when the current Coronavirus pandemic allows, I will travel Britain on my eightieth-birthday tour: a look back at, and celebration of, more than sixty years in music. It will feel like the latest adventure in a truly extraordinary dream. Which I *still* don't want to wake up from.

All my life I've been a dreamer, some might say a lucky one . . .

Yes – you can say that again! So, here, in these pages, is the story of my dream to date. Of course, any story has to start somewhere and mine began a long while ago, back in the mists of time (!), on the other side of the world . . . in India.

ONE

A PASSAGE FROM INDIA

Sometimes dreams can be hard to recall and memories of my early boyhood in India are so hazy now. It's a fact that everybody knows about me: *Cliff Richard was born in India*. Yet when I try to cast my mind back more than seventy years to those days, they are like a blur, a faded half-memory.

My grandfather first took my family out there. Frederick William Webb, my dad's dad, was born in Woolwich, in south London, and taken to India in Victorian times, at the height of the Raj. As a young man, he moved to Rangoon, in Burma, to become an engineer and make his fortune. I don't think he ever achieved that.

Frederick Webb and his wife, Donella, my grandmother, got very busy making a family. They had no fewer than eleven children. My dad, Rodger Oscar Webb, was one of the middle ones: he was born in Rangoon on 23 December 1904. The Webbs moved back to India ten years later.

If I were ever to go on the BBC's family-history show, *Who Do You Think You Are?*, they would have a great episode, because my mum's side of the family had a very chequered history. Her dad, William Dazely, was a soldier who met and married Dorothy Bridgewater in India. My mum, Dorothy Marie Dazely, was born nine months later, in 1920, in Lahore.

William Dazely vanished four years later, presumed killed, fighting in the Indian army against Afghan tribesmen. Yet decades later, a writer – Steve Turner, who was writing a book about me – did some digging and found my grandad had later resurfaced, back in the UK and living in Birmingham with a second family. He was a bigamist!

Knowing none of this, in 1926 my grandma, Dorothy, remarried Richard (Dick) Dickson, who raised my mum and her sister, Olive, as his own. They settled in Asansol, a city in West Bengal. And that was where my parents met.

My father was then an area manager for Kellner's, a catering firm with the concession for the restaurants in all the Indian railway stations. He used to visit one of his sisters, also called Dorothy (there are a lot of Dorothys in this story!) in Asansol, and in 1936, she introduced him to a friend: Dorothy Marie Dazely.

They weren't an obvious match. Rodger was thirty-one, Dorothy was sixteen. My dad lived 125 miles away in Calcutta and rarely went to Asansol. Yet they embarked on a three-year courtship, mostly – through necessity – conducted by post. On 26 April 1939, they married and moved north to live in a town called Dehradun.

Which is where I come in . . .

I was born, eighteen months later, on 14 October 1940, in the King's English Hospital in Lucknow, in what is now Uttar Pradesh. My mum and dad christened me Harry Rodger Webb.

It was a name that I was only to keep for seventeen years.

I was much too young to remember but when I was one, my parents had a second son, Freddy. He was born with a blood problem and was what they used to call a 'blue baby': he literally turned blue. He died while he was still a babe-in-arms. Poor Mum and Dad.

When I was a boy, my parents rarely mentioned Freddy, but I have often wondered to myself, over the years, what it might have been like to have grown up with a brother. Who knows? We might even have turned into a British version of The Everly Brothers!

While I was still a toddler, my dad got promoted at work and we moved to Howrah, a small town in West Bengal on the outskirts of Calcutta. And this locale was where I was to spend a happy and carefree early boyhood.

What do I remember about Howrah? The heat; lots of stone walls; messy roads, full of potholes. I particularly remember that our first-floor apartment was right above a chocolate factory. I adored the delicious smells that used to waft up from downstairs.

Our life in India was comfortable. Kellner's paid for our home and we were very well looked after. We had servants and one boy, Habib, took care of me. I remember once watching him, under the one tree in our garden, killing chickens for us to eat. I was shocked . . . but not enough to lose my appetite!

When I was three, my sister Donna came along. She was a sickly child who used to get high fevers, so Mum and Dad would fill a hot-water bottle with ice and hold it to her face. The bottle had a leak and water ran into her ears, giving her hearing problems in later life.

Dad would be away working for weeks at a time, visiting all of the train stations to check on Kellner's restaurants. The British railway in India had fabulous restaurants – people would go there to eat even if they weren't catching a train.

I can still picture my dad heading off to work, immaculate in his suit and tie. He always was a neat dresser. Years ago, I found a photo of him in India, wearing a white suit. He looked so cool! He used to play the banjo in a local jazz band.

When I was five, I started going to the local Howrah school. It was an Anglican church school, mostly for expats but with a few Bengali kids. It was a bit too far from our house for me to go home for lunch, so Habib would turn up every day with food and a napkin.

That school was the first place that I ever sang. The teachers put me in the church choir. I've no idea if I was any good, but I still remember feeling embarrassed changing into a cassock, because it felt as if I was putting on a girl's dress.

The school taught me some Bengali and Mum said after a year or so I could speak it pretty well. More than seventy years on, it's all long forgotten, except for a handful of phrases. Dad used to tell me: *'Darajā bandha kara!'*: shut that door! Or he would give me a *jhap*, a cuff around the head, if I was playing up.

My best friend didn't go to my school; he was a lad who lived in our street. He was called Lal – 'red' in Bengali – and we'd dip our fingers in the trays of cooling chocolate on the factory's windowsill. Every monsoon season, Lal and I would play in the road as it flooded up to our waists. It was so exciting, but the water must have been filthy!

I wonder what happened to little Lal? I wonder if he is still alive, and if he knows what I became?

Dad was the disciplinarian in our family. He made the decisions and kept us in line. I remember the first *jhap* he ever gave me. I forget what I'd done, but he picked up a little cardboard toothbrush case and slapped me on the back of the neck with it. *Ow!* It didn't hurt much, but I definitely didn't like it!

My father could also be a lot of fun. There was a wonderful novel published in 2003 by Khaled Hosseini, called *The Kite Runner*. Set in Kabul, it was about two young Afghan boys who grew up flying kites and having kite battles. We did the same in India and it was fantastic.

Kite battles are an art form in India. The object is to cut the string of your opponent's kite. Dad was great at it. He would put on a gardening glove, mix up ground glass and egg whites, and glue them all along the string, so the kite was effectively attached to a hundred-foot-long knife edge.

We'd go up on the flat roof of our house and my dad would fly a kite against his pal. He would get his kite high in the sky above the other one, then pull his control down *QUICK!* so that his string would cut the other cord and send his mate's kite soaring up, up and away. It was amazing, poetry in motion. A lifetime on, I have never forgotten how exciting it was to watch.

We ate curry every day in Howrah. I never saw roast beef, or egg and chips, until I was eight. At home, we ate with knives and forks, but a big treat for Donna and me was getting packed off to stay with my dad's sister, Aunty Marjorie, a mile away.

Aunty Marjorie was the classic cool aunty and let us eat curry with our hands, like the locals. She made us swear to keep it our secret: 'You can't tell your mum and dad I let you do this!' Donna and I never did. Our lips stayed sealed (and covered in curry).

When I had just turned seven, my second sister, Jacqui, arrived. My parents also decided that we had to leave India. They had no choice. By the second half of the 1940s, the Indian independence movement was building to a peak. In 1947, the British government granted India independence and partitioned it into India and Pakistan. Suddenly, British expats were far less welcome there.

There was a lot of fighting going on in different parts of the country between the Hindus and the Muslims. I was more concerned with flying kites and nicking chocolate from the shelf with Lal, but at nights, we would sometimes hear gunshots. And then, suddenly, the trouble was right on our doorstep. There was a derelict building next to our apartment. One day, one of our staff came in and told my father, 'There's a Muslim hiding next door. He says he needs help!'

My dad talked to the young guy and told him to hide out in the top floor of the abandoned building and we would look after him. 'We'll send food up to you,' he told him. For six months, he fed and took care of him – I guess it was a bit like Anne Frank. Then, one day, the guy was gone. We never knew what happened to him.

It began to get difficult for British women to walk freely in the street. I don't know if Mum ever got jostled, as some women did, but when an annual religious ceremony came around that involved local men splashing paint over themselves, they were keener to splash it over English women.

I was vaguely aware my parents seemed distracted and worried. I realise now how stressful it must have been for them, trying to raise a family in a land that no longer wanted them and that was near to civil war. Unknown to us kids, they began to argue over where they should go.

Mum told me later that Dad argued long and hard for us to move to Australia. One of his senior colleagues in Kellner's asked him to go Down Under with him and start a restaurant business. 'It's a new, growing country,' he urged. 'Australians love their food and wine. We could make a fortune!'

But it wasn't to be. It's strange, because my father always took all of the major decisions in our family, but on this one, my mother simply put her foot down. She said her mother and her sisters and brothers had all recently left India for England and she was going to join them.

'If you want to go to Australia, you go,' she later told me she had told my dad. 'I'm taking the kids back to Blighty.'

Blighty. To this day, I have no idea where the word comes from, but that was what we called England when we talked about it, as all the expats in India did: *Blighty.* I'd never been to England in my life, yet we talked of it as if it were our long-lost home.

So, when Mum and Dad broke the news to us, I didn't feel upset or scared that I was about to leave the only place I had ever known, and my school, and Habib and Lal. I felt excited.

We're going home to Blighty!

It took a while to arrange. It was an expensive business to transport five people from India to London, three years after the end of World War II, and Dad sold off all of our belongings in Howrah to help cover the cost. But on 24 August 1948, my family set off on our epic journey.

It was to take nearly a month. First came three days on a train across India, which I thought was fantastic. Then, when we arrived in Bombay, we boarded the steam-driven P&O liner the SS *Ranchi*. For the first week, it felt like hell on earth – or, rather, on water. The five of us were in one cabin and Mum and I got horribly seasick. I'd never been on a ship before and spent the first few days throwing up as the waves hurled the *Ranchi* from side to side. It was nothing like taking a cruise liner nowadays – those old boats were all over the place.

Dad took me for a walk on the deck and taught me the best trick for avoiding seasickness: *never sway the same way as the boat.* 'If the boat sways one way,' he explained, 'you sway the other one, so that your head stays level with the horizon.' Once I got the hang of *that*, I enjoyed the voyage.

We sailed through the Suez Canal. It was where I learned to whistle. The banks of the canal were close to the ship on both sides and people were waving and whistling to us. I was waving back at them and I found that I could whistle, too. *Cool!*

After three weeks at sea, the SS *Ranchi* pulled into Tilbury Docks, in Essex, at six in the morning on 13 September 1948. It was almost three months after the now-famous, and notorious, *Empire Windrush* had arrived from Jamaica. I walked down the gangplank with my family and looked around, wide-eyed, at this new land.

So, this was Blighty. This was England.

This was *home*.

TWO

'WHERE'S YOUR WIGWAM, INDI-BUM?'

People have often asked me what my first memory is of arriving in Britain. I think I'd have to say the cold! We disembarked from the liner at sunrise on a sharp autumnal English morning. I'd never felt that kind of chill before.

Before we left India, our parents made a plan for us to stay with our gran, Mum's mother Dorothy, who had left India a few months earlier. She and her second husband Richard, known to us as Grandpa Dick, had settled in Carshalton, Surrey, ten miles south of London.

I still have vivid memories of getting off the train for the first time in Carshalton. I was amazed that the railway station was full of green trees and plants – it even had roses growing up the station walls. I had certainly never seen that in dusty, arid Howrah.

Kids can adapt to pretty much anything and I got used to the cold weather very quickly. One exciting thing was that soon after we arrived, it snowed. It was the first time I'd ever seen snow and I pressed my nose to Gran's window to stare out at this magic white powder falling out of the dark night sky. It felt mystical.*

Grandma Dorothy was a lovely, big woman – she had put on weight eating English food! – and she was very kind and welcoming to us, but our first months in England were not easy. My family and I were refugees and, like so many people forced by political events to flee their homes and migrate across the world, we had it hard.

My granny lived in a three-bedroomed, semi-detached house in a street called Windborough Road, but she still had seven of her own children living at home and she didn't really have space for five new arrivals. We all slept on the floor in her front room for a few days until she hit on a plan. Her next-door neighbours had a spare room, an upstairs front bedroom, and they agreed to rent it to us.

So, a routine began where we would spend the days in Gran's house and then, after we had eaten our evening meal, we would all go next door to sleep. Baby Jacqui would sleep in the bed with Mum and Dad, while Donna and I kipped on mattresses on the floor.

When you are a kid, everything is just a great adventure and I didn't mind this new hardship too much, but I realise now how difficult it must have been for Mum and Dad. They were used to our privileged life out in India and now, all of a sudden, here we were, homeless and living like paupers.

---

* I still think of this childhood memory when I sing my Christmas hits.

My dad had arrived in good old Blighty with £5 to his name (just under £200 today). We landed at a time of post-war rationing – I can still picture Mum's little ration book, with its green cover and the serrated tokens to tear out each week for milk, sugar and butter. Our biggest problem was that Dad couldn't get a job so £5 was not going to last us very long.

My father was a very proud man but he didn't think that any jobs were beneath him. Week after week, he applied for anything and everything, heading off for interviews but returning home unlucky. Yet he put on a brave face: I never once saw him with his head in his hands, moaning, 'What are we going to do?'

His pride meant that he wouldn't sign on the dole. He was entitled to unemployment money from the British government, which would certainly have helped tide us over until he found work, but he just wouldn't do it. He was from that generation that will not take state handouts – and, I must admit, I admire that.

After a few weeks, Dad got a job pushing sick patients and medicine trolleys around a hospital. It was quite menial work compared to his role in India, but every day he left the house at dawn, returning late into the evening. Again, I never once heard him complain.

When you are a young lad, your dad is your role model and I soon had to copy my father's stiff upper lip, because my first few weeks of school in England were awful. My parents put me into Stanley Park Primary School in Carshalton. I arrived there knowing nobody, a total outsider, and that was precisely how the other kids treated me.

There were a few good things about the school. I liked the fact that it had a playground, unlike my school in India. I also liked that we were given free milk every day, even though I wished it were full of sugar like it was in India. But, outside of the class-room, my school life was an ordeal.

Children will seize on any kind of difference to give each other a hard time and with me, they had plenty of scope. My years in the Howrah sunshine had made me a lot swarthier than the pale-skinned English boys and girls – and when they heard I was from India, they went to town.

'Oi, Webb, where's your wigwam?' they taunted me. 'Where's your horse?' They would make whooping sounds with their hands cupped over their mouths, like they'd seen in Western films. Then they made up a nickname for me: *Indi-bum*.

'Hey, Indi-bum, are you going to scalp us?'

'Do you want a pow-wow, Indi-bum?'

No matter how much I tried to explain that they were think-ing of Native Americans, or 'Red Indians' as we used to call them, not people from India, they couldn't have cared less. The abuse got violent and I soon found myself in a lot of nasty fights in the play-ground at lunchtime.

Boys would be punching me all over the place . . . *but I would fight back*. I quickly realised that if you are being bullied by some-one bigger than you, like I was, the best thing to do is flail right into their stomachs. It's the easiest place to reach, and it would rock them back on their heels.

It might surprise people, because I've always had this public image of being a wet Goody Two-Shoes, but I was tough at school.

I had to be. If the other boys went for me, I would get them on the floor and punch them until the blood flowed. In fact, I don't remember ever losing a fight.

When the bullying first started, I told my parents. Dad was disgusted: 'If those boys really think you have come from a wigwam, they must be stupid!' he said. 'They have no sense. It's beneath you. Just ignore them, because they're not worth bothering with.'

I would have loved to do that . . . but it was impossible when they were punching me in the face. After the first few fights, I didn't tell my dad. And after a few weeks, when the boys realised that I would hit them back, the bullying stopped.

I loved my dad, but he could be frustrating, and the natural respect I felt for him could border on fear. One day at school, I got the cane. I can't remember now what for, but I'd deserved it. I came home and complained to Mum and Dad about how much it had hurt. My father was furious – but not for the reason I wanted. He grabbed a wooden ruler and whacked me hard on the legs.

'How dare you!' he told me. *Whack!* 'Don't you realise your teachers know that you are my son?' *Whack!* 'You will give me a bad name!' *Whack!* 'They will think I cannot bring up my children properly!'

It was one of the worst *jhaps* he ever gave me and it hurt me more than the caning at school, physically and emotionally . . . and yet I can see why he did it. This may sound strange, seventy years later, when the world is a very different place, but I think he was right and I deserved what I got for behaving badly at school.

Parents hitting their kids is seen as wrong today, and I agree it should never go too far, but a little slap now and then won't harm a child. It makes them think what they did to deserve it and decide, *Oh, I don't like being hit – I won't do THAT again!* I never once doubted that Dad loved me: he was teaching me a lesson and I learned it.

My mum loved us in a very different way, all kisses and warmth. If Dad gave me a *jhap* and I went crying to Mum, she would give me a hug and calm me down, but she would never say anything against him: 'Well, Harry, what did *you* do? Your daddy would never hit you if you had done nothing wrong. You must have done something bad . . .'

My parents were yin and yang. Between them, they were the perfect balancing act and gave us all we needed. I'm sure they fell out sometimes – what couple *wouldn't*, given the pressure they were living under? But they sorted things out in private – they never argued in front of us kids.

Things were hard in Carshalton. Even with Dad working, we didn't have much money and my parents must have felt they were a burden on my gran. They longed for us to have our own home, but the waiting list for a local council house was five years – a lifetime.

I sensed that Mum and Dad were tense and worried, and like any kid, wanted to make them happier. I still remember, one day, telling my mum very seriously: 'Mum, when I have one hundred pounds, *I'll* buy you a house!' She smiled and gave me one of her kisses.

We had been in England for a year when a temporary solution presented itself. My dad's sister, Dorothy, who had first introduced him to Mum in India, was by now living with her husband and their two boys in Waltham Cross, in Hertfordshire. The council-house waiting list was shorter there and she said she could put us up for a bit.

On my ninth birthday, we moved up north of London, but when we got to Waltham Cross, our situation was no better. We were still crammed into one smallish room, which became even more crowded when our family expanded after Mum had my youngest sister, Joan, in February 1950.

In some ways, things were slowly looking up for us. My father left his hospital work and got an office job in the City. It meant a two-hour daily commute for him but it paid a bit more. My new school was also far better for me than Stanley Park had been.

When I started at Kings Road School in Waltham Cross, I was bullied again for looking and sounding different from the other boys, but this time it wasn't as bad and it didn't last as long. Everyone was a year older, a bit more grown-up – and I was good at football, which helped me to make friends.

I started doing well in the lessons. In fact, at the end of my second year at Kings Road, the teachers gave me a prize of a book for being top boy in the school. I was the second-best student over-all, behind a girl (how I wished I'd beaten her – it's like the Top 40, I've always loved being Number 1 more than Number 2!).

So that was all good, but life in Waltham Cross was tough. All six of us slept in one small room that would just hold two mattresses. It was claustrophobic, especially as baby Joan's washed nappies had to be left to hang out to dry on a washing line inside the room. Dad had put us on the council-house waiting list, but nothing was happening.

The only way that Aunty Dorothy's place was better for us than Gran's was that we no longer had to sleep in a neighbour's house – at least we were actually staying with family. But, funnily enough, it was Dorothy's next-door neighbour who helped us finally to get on our feet.

Chatting over the garden fence, Mum became quite friendly with this neighbour, a lady called Marcelle, who invited her round for tea. Mum went round, had the rare pleasure of seeing people actually living in a proper house, and asked Marcelle back to ours the next day.

Aunty Dorothy would only allow us to use our room, the kitchen and the bathroom, so my mum made Marcelle a cup of coffee and took her into our crowded bedroom. Marcelle was surprised: 'What other rooms do you have here?' she asked her.

'None,' admitted Mum. 'We all live in this one.'

'You can't live like *this*!' Marcelle told her, horrified. She took it upon herself to tell a friend who worked at the local council about our plight. When this guy came to have a look at our living conditions for himself, it finally spurred the local authority into action.

Two weeks later, and two-and-a-half years after my family disembarked from the SS *Ranchi*, we were given a new council house in Cheshunt, just under two miles away. The house had three – *three!* – bedrooms, a kitchen, a bathroom and a big sitting room. It may have been public housing, but to us it felt like a palace.

Cheshunt was a small, typically English suburban town, mostly full of City workers who caught the train into London's Liverpool Street station each day. We were given the keys to 12

Hargreaves Close on the new-build Bury Green Estate. It had green spaces to play and wide roads, not that there was a single car on the estate – nobody could afford them.

On the afternoon we moved in, we got the bus over from Waltham Cross and carried our meagre belongings into the house. We'd had no lunch and were starving. I remember we ate plain bread, with no jam or butter, yet I told my sisters, '*This* tastes fantastic!' I loved it because I could walk from room to room as I ate it, and *anything* tastes good when you're starving.

We had more than one room now but they were all empty. We had no furniture and no money to buy any, so Mum and Dad slept on a mattress on the floor in their bedroom, we four kids did the same in our room and we kept the few odds and ends we had in a tiny box room.

Dad quickly found a new job as a clerk at a firm called Atlas Lamps. A lighting company owned by Thorn Electrical, it was based in Enfield, only five miles from Cheshunt. To bring some extra money into the house, and now that we were older, my mother also got a job there, in their factory.

Mum said it was boring work, putting a filament into every light bulb that passed by on a conveyor belt, but off she went to do the same thing each day. She was always so stoical, which was why I was horrified the day she came home from work in tears. I had never seen her cry! What was wrong?

Mum explained that the other conveyor-belt workers had complained to her that she was working too fast. If she slowed down a bit, Atlas would have to give them overtime to finish the work. Mum thought that would be cheating the company, but when she carried on working at the same speed, the other women sent her to Coventry. She was really upset – but she didn't give in.

I started yet another new school and, in 1952, I had to face up to a British rite of passage – the 11-Plus exam. This was the nationwide paper all kids aged eleven took, and the result determined whether they would go on to prestigious, academic grammar schools, or the rather lesser secondary moderns.

I had been doing OK at school so I wasn't nervous going into the exam. I can't remember anything about the questions, or how I felt coming out, but when I got my result a few weeks later, it was a total bucket of cold water in the face.

I had failed.

To this day, I don't know why, or what I did wrong. I have since met teachers who tell me that some pupils are good in the classroom but don't do well in exams, so I guess I'll cling to that explanation (or should I say excuse?). But as I absorbed my result, one thought went through my head: *Dad isn't going to like this.*

I was right. I'll never forget standing in front of our fireplace at home, the flames hot on the backs of my calves, as I broke the news that I had failed. Dad was *so* disappointed.

'Harry, you have let me down,' he said, shaking his head. 'How *could* you do this to me? What have you done?'

I had no idea what to reply. I just felt so ashamed.

I have always been competitive, so this debacle really upset me and I felt even worse that September, when I was packed off to the brand-new Cheshunt Secondary Modern School. On my first day, I was told that I would be in class Lower 1B. *Lower!* I wasn't even in the middle group. *Oh no!* But there it was.

I was sitting in my new Lower 1B classroom, totally demoralised, when a teacher walked in. I can even remember his name: Mr Faid. He glanced at a piece of paper in his hand and asked, 'Is there a Harry Rodger Webb here?'

I put my hand up.

'There's been a mistake,' he said. 'Follow me.' He led me to the class that I should have been put in: Upper 1A.

Now *this* was more like it!

After that, I settled pretty well into secondary school. I wasn't academically brilliant, although I did my work OK and never really got into trouble, but I did turn out to be good at sport. I enjoyed sprinting, set a new school record for throwing the javelin and got hooked on basketball for a while when the school started teaching that.

Yet my big thing was football. I started playing for the school team, as a defender, and I remember one day flabbergasting the PE teacher. A ball came at me really hard and I raised my foot in the air, trapped it and, in one skilful movement, passed it to a teammate on the far side of the pitch.

The teacher thought it was brilliant. I didn't dare confess that it had been a sheer fluke and I couldn't have done the same thing again if I'd tried for a year! But I went on to play football for the Hertfordshire Under-14 team, so I must have been reasonably good.

In most ways I was a pretty average boy, yet I did one very remarkable – and prescient – thing. The school encouraged us to have pen pals and arranged for us to exchange letters with pupils the same age at a school in Australia.

I did so, immediately forgot about it and had no memory at all of what I wrote to my pen pal. Years later, when I had got famous and was on tour in Australia, this girl wrote to me and enclosed the original letter that I had sent her. This was what it said:

> Dear Catherine,
>
> My name is Harry Rodger Webb. I go to Cheshunt Secondary Modern School in Cheshunt in Hertfordshire. I am twelve and a half years old. My ambition is to be a famous singer.

Now, *why* did I write that? I have absolutely no memory of thinking such a thing, or having any interest in music or singing, until I hit my mid-teens. But deep in my subconscious, something must have been brewing . . .

I can clearly remember the Queen's Coronation on 2 June 1953. There was a huge street party just down the road from us in Cheshunt and I recall lots of cheering, shouting and, most important of all, eating! It was fantastic, not least because we got a day off school.

Two years after my father started work at Atlas Lamps, we finally got some furniture. He made it himself. The firm used wooden crates to store and deliver its electrical appliances and let employees buy unwanted ones for a few bob (as we used to call shillings then) each. Dad bought some and brought them home.

Carefully, diligently, he took them to pieces, planed them down, re-shaped them and screwed them into place to make armchairs and a table. Yet we were still sleeping on mattresses on the floor and certainly couldn't afford a television or a telephone.

We were properly poor. A few memories emphasise that. Our gas and electric were on meters and every few months a man knocked the door and came in to read them. If he said we had a rebate and gave my father a few bob, it was *such* a big deal. My dad might even give us a few pennies each for pocket money – a rarity.

Post-war rationing was coming to an end, but you would never have known from looking at our (homemade) dining table. Three days a week, our main meal was two pieces of toast, soaked in tea, with sugar sprinkled over the top. Luckily, I had brought my sweet tooth from India with me!

My father always said grace before meals. He and Mum were both Christians, but they never forced their faith down our throats. In my early teens we went to church as a family every Sunday. I found it boring, because I didn't understand it. I was equally unenthused when Dad occasionally suggested I read the Bible at home: 'Why? Do I have to?' He never forced the issue.

When I was fourteen, my parents asked me to attend confirmation classes at church. I went for two weeks, came back and said, 'Look, I don't want to go! I'm not interested at all.' They said, 'OK, don't worry about it.' The best thing they ever did was to not *make* me go.

Religion didn't do anything for me back then, but acting was starting to interest me – and that was down to one woman. Everybody can remember their favourite teacher who inspired them at school and mine was Mrs Norris. For me, she was a Wonder Woman.

Jay Norris was a young English teacher who was small but had a huge personality. Her dark hair was swept back, she was always well turned out – and, most importantly, she loved what she was doing. She loved teaching us.

Mrs Norris helped to bring alive the texts and books that we read in class. Each week, she would pick kids to read plays and dramas aloud, record us and then play our voices back to us. She was so talented – and she inculcated her love for literature in us.*

Mrs Norris started an after-school drama society and asked me to join as she thought I'd really enjoy it, and I was delighted. I was shy as a boy, so I thought I might be nervous, but I soon took to being on stage and found that I loved acting and theatre. Initially, my father was not quite so keen on my new interest, mainly because on drama society nights I didn't get home from school until after tea-time. He visited the school to outline his grievance to my teacher.

'My son is not coming home until late at night,' he moaned. 'It is seven o'clock some evenings.'

'Yes, I'm sorry, but Mr Webb, your son is just *so* talented,' Jay Norris replied, sweetly. 'We really need him in rehearsals!'

'Oh, really?' replied my father, totally mollified. 'Well, I suppose that's OK, then.'

She knew how to work him.

At first, I had small parts in a couple of productions. I played a chancellor in a play by A.A. Milne called *The Ugly Duckling* (nothing to do with the Hans Christian Andersen fairy tale) and I was

---

* Jay only registered one failure with me, in no way her fault: William Shakespeare. I found him wordy, impenetrable and boring. It was only Sir Kenneth Branagh's films, years later, that brought home to me just how brilliant Shakespeare was.

in a play called *Willow Pattern*, which actually won a prize at a youth drama festival. Then Jay Norris had another idea – one that filled me with dread.

It was 1955 and she wanted to put on a Christmas production of another A.A. Milne work, *Toad of Toad Hall*, based on Kenneth Grahame's novel *The Wind in the Willows*. She asked me to play Ratty. I thought it sounded great and I wanted to do it, but there was a big drawback – Ratty had to sing a song. Yikes!

'I can't sing to people,' I told her flatly. 'Sorry, I just can't do it.'

'Well, I'm afraid it's quite simple, Harry,' she replied. 'If you won't sing the song, you can't be Ratty.'

I couldn't bear to lose such a good part, so I spent weeks of rehearsal diligently learning Ratty's song, which was called 'Ducks' Ditty'. I can still remember it now:

All along the backwater,
Through the rushes tall,
Ducks are a-dabbling,
Up tails all!

We put on the play at the school for three nights and before the first night, I was terrified at having to sing in public. When the moment came, it went well and I enjoyed it – especially when the audience clapped me at the end.

Hmm. Now, here's a feeling that I like . . .

My teacher opened my eyes to literature and to theatre. As I grew into my mid-teens, I also got into cinema. I would go to the pictures as often as I could, sometimes with Donna, although Dad always gave us a strict curfew.

One evening, he told me we had to be home by ten but the film was longer than usual so we missed our bus and got home thirty minutes late (oh, for a mobile phone in the 1950s!). The house was in darkness. Donna and I didn't dare wake the family up, so we decided to sleep in the coal shed in our back garden.

It was cold, dark and dirty and we sat there, miserable and scared, for fifteen minutes until Dad appeared at the shed door.

'When I tell you to get you and your sister home by ten, you get home by ten!' he chastised me, with a brisk *jhap*. 'Now, come in the house.'

We did so eagerly, to find Mum up and waiting for us in the brightly lit kitchen. They had been teaching us a lesson and, kindly but firmly, she explained how worried they had been when we were late. I apologised profusely and the lesson hit home – I never did it again.

Thankfully, not every trip to the flicks was so traumatic. In 1956, one of the big films was Roger Vadim's *...And God Created Woman*, starring Brigitte Bardot. I was desperate to see it, but it was pretty sexually charged and, at fifteen, I was too young to watch it without an accompanying adult.

There was no way my parents would take me, and I would have been far too embarrassed to watch it with them anyway, so I went to the local cinema and hung around outside. When I saw a guy going in, I stopped him and asked, 'Excuse me, but can I come in with you, please?' He agreed. Can you *imagine* trying to do that today? I don't think so!

I thought Brigitte Bardot was *so* beautiful. When I stopped sharing a bedroom with my sisters and moved into the tiny box room, I dragged my mattress in there and decorated a wall with her pictures. My father used to read a newspaper called *Reveille* and they had a special promotion where, for three days in a row, their centrespread photo was a different section of Brigitte: her head, then her torso, then her legs. I collected all three, sellotaped them together and put the picture over my bed.

The other big thing that I was getting into at the age of fifteen was music. If we had music around the house at all, it was my parents listening to stuff like the Stan Kenton Big Band. My mother would listen to the radio and had her own technique of deciphering song lyrics. It was quite amazing and I was always very impressed by it.

When a song came on that Mum liked, she would write down any words she could hear. If she missed a word, she would write the initial. The next time the song came on, she'd listen hard and fill in the missing gaps. Eventually she would have the whole lyric and would be able to sing along.

My dad built me an old-fashioned crystal radio and I began listening to Radio Luxembourg on headphones in the evenings: DJs like Barry Alldis, Keith Fordyce, Pete Murray. I enjoyed it, even though listening to Luxembourg was frustrating: the broadcasts were faint, crackly and always fading in and out.

So, I had a developing interest in pop music but it certainly wasn't a full-blown love affair. That all changed for ever one fateful Saturday morning in May 1956, when I was fifteen.

I was living in Cheshunt but I still used to hang out over in Waltham Cross a lot. I think, for some reason, my school friends and I figured it was a more happening place than Cheshunt, so it was a sort of hub of our social scene. That Saturday morning, I was mooching down the road in Waltham Cross with Norman Mitham and a lad called Terry, two of my best mates from school. Suddenly, a dark-green Citroën screeched up next to us and the driver jumped out and ran into the newsagent's, Asplands.

He had left his engine running and the radio on. It was a sunny day and so his window was wound down. As we passed the car, an extraordinary piece of music came blasting out of the interior.

It was like nothing I had heard before in my life. Terry, Norman and I stopped dead in our tracks, craned our heads towards the noise . . . and the driver ran back out of the newsagent's, jumped in the car, threw his newspaper and fags onto the passenger seat and sped off.

They call those moments epiphanies. Well, you can say that again! As the Citroën vanished down the road, the three of us stared at each other, our mouths hanging open. The same thought was written across each of our faces: *What. Was. That?*

It was the precise second that my dream began.

THREE

'I CAN MAKE YOU A STAR!'

That chance blare of amazing music through a car window turned our lives upside down. From the second that we heard it, Norman, Terry and I were on a mission to discover what and who it was, so that we could get hold of it and listen to it again and again and again.

Today, of course, it would be easy: you would pick up your iPad, type the lyric into Google and know the answer in ten seconds. In 1956 the process was not so straightforward and all we could do was glue ourselves to the radio and hope that a DJ would spin that magical song again.

I listened in vain to Radio Luxembourg but it was Norman Mitham who solved the mystery. After a day or two, he tracked it down via the American Forces Network (AFN), who broadcast out of Germany. Next time we met up he was triumphant.

'I've heard it again and I know who it is!' he proclaimed. 'It's called "Heartbreak Hotel" and it's by a guy called Elvis Presley.'

Terry and I fell about.

'Elvis Presley?' I laughed. 'I've never heard of him! What kind of a name is *Elvis*?!'

Now I knew what it was, I had to own it. I saved up my pocket money then went straight to the little record shop in Waltham Cross and bought the single. I played it and played it and played it on the little family Dansette. It sounded more amazing every time.

All my life, people have asked me so many times why I was so blown away when I first heard Elvis. Of course, the correct answer would be for me to say, 'Just listen to it and you'll know!' – but I'll try to explain here.

'Heartbreak Hotel' was completely different from anything we'd ever heard before – different from Frank Sinatra, Dean Martin, or Perry Como, or even Fats Domino. It was a million miles from 'Greensleeves', or Max Bygraves singing 'You're A Pink Toothbrush'. I mean, I'm not disrespecting those guys and I love listening to Sinatra or Fats Domino (Max, maybe not so much . . .) but this was the real deal.

The music echoing from that Citroën window sounded like it came from outer space. Elvis changed the world overnight. I don't believe there has been a shift like it in music ever since. It came down to this. Ordinary British kids like me were neither inspired by, nor wanted to be like, Frank Sinatra, but we did want to be like Elvis. In fact, we *dreamed* of being like him.

'Heartbreak Hotel' was fantastic but I had fallen in love with America because of Elvis and I wanted more – I *needed* more. I started saving up my pocket money to buy his album. It took me a few weeks, but eventually I had the 4/6 (a mighty 22½p in today's money!). I needed to go back to the Waltham Cross record shop and buy *Elvis Presley*. They used to give you your record in a bag, but I took the album out and held it in full view all the way home, so that people could see it.

It was amazing! I loved every track, from 'Blue Suede Shoes' to 'I'm Left, You're Right, She's Gone' to 'Lawdy, Miss Clawdy'. I played the album to death. It must have driven my mum and dad nuts but they didn't seem to mind, even though they made a few parent-type comments: 'Huh! I can't tell a word he's singing!'

I say that I wanted to be like Elvis, but that isn't really true: I wanted to *be* him. Now that I had seen a few photos of him, and knew how cool he looked, I began to change my appearance to look as much like him as possible. I became a walking one-man Elvis homage.

Everything about him fascinated me: his look, his voice, the way he moved . . . and also the fact that he always had girls screaming at him. I tried to imagine what that must feel like. I decided that it must be like having the best dream in the world.

I started combing my hair back into a bouffant quiff, which meant hours carefully sculpting it into place with Brylcreem. It was such messy stuff and it always came off onto my clothes, to my mum's horror. But I persisted. It just felt so important.

There was one other boy at school who was also aping the Elvis look – a lad called Ian Minchin. He had his blond quiff and I had my dark one and it made us quite a hit with the girls (the dinner ladies went for it, too, and would sometimes sneak us a bit of extra pudding).

At home, in the privacy of my bedroom, I would sing along to Elvis and practise curling my lip in the mirror. I had one tooth that was growing inward and it would spoil the effect slightly. That used to bother me far more than it should.*

Yet the desire that Elvis Presley awakened in me went beyond wanting to copy his hair, or trying to look like him. It sounds crazy, but Elvis showed me what I wanted to do with my life. I now knew I wanted to make music – or, rather, I wanted to be a rock and roll singer.

Really, it's impossible to overstate his influence on my life. I have always said if there had been no Elvis Presley, there would be no Cliff Richard. It's not hyperbole, or sycophancy, or false modesty, or anything else: it's simply a stone-cold, incontrovertible fact.

Elvis gave rock and roll a shape, an attitude and a face and I guess he opened the floodgates. Suddenly there was this wave of cool music on AFN and Luxembourg: Jerry Lee Lewis, Little Richard, The Everly Brothers, Buddy Holly . . . I loved all of it.

Ricky Nelson was another exciting new American guy. To me, he seemed different from Elvis, but he also had a fantastic band and was playing rock and roll. Ricky was a great-looking guy. I was jealous of the fact that he had dark hair and blue eyes – the dream combination!

It was all so new, and these guys were rewriting music history and inventing the future, yet I didn't know this then. I wasn't thinking that way or trying to figure it all out, I just knew that I

---

* As soon as I made some money and could afford it, I had that rogue tooth capped.

had a huge emotional response to the music and was desperate to be part of it in any way I could.

My first musical baby steps weren't very spectacular, but they were fun. On Saturday nights, I started going with school friends to a dance at a youth club in Waltham Cross. We used to dance to records that were in the chart and a few of us began singing along to them. It was me, a guy called John Vince and three girls: Betty Clarke, Freda Johnson and Beryl Molineux (Betty became my sort-of first girlfriend for a while, although we didn't do much more than go for long walks and hold hands). We called our group The Quintones.

Mrs Norris helped us along. By now we were in the fifth year and she spoke to the headmaster and got permission for us to use one of the classrooms as an after-school club. But it came with conditions: 'I am still your teacher after school, so if I walk in, you need to stand up,' she told us. 'And don't make too much noise.'

One or two nights per week, the five of us would get together and sing harmonies on songs like 'Eddie My Love', a doo-wop song by The Teen Queens, and Paul Anka's 'Diana'. I liked the vocal harmony stuff that was largely coming out of New York.

We even sang in public once or twice, at the youth club and in our school hall. We'd do three or four a cappella numbers, then people would say, 'Come on, Harry, do your Elvis bit!' and I'd start going *Uh-huh-huh!'* and wobbling my knees, and sing 'Heartbreak Hotel' and 'All Shook Up'. My friends loved me doing that.

Singing in The Quintones was fun, but it wasn't my dream. It wasn't rock and roll.

It wasn't Elvis.

Elvis was playing a guitar on the sleeve of his first album and I knew I wanted one. It wasn't so much that I wanted to learn to play guitar – I was just keen to have one hanging off me, the same as he did. And on my sixteenth birthday, I got my wish.

My parents were tolerant of my new obsession with rock and roll and Dad bought me a guitar for my birthday. Looking back, it's remarkable that he did. He was a cautious man who would never buy stuff on 'tick' or 'the never-never', as they used to call hire purchase. Dad always told me, 'You can't have anything that we can't afford!' – but he made an exception for my guitar.

I didn't get to choose it and it wasn't anything fancy, but spread over weeks of payments, it cost my dad £27. I looked it up recently, out of interest, and that was the equivalent of more than £650 today. I guess he must have had faith in me.

Maybe Dad was also vicariously reliving his own past, playing banjo in the jazz band in India? He taught me my first three chords – G, C and D – and how to play the first song that I ever learned on a guitar: 'The Prisoner's Song', later sung by Fats Domino.

Yet I never took a single guitar lesson. When I played guitar, I was always busking it, or faking it. Like I said, my dream wasn't learning how to be a guitarist: it was all about *how it looked*.

Desperate to add to my tiny record collection, I got a part-time job at weekends picking potatoes on a local farm. It was back-breaking work and I would spend four hours filling up a big basket with spuds for a shilling an hour (it would be £1.20 today – less than the minimum wage!). Still, four shillings – that was nearly enough for another Elvis album!

I was still obsessed with American rock and rollers and I finally got a chance to see one. I liked Bill Haley & His Comets' 'Rock Around the Clock'. It had been a huge hit and when I learned he was coming over and was even going to play a local gig, there was no question: I *had* to be there.

Now, Bill Haley was a funny one. An older guy, and a little bit tubby, he was no heart-throb, unlike Elvis. Even so, he was *American*, and *rock and roll,* and the newspapers all reported that when his ship from the US docked at Southampton, he was met with hysteria.

He was to play the Regal in Edmonton, just down the road from Cheshunt, on a Sunday night at the start of March 1957. Tickets went on sale a few weeks earlier and Norman, Terry and I, plus another couple of mates from school, went down and queued outside the venue at six in the morning to make sure we didn't miss out.

We'd planned to go straight into school from there but by the time we got the tickets it was past lunchtime, so we decided to hang out at Terry's house instead. Big mistake! Somebody had spotted us in Edmonton and snitched on us, and we got called before the headmaster.

He tore a strip off us. I was a prefect at school by then, which I liked, but I got my badge taken off me as a punishment. I was quite upset by this, but not as upset as my favourite teacher.

Jay Norris was really disappointed that I'd skipped school to buy a ticket for a pop concert and gave me a gentle scolding. 'What a silly thing to do!' she said. 'Ten years from now, I bet you won't even remember who Bill Haley was.'

How wrong could she be!*

The Bill Haley show was a blast. It was my first dose of live rock and roll, the first time I had heard the rockabilly shuffle beat at close quarters and it blew me away. We were up in the circle and had to stand up to see when Bill strode on, playing 'Razzle-Dazzle'. Was it my imagination, or was the whole balcony shaking beneath us?

I knew rock and roll from my records and from Radio Luxembourg, but suddenly *here it was*, right in front of me and more exciting than I had dared imagine. Even if Bill was no looker, the girls were all screaming at him. His bass player was the real extrovert, though: he would twirl his double bass, then lay it on the floor and play it as he lay across it.

If I had any remaining doubts about my dream for my life, they died that night. But I was a schoolboy. In Cheshunt. How could I begin to make it happen? It felt as likely as flying to the moon.

When I came to leave school that summer of '57, it became clear to me – and everyone else – how much of a toll my obsession with Elvis and music had taken on my academic work. I had been too distracted to concentrate in lessons and I failed all of my O-levels except for English Language.

By now, if I'm honest, I wasn't that bothered. All I cared about was being a singer and *that* didn't need good exam results. My dad took it harder. As I stood in front of the fire at home again and

---

* I have always kept in touch with Jay. Ten years after this incident, I drove to her house in Cheshunt. When she opened the door, I gave her a box of chocolates and said, 'Bill Haley!' She is due to turn 100 in 2020 – sadly, the Coronavirus lockdown means I'm unlikely to be able to visit her.

confessed my latest failure, he made it clear how disappointed in me he was. *Again*.

Dad was never going to let me sit around doing nothing now that I'd left school and he set about finding me a job. To keep me busy in the meantime, he got me part-time work picking tomatoes in a nearby nursery – I suppose it was a promotion from potatoes!

But it wasn't for me. In fact, I found it thoroughly depressing, not to mention dull. I had to spend all day walking up and down between tomato vines, squeezing the knuckles on coarse green stems to release the fruits. *I can't spend my life doing this*, I thought. The idea was totally terrifying.

Luckily, I had been a tomato-picker for just two weeks when Dad found me a full-time job. He didn't have to look too far, it was in his office at Atlas Lamps. He got me in there as a lowly full-time credit-control clerk.

Dad had also bought me a second-hand bike, and so every morning I had a half-hour cycle ride down the A10 to Enfield. I used to pray the wind wouldn't be against me because it made it hard work and, far more importantly, it used to seriously mess with my quiff.

I didn't really like it at Atlas Lamps. There were only a couple of other teenagers there and most of the staff were my dad's age. The work was pretty boring and, more to the point, it just wasn't what I wanted, what *I needed*, to be doing. I simply felt like I was in the wrong place.

The company sold lamps, televisions, radios and general electrical goods to people all over the country and my job was to keep a note of which counties the orders had come from. I wasn't very good at it. Geography was one of the many subjects I had neglected at school and I hadn't even heard of half the places.

An order paper would land on my desk. I'd read it, then walk over to one of the other young guys. 'This says it's from Cumbria,' I'd whisper to him. *'Where's Cumbria?'* He would have no more idea than me.

I think it's fair to say that I wasn't one of life's natural credit-control clerks. The only thing about the Atlas Lamps job that I liked was that I got to play badminton with Dad in the company's sports and social club. We got quite good, even winning the 'Father & Son' Championship, which I was pleased about – as I say, I like winning!

And yet in a funny way, this mundane job – or, rather, the commute to it – was to give me my first opening into music. One autumn morning in 1957, my bike had a flat tyre, so I had to get the bus into work. On the top deck, I bumped into an old friend from school.

She told me that her boyfriend, Terry Smart, who I also knew from school, was playing drums in a local skiffle group led by a guy called Dick Teague. Their singer had just been called up to do his National Service and so they were looking for a replacement.

I told her that I could be interested in trying out for that, and Terry came around my house to see me. He arranged an audition for me to join the group. I turned up and nervously sang a couple of songs – for the life of me, I can't remember what – and, just like that, I was in!

It was a break, yet I wasn't totally blown away. Skiffle wasn't my thing. The good thing about it was that it was cheap and easy to do. The bass was a tea chest and a broom handle, with a bit of string tied between them, so anybody could play it. Families could have fun playing it at home.

Skiffle had its place. It was a crucial part of the British pop scene at the time, with big hits like Lonnie Donegan's 'Rock Island Line', 'Don't You Rock Me Daddy-O' and 'Gamblin' Man', and Chas McDevitt's 'Freight Train'. I respected it, but I could never compare those guys with Little Richard or Buddy Holly – and they sure weren't Elvis!*

Still, it was my first chance to sing in a band in front of a crowd and it was the only offer I had. I started to rehearse with them at their houses in Cheshunt, singing mostly Lonnie Donegan songs with a few numbers by American folk singers like Woody Guthrie.

Dick Teague, who ran the group, was about five years older than me and a fairly serious soul. He was also somewhat devout about skiffle. Like me, Dick spent his weekdays working as an accounts clerk. However, unlike me, he seemed actually to enjoy it.

I picked up the songs pretty quickly and we started to do quite a few local shows. We played youth clubs, boy scout halls and social clubs. To my delight, I found that I took to performing live well – I would be a bit nervous before we started, but once on stage I loved singing in front of a crowd.

I'm not sure how well I fitted into the skiffle ethos, though. I was still firmly pursuing my Elvis fixation. By now my quiff was

---

* Of course, while I was signing up to the Dick Teague Group, John Lennon had formed his own skiffle group called The Quarry Men in Liverpool. Paul McCartney was to join soon afterwards.

abetted by a pair of Presley sideburns and I had also picked up a lot of moves from his repertoire of hip shakes, leg wobbles and pelvic gyrations.

Dick was more of a traditional skiffle purist and every now and then I saw him looking at me askance. When I asked him if I could do a solo spot during the gigs, singing 'Heartbreak Hotel' and 'All Shook Up', he was horrified – it wasn't how he saw his band.

It was a strange time of my life. I was just turned seventeen, doing a routine, dead-end desk job and consumed by rock and roll. In theory, singing with Dick's band should have been a godsend and incredibly fulfilling, but they were just so far away from the music I loved.

In 1957 alone, Elvis had Number 1s in the US with 'Too Much', 'All Shook Up', '(Let Me Be Your) Teddy Bear' and the brilliant 'Jailhouse Rock'. This wave of fantastic rock and roll washing over the Atlantic was the music that excited me. It was the future – so why was I singing corny stuff like 'Don't You Rock Me Daddy-O' in local scout huts?

It turned out I was not alone in my musical frustration. One day after rehearsal, I went to a café for a coffee with Terry Smart. Suddenly, he asked me a very pertinent question: 'Harry, what's your favourite type of music?'

'I like rock and roll,' I told him.

'So do I,' Terry agreed. 'You don't like skiffle, do you?'

'I don't *mind* skiffle,' I said. 'But I'd rather play rock and roll.'

'Well, let's start a rock and roll band, then,' Terry suggested.

'OK,' I nodded.

It was as simple as that. We had one last attempt to talk Dick Teague round to doing edgier, rockier material, but when he wouldn't budge, that was it. Terry and I quit, amicably. Dick seemed a little sorry to see us go, but I think we all knew it was time for a parting of the ways.

So, what now?

The first thing we needed was a guitarist. I asked Norman Mitham, my old schoolmate who had been with me on that fateful day I first heard Elvis, if he would join the band. He had never played guitar in his life, but he had an uncle who used to be a professional guitarist and gave him a few tips.

Norman, Terry and I began rehearsing at my house. We took over the front room. At that stage we were only playing acoustically, so it wasn't too noisy, but even so I still marvel, thinking back, at how tolerant and supportive my parents were.

They were great, really. My mum was behind everything I was trying to do and completely enthusiastic. She was always discovering local talent contests she thought I should enter: 'Harry, I'm sure you're going to make it!' she would tell me on a fairly regular basis.

Dad was also encouraging, but as was his nature, more cautious: 'If you make it, that's great,' he would say, 'but, don't forget, if you don't, you can still have a life.' He definitely wanted me to keep the safety net of my day job. I suppose they were just doing their yin and yang thing again.

Free from the limitations of skiffle, Terry, Norman and I could now play whatever music we wanted. We covered Ricky Nelson, The Everly Brothers and, of course, lots of Elvis – by now,

I was doing a pretty precise impersonation. We'd buy his new singles like 'Party' and 'Don't' and pore over them, learning the chord changes.

What with dispatching televisions to Cumbria (wherever that was!) during the day, and rehearsing with Terry and Norman every spare minute we could, I had no time to think about getting a girlfriend. So, that was exactly what I did.

Janice Berry was a lovely girl. I had been in the same class as her at school, but we had never dated because she was seeing one of the other lads. After we left, when I heard they had split up, I summoned up the courage to ask her out and we started seeing each other.

We got on great, but I'm not sure how good a boyfriend I was. I was always busy with the band and I didn't get paid much by Atlas Lamps, so I never had any money. We couldn't afford to go to restaurants and if we went to the cinema, I'd always meet her inside because I was too skint to pay for two tickets. Still, we got along well and I liked going out with her.

Had I been asked to give my life a mark out of ten at the end of 1957, I would probably have given it a seven: I had a loving family, a cool girlfriend, a boring job, a fun hobby band with good mates, and an Elvis obsession. There wasn't the slightest hint that, by the end of a roller-coaster and breathtaking 1958, my life would be utterly unrecognisable and even my name would have changed.

My dream would have begun.

But that was exactly what happened.

* * *

By the start of '58, Terry, Norman and I were hankering to get out of my mum and dad's front room and play a few shows, but we knew we needed a band name. We thought of calling ourselves The Planets, but it was too much like Bill Haley's Comets. I looked up the word 'planet' in a dictionary and found the phrase 'cosmic drifter', which I liked. 'Cosmic' sounded over the top, so we just became The Drifters.

Our first gig under that name was in March, at the local badminton club where Dad and I played. We did what I thought was a cool set of chart hits. Liberated at last from Dick Teague's disapproving stares, I could finally start trying to be a proper rock and roll frontman.

There were maybe three hundred people and we went down well. Then again, a lot of them were friends and family. I think my parents and Janice were clapping the loudest! The night had a real 'Local boy done good' feel – not that I had really done anything yet – and I loved every minute.

Heartened by this mini-success, we tried to pick up more local shows. We heard that a pub called the Five Horseshoes, five miles down the road in Hoddesdon, had started putting on live music and we went to see the landlord. He agreed to try us out on a midweek night, when the place was quiet.

So, a week or so after rocking the badminton club, The Drifters took to the stage at the Five Horseshoes. It was a bit empty and probably a harder audience, being as this time we were neither related to, nor friends with, most of them, but we thought it went OK. We even got an encore.

I'd worn glasses since I was eleven but I wouldn't wear them on stage. It was pure vanity – I guess I thought that, Buddy Holly aside, specs weren't very rock and roll! Yet, despite not having my glasses, I had half-noticed a big, stocky, Teddy Boy-looking guy in a leather jacket, leaning on the bar and drinking while we were playing.

After we had finished, and were packing away our gear, this character wandered over to us. We looked at him, and he said something to me that I had previously assumed people only ever said in movies:

'I can make you a star!'

FOUR

'IT'S NOT CLIFF RICHARDS – IT'S *RICHARD*'

We absolutely cracked up. Terry, Norman and I fell about even more than I had when I learned that 'Heartbreak Hotel' had been sung by somebody with the weird name of Elvis Presley.

I mean, that had been funny, but *this*? Some big, burly rocker in a pub in Hertfordshire coming up and talking to us as if he were Cecil B. DeMille addressing a hopeful movie starlet on Hollywood Boulevard? Come on, this was even funnier!

Except that he actually seemed to mean it.

The guy introduced himself. His name was John Foster and he said he had really enjoyed our set and, if we didn't have a manager, he'd like to manage us. He added that he knew the manager of the 2i's Coffee Bar in London and he could get us a show there.

We didn't know what to make of this guy, but our ears pricked up at this last comment. We knew all about the 2i's. It was a hip and happening hangout and live music venue in the heart of London. Tommy Steele and Terry Dene had both played early shows there.

Steele and Dene were the nearest thing Britain had to Elvis-style rock and roll stars back then. Tommy had had a Number 1 with 'Singing the Blues' followed by a Number 1 album and was big news. Terry was in the charts with a cover of Marty Robbins's 'A White Sport Coat' and was being dubbed the 'English Elvis'.

I was interested in them both because they were current and Tommy was almost Britain's first proper pop star, but I wasn't a big fan. Tommy's hits such as 'Rock with the Caveman' just sounded too *English* to me, so I wasn't that impressed. Terry was a little bit more rock and roll, I suppose, but ultimately, the wild sounds coming out of America were what did it for me. *They* were what floated my boat.

Even so, a chance to play the 2i's was not to be passed up, even if John Foster seemed an unlikely way in. As we chatted, it became clear that he had nothing to do with the music industry – he drove a lorry at the local sewage works! Still, he was adamant he could sort us a gig, and he seemed like a nice guy, so we agreed.

OK, he could manage us. Why not? What had we got to lose?

John told us to meet him on Saturday afternoon and we would get the Green Line bus together up to London. I went home and told my family the exciting news. My parents' reaction was the same as it always was: 'Great! Good luck – but be careful!'

I'd been to London with school friends once or twice before but that Saturday felt different. As Terry, Norman and I got off the bus with John at Oxford Circus and walked through the crowds to Soho, our guitars hanging on our backs, we felt like real rock and rollers – The Drifters, up in London town!

The 2i's was in Old Compton Street in the heart of Soho, which was easily the most exotic place I had ever seen (I'm not counting India here!). It felt chic, vibrant and *young*, and the trendy clothes shops, international stores, coffee bars and clubs – not to mention the odd striptease joint – seemed to hum with life.

The 2i's itself was nothing like a staid Cheshunt café doing Typhoo tea in chipped mugs. It didn't serve alcohol, but the hum of Gaggia coffee machines filled the air as bohemian types hung out sipping espressos. A rich coffee aroma suffused the place.

The venue was basically their cellar. It was a long room shaped like a tunnel, with a small stage at the far end. Terry, Norman and I set up and played two songs for Tom Littlewood, John's mate who owned the place. He liked us and said that we could come back and do a few numbers that night.

That afternoon, we killed time walking around and soaking up Soho, attempting to act cool and ignore the mounting excitement inside us.

This is it! We're about to play a gig in London!

Our set that evening went well. As the opening act, we only got to play four or five songs. The audience didn't scream but they listened and applauded. Tom was pleased as well: when we were done, he offered to let us play every night of the next week, if we wanted to. He would even pay us £25!

Of course we wanted to – more than anything in the world. When I got home very late that night, I couldn't resist waking up

Mum and Dad to tell them how well it had gone. They were nearly as delighted as I was.

For the next week, I was busy, busy, busy. I was still misdirecting customer orders at Atlas Lamps, so each day I had to quickly cycle home from work, pick up my guitar and jump on the bus in time for the show. I'd get home after midnight, fall into bed, then be up early for work and do it all again.

It was no problem! I was seventeen, full of energy and adrenalin and chasing my dream. Norman, Terry and I were totally confident about what the week in the 2i's would hold for The Drifters. Tommy Steele and Terry Dene had both been discovered there and we were confident that we were better than either of them.

'It's bound to happen for us,' we told each other. 'All we have to do is turn up!' *Ha!* The confidence of youth, or what?

How wrong we were. We didn't meet any record label executives during the week. We enjoyed the shows and got a good response every night, but zero A&R men brandishing contracts turned up to whisk us off to fame and fortune. We just did the gigs and went home.

They were an invaluable experience, though. We knew we could do OK in Cheshunt scout huts, but rocking a hip joint in the heart of London was a real step up. It was stiflingly hot in there every night, but looking out at the sea of faces, the kids getting into us, I was exactly where I wanted to be; doing what I wanted to do.

And we *did* have a couple of important encounters in the course of that heady week. One night early in the week, a guy a couple of years older than us came over after our set and introduced himself. His name was Ian Samwell and he was on leave from the RAF, where he was finishing National Service. (I never had to do this as, by 1957, males born after 1939 were no longer being called up.)

Ian explained that he was a guitarist who was currently in a skiffle band but he loved what The Drifters were doing – might we need a lead guitarist? He seemed keen, and serious, so I asked him to bring his guitar down to the 2i's that Saturday afternoon and have a play – well, it was an audition, I suppose – with us before our evening set. When he did it, he was great, so Ian was in.

On the same night that we met Ian, a girl called Jan Vane said hello to us. She was celebrating her sixteenth birthday with her boyfriend. 'I think you're great!' she told us. 'Can I start your fan club?'

We fell about again. I explained to Jan that we had only been playing for a few weeks and our only 'fans' were our family and friends, but, sure, she could start a fan club for us – why not? Jan's boyfriend had a car and gave us a lift home to Cheshunt, which made a nice change from Green Line.*

We didn't meet any record label people during our stint in the 2i's but we *did* meet a concert promoter. Harry Greatorex was a guy in his thirties who ran a dance hall called the Regal Ballroom in Ripley in Derbyshire. He came down to London a lot to find new talent to book.

Harry caught our set in the cellar, liked it and told John Foster he wanted to book us. He would pay us a fiver to play a Saturday night show in Ripley – but it would be on one major condition.

---

* Jan might have thought twice before offering, had she known what she was taking on. She went on to run my fan club for years, including when it became the biggest in Britain. She was certainly there from the start!

Harry wanted us to amend our name. He didn't want us just to be The Drifters. A lot of American rock and roll bands had their singer's name upfront – Bill Haley & His Comets, Buddy Holly & The Crickets, Hank Ballard & The Midnighters – and he wanted us to do the same thing.

'What's your name, son?' he asked me.

'Harry Webb.'

'OK, we'll bill you as Harry Webb and The Drifters.'

No way! As soon as he said it, I knew I was never going to use my real name. Rock and roll stars were called Elvis, or Chuck, or Frankie, or Buddy. They certainly weren't called Harry!

I had never really been that keen on my first name. There had also been a recent Alfred Hitchcock comedy film called *The Trouble with Harry*: people would sometimes jokingly say the title to me, which used to annoy the heck out of me. Harry just sounded too ordinary; too plain; too *British*. It didn't sound right.

'No, I'm sorry, I won't use my name,' I told Harry Greatorex (I didn't say why, in case it offended him – after all, it was *his* name, as well!).

'Well, if you want to play my club, you'll have to have a name,' he frowned.

'Don't worry, we'll think of one,' John assured him, then turned to the band: 'Come on, let's go to the pub.'

* * *

We sat in The Swiss Tavern, a pub around the corner from the 2i's, and set about renaming me. *What was I to be called?* Somebody said they liked the name Russ, after a singer called Russ Hamilton, who had had a big hit the year before with a single called 'We Will Make Love'.

'How about Russ Clifford?' somebody else suggested.

'I'm not sure,' I said. 'It sounds a bit like a lawyer.'

'Could we turn it around?' wondered John. 'Cliff Russard?'

'I like Cliff,' I agreed. 'Cliff, a cliff face made of rock, rock and roll – yeah, that's good. But I'm not sure about Russard . . .'

As we sipped our drinks, the ideas kept coming: 'Cliff Richardson?' 'Richards?'

'Yeah,' I said. 'Cliff Richards. Not bad . . .'

Ian Samwell was a full member of The Drifters by now and it was he who had the final brainwave: 'Let's call you Cliff Richard,' he said. 'It sounds a bit like Little Richard, which is cool, and also, when you do interviews, they are bound to call you "Cliff Richards" and you can correct them. It means they will say your name twice and it will stick in people's minds.'

Well, who could argue with logic like that?

I had walked into the Swiss Tavern as Harry Webb and I walked out as Cliff Richard. I liked the name. It felt like it suited me and fitted me already. Harry Greatorex was happy too, and went back up north to start promoting the gig.

Over breakfast the next morning in Cheshunt, I broke the news to my family and asked them not to call me Harry anymore: from now on, I was to be Cliff.

My mum and sisters were fine with this, and they got used to it quickly, although Joan, my youngest sister, was always forgetting: 'Can you help me with my homework please, Harry . . . Oops, sorry, I mean Cliff!' Dad liked it as a stage name but rarely called me Cliff at home. As far as he was concerned, his son would always be Harry.

* * *

Cliff Richard made his live debut outside London on a Saturday night at the Regal Ballroom in Ripley, just after our 2i's residency. If our London shows had felt like a big deal, so did this first gig in a different part of the country.

I wasn't even sure where Derbyshire was. As I had learned at Atlas Lamps, geography wasn't my strong suit, partly because my family were so poor that we never took holidays or went anywhere. I had never been to the North or the Midlands before – I was very unworldly.

This made getting a train to Derby an adventure, especially when we arrived to find Harry Greatorex had been splashing my new name on posters all over town. Seeing them was a real buzz:

REGAL BALLROOM, RIPLEY

3 MAY 1958

DIRECT FROM THE FAMOUS SOHO 2I'S COFFEE BAR:

CLIFF RICHARD & THE DRIFTERS!

The Regal was a converted snooker hall and, on the night, it was packed. People were sitting on wooden benches around the edge of the room but as soon as we walked onto the stage and began playing, everybody got up and started dancing. They were totally into us from the start.

We did our normal Elvis and Ricky Nelson stuff and we played for an hour, by far the longest show we had ever done. It was a totally exhilarating experience and I loved every single minute of it.

We had missed the last train back to London so Harry Great-orex let us sleep on the ballroom benches — not that we got any sleep! There was too much adrenalin pumping for that! I hoped Mum and Dad weren't worrying that I hadn't come home, but I had no way to ring them. We didn't have a phone. Nobody did, in those days.

It felt like things were beginning to happen for us a bit, but we were still primarily music *fans*. When we got home, I was delighted to learn Jerry Lee Lewis was about to play his first British tour. The Drifters often played 'Breathless' and 'Great Balls of Fire' in our sets, so we all bought tickets for his show at Kilburn State Theatre.

Things weren't going well for Jerry Lee. The press had just discovered that he had married his 13-year-old third cousin, Myra Gale Brown, and turned it into a major scandal. Fans were boy-cotting his shows — in fact, the tour got pulled after three shows — and the Kilburn venue was pretty empty.

This didn't seem to bother Jerry Lee, who played a blistering set of rock and roll: we were truly watching a master. Afterwards, our gift-of-the-gab manager John Foster pulled a fast one and managed to arrange for us all to meet him.

I was pretty nervous going backstage — *Oh my God, this is Jerry Lee Lewis! A proper American rocker! I've got his records at home!* — but he was friendly and seemed happy to meet anyone who liked him, given the grief he was getting. The band got a photo with him. I still treasure it.

For a guy who drove a sewage lorry and was making it all up as he went along (as we all were!), John Foster was proving surprisingly resourceful as our manager. A week after getting The Drifters in to meet Jerry Lee, he had us playing another London gig.

This time, he had booked us in to a Gaumont Teenage Show at the Gaumont Theatre in Shepherd's Bush. It was a Saturday morning entertainment show for teenagers that featured a film and a talent competition. We got the gig because we said we weren't entering the talent show but we'd play for free – always an attractive word for promoters!

And when we played there, on 31 May 1958, something strange happened.

I knew I'd been getting better on stage. In normal life, I was still a polite, very shy 17-year-old, but in front of an audience I grew far more confident. The shows at the 2i's and in Ripley had helped – I suppose they made me feel like a star, so I behaved more like one? A little success had given me more confidence.

We took the stage at the Gaumont and I began singing – and the crowd started screaming. *Really* screaming. Not just at the songs, and the music, but at *me*: 'Cliff! Cliff!' I looked out into the audience and I could see excited young girls shrieking and waving at me.

I was absolutely thrilled. A very, very major part of my dream was coming true!

The screaming was exactly like I had seen happening on footage of Elvis gigs in America, or that I had heard at the Bill Haley show. It was precisely what I had wanted to happen from the very first second I heard Elvis, and it felt exactly like I hoped it would: *fantastic*.

It was my first taste of being a real rock and roll star.

We only played for a short while but the noise went on through the entire set. Afterwards, and for the next few days, I only had one topic of conversation with everybody I met: 'I've been screamed at! People screamed at me!'

I loved it more than I had ever loved anything before – and I knew that I wanted it a whole lot more. But if this was going to happen, we needed to start making records. For one thing, it might finally get me away from my desk job at Atlas Lamps.

John Foster felt the same and began scanning entertainment trade newspapers like *The Stage* to try to find us an agent. He called – at random – a guy named George Ganjou and met him at his office. Ganjou suggested we should make a demo record that he could tout around record labels.

There were obviously no recording studios in Cheshunt, so John booked us into a tiny studio above the HMV store on Oxford Street in London. It was my first time in a studio and it felt like a taste of what lay ahead. We recorded a two-song acetate of Elvis's 'Lawdy, Miss Clawdy' and Jerry Lee Lewis's 'Breathless'. It cost us £5.*

The Shepherd's Bush Gaumont noted how well we'd gone down at their Teenage Show and so were happy when John offered

---

* I would love to still have a copy of this acetate, but I'm hopeless at keeping souvenirs and I have no idea where my copy went. I hear things like that occasionally come up on eBay – I should really take a look!

for us to return as 'special headline guests' at their talent show a week later (or maybe they were just pleased when he said we'd do it for free again!). This gig was utterly wild.

The kids that had gone crazy at us a week earlier had come back for more – and brought friends. We could hardly hear ourselves play during our set. The screaming was a white wall of noise throughout: deafening. Everywhere I looked, there was hysteria.

After the show, some three hundred fans hung around outside the theatre chanting my name: *'We want Cliff! We want Cliff!'* When I left, they chased me down the street and I had to take refuge in a men's toilet on Shepherd's Bush Green. The police helped get me out of there. Some of them were on horseback.

How the heck had THIS happened? We were still totally unknown!

After this show, Janice and I finished. We had been going steady for a year, she was a lovely girl and I really liked her, but the truth was if I *was* in love, it was with rock and roll. She hated the mad crowd scenes after the show and didn't want to be around that – so, although it was upsetting at the time, the decision was mutual.*

George Ganjou had come to our second Gaumont show. He wasn't the right agent for us – he handled mostly variety acts – but he could see something was happening. He took our two-track demo to Norrie Paramor, head of A&R at Columbia, a record label run by EMI.

---

* More than sixty years after we split up, I am still close friends with Janice. She married a great, arty guy named Mike, who had nothing to do with rock and roll, and I don't blame her! He's perfect for her.

Norrie was also not steeped in rock and roll. He was an ex-band leader and worked mainly with old-fashioned crooners like Ruby Murray: his latest hit was a novelty song, 'Lollipop', by The Mudlarks. But when Ganjou told him about the pandemonium at the Gaumont, he took our demo home to play to his teenage daughter, Caroline.

Norrie also gave her a copy of the photo of me and The Drifters meeting Jerry Lee Lewis. Apparently, Caroline liked the music, and liked the photo even more! His daughter's thumbs-up was good enough to persuade Norrie to ask us to London for a meeting.

He invited us up to his office to audition for him. Norrie was a friendly, welcoming, middle-aged guy, and I liked him straight away. We set our gear up in his big office and played: Ian, Norman and I plugged our guitars into our tiny Selmer amp and Terry patted a little drum.

Norrie smiled, nodded and didn't give too much away. He told us he was going on holiday and would let us know when he came back. We stewed for a couple of weeks while we waited for his decision, and did a gig at Freight Train, skiffle star Chas McDevitt's Soho coffee bar.

A few days later, John called with some good news: Norrie Paramor was back from his holiday and had decided to offer us a record contract with Columbia. He had even chosen our debut single.

A music publisher called Franklyn Boyd had played Norrie a song called 'Schoolboy Crush'. Previously a hit in America for Bobby Helms, Norrie wanted us to cover it for Britain. He sent me an acetate of the song and we learned it very quickly.

Yet, far more importantly, magic happened for us on a Green Line bus. *Life-changing, career-making magic. The kind of magic that dreams are built on.*

Ian Samwell used to get the bus over from his parents' house in London Colney to Cheshunt for band rehearsals. He would have his guitar with him, and a notebook for jotting down ideas. One day he arrived at the house looking unusually excited.

'Hey, guys, I started writing a song on the bus over here!' he told us. 'It's called "Move It".'

In the front room, he plugged his guitar into our amp and played us the basic song. Even through that puny equipment, we could tell it was special. It had attitude, and drive, and energy. The riff throbbed and yowled like Chuck Berry at his finest. It sounded pure rock and roll.

It sounded . . . American.

Ian had even scribbled down some lyrics:

C'mon pretty baby, let's a-move it and a-groove it . . .

'Wow! Did you really do this on the Green Line?' I asked, nonplussed.

'Yep,' nodded Ian. It was rough and ready, but I could tell there was the germ of something special there.

* * *

We asked Norrie if we could meet him again and play 'Schoolboy Crush' to him. On that fateful day, on the Green Line up to London, we all sat at the back of the bus around Ian and finished off 'Move It', tapping on drums and working out the chords and lyrics as we sped along.

We played both songs to Norrie. He liked our version of 'Schoolboy Crush' . . . and agreed that 'Move It' could be the B-side. This was very unusual. In those days, record labels told artists what songs to cover. Bands writing their own material was unheard of – especially young, wet-behind-the-ears bands like us.

Because we *were* so young, and so wet behind the ears, Norrie had a few stipulations. He wanted an orchestra to record the song, with me singing over the top. Now, I was only seventeen, a boy in a music industry of men, but I knew this was wrong and so I stood my ground.

'No, sir, this is a rock and roll song and it needs a rock and roll band sound!' I told him. 'You have just heard us, we can play it fine!'

'I can't chance it,' replied Norrie, shaking his head. 'I need to get professional players in – making records is expensive!'

In the end, we reached a compromise: we would record 'Move It' as a band, but Norrie would draft in two session musicians to help us out. He booked us in for the session at the EMI Studios in Abbey Road, two weeks later.

Wow! We had a record deal, and we were making a single! It was all incredibly exciting and I even felt as if my dream might really be beginning to take shape – but, sadly, one of The Drifters was not to make it to the studio.

As a slightly older guy, and the writer of 'Move It', Ian Samwell was kind of a musical band leader for us, and pointed out to me that we didn't really need Norman Mitham in the group.

Norman was no virtuoso, and with Ian on lead guitar and me playing rhythm, he was kind of superfluous.

I could see that Ian was right. Still, it was a hard conversation to have, because Norman and I went right back to school days: he had even been with me that fateful day when I first heard Elvis. And yet I knew it had to be done.

It may surprise people, but I have always been tough enough to do whatever is needed for my music and my career. This was a musical decision, and a business decision, and I knew I couldn't let friendship get in the way. Thankfully, Norman and I stayed friends.

Getting a record deal also enabled me to make a happier, far easier decision: I quit my job at Atlas Lamps. When I gave them a month's notice, my boss told me that if I hadn't done so, they were going to get rid of me anyway. Was it my lack of geographical gumption?

I worried slightly that my dad might be disappointed at me resigning my job but he was fine with it. I had stuck it out for nearly a year and now he could see I was getting somewhere in music – and that it was my heart's desire. Much to my relief, I left with his blessing.

Atlas Lamps was the last full-time job that I was to have in my entire life (so far, anyway!). And now, it was time to make a record.

* * *

After the little studio over HMV, which was all we had known previously, Abbey Road studio two seemed vast and swish. Norrie Paramor produced the single himself and the sessions were successful. I wasn't really in love with 'Schoolboy Crush' but the recording went well enough.

However, it was when we recorded 'Move It' that the session really came alive. Ernie Shear, one of the professional session men that Norrie had drafted in, played lead guitar and did the solo. The other session guy, Frank Clarke, pumped us along on bass, and Ian Samwell played the monster, driving riff that he had dreamed up on rhythm guitar.

I was strumming along as well at first, but Norrie – quickly realising my guitar was largely for show – told me through my studio headphones that I didn't need to play as Ernie and Ian had the guitar parts covered, so I put it down and concentrated on my singing. Three or four takes later, Norrie came on my headphones again:

'Cliff, can you pick up your guitar again, please?'

'I thought you said we don't need it?' I asked, puzzled.

'We don't,' he said. 'I don't want you to play it – just hold it! When you are holding it, you sing better.'

I'm still not sure if that was an insult or a compliment! Maybe both! Once I was holding the guitar again, I couldn't resist a few strums as I sang. So, I do actually play guitar on 'Move It' – it's just that nobody can hear it.

The single was due out a month later, at the end of August 1958, and so it was time for Columbia to promote it. As I worked my notice period at Atlas, Franklyn Boyd, the music publisher, was playing test pressings to people – including one particularly influential figure.

FIVE
ENTER HANK AND BRUCE

Jack Good was a young, very driven TV producer. He had launched the BBC's early-evening pop music programme *Six-Five Special* the year before and was now developing a rival show for ITV, *Oh Boy!* Franklyn Boyd managed to secure a meeting and played Jack our acetate.

Jack was lukewarm about 'Schoolboy Crush' (in fairness, so was I), but when Franklyn played him the flip side he, well, flipped! He loved it – and even wrote about it in a column in a pop magazine called *Disc*. I can still remember how the headline ran:

**JUST ANOTHER BEGINNER? NO – THIS BOY IS
REALLY TERRIFIC!**

Jack went on to say that 'Move It' could have been recorded at Sun Studios in Memphis and deserved comparison to Elvis and Jerry Lee Lewis. He finished off by saying, 'When one considers that this is the product of a 17-year-old boy from Cheshunt, Hertfordshire, the mind just boggles.'

Other papers picked up on the record as well and Jack booked us in for the first episode of *Oh Boy!* the following month. Suddenly, it was all going amazingly well – and The Drifters and I celebrated by going to Butlin's.

No, not for a holiday! George Ganjou, our agent, had booked us in to play two weeks of shows at Butlin's holiday camp in Clacton-on-Sea, Essex, entertaining holidaymakers during the high season. It filled in the gap before 'Move It' was released and was the first time I had ever stayed away from home.

That Butlin's fortnight was a hoot. On the day we arrived, the camp managers said that they wanted us to play in their famous red coats. Being a Butlin's Redcoat did *not* figure in my rock and roll dream, and I was horrified: 'We're not wearing *those*!' So, they gave us white T-shirts with a red V on them. A guy called Ken Pavey, whom we met at the camp, played guitar with us at these shows, and Ian Samwell switched to bass.

The managers moved us around the site. We started off in the camp pub, The Jolly Roger, but it was a boozers' refuge so they switched us to the cocktail bar. That was too sedate for us, so they put us where we should have been all along: the main Rock 'n' Roll Ballroom.

The shows were a good learning curve. We'd had kids screaming at us as if we were pop stars at the Shepherd's Bush Gaumont, but now we were jobbing musicians, entertaining people of all ages. It was fun to watch families letting their hair down on holiday and jumping around the ballroom.

We kicked off with 'Twenty Flight Rock' by Eddie Cochran then ran through our usual Elvis and Jerry Lee Lewis standards. But the biggest thrill was playing our own tune, 'Move It', and seeing the dancing campers get just as much into it as they did to 'Hound Dog'.

Norrie Paramor had given the site manager a pre-release pressing of our single and first thing every morning, right after 'Good morning, campers!' they played 'Move It' over the camp loudspeakers: 'That's our boys, Cliff Richard and The Drifters, and you can see them in the ballroom tonight!' It was a great start to the day.

We were paying our dues at Butlin's, as bands did in those days, and now things were really happening. I had to pinch myself when I first heard 'Schoolboy Crush' on Luxembourg – *is that really me they're playing? On the radio?* – and when I got home from Butlin's, things got even better.

I was at home in Cheshunt when I heard BBC Radio spin 'Move It'. It was so exciting! Hearing our song, and knowing millions of people were hearing it at the same time . . . My sisters and I were leaping up and down. Mum and Dad weren't leaping up and down, but they couldn't have looked any more proud.

I certainly felt proud when I got my first cheque from the single: £60! It was a small fortune, especially as my dad only earned about £10 a week at his full-time office job. I spent it on a TV for my parents – I couldn't think of anything I would rather buy.

It also meant that they would be able to watch me make an important debut. Because Cliff Richard & The Drifters were about to go on the telly.

Jack Good's new show, *Oh Boy!*, was a big deal and we spent a week rehearsing for it. It was to be broadcast on ITV live from the Hackney Empire on a Saturday night, but Jack drilled us for days first in a rehearsal room in Canonbury Lane, Islington.

Jack was an imposing and quite inspiring character. He was only in his late twenties and was an Oxford University graduate, which was impressive and a bit intimidating for us secondary modern rabble. He also knew exactly what he did and didn't like about me and my stage act.

Jack quite correctly twigged that at that stage I was basically an Elvis Presley tribute act. He didn't want an Elvis impersonator on his show and made it clear exactly what I had to do: 'Get rid of your guitar and lose your sideburns. Stop trying to be Elvis!'

I guess some people might have bridled at being ordered about like that, but . . . I was fine with it. I understood that I was raw and young, and didn't know what I was doing, and I trusted Jack – he was very driven, with an air of competence and confidence that made you believe in him.

It was just as well that I did, because Jack totally micromanaged me. In rehearsals, he coaxed me through every single move: 'When you sing *this* line, I want you to turn slightly sideways to the camera,' he would tell me. 'On *this* line after, grab your shoulder.' His attention to detail was complete. He taught me how to look at the camera (while hiding my uneven tooth); how to dance; how to tease a crowd and get them screaming. I take my hat off to him: he had a vision for me, and he realised it.

Given the raw material of a gawky teenager who was keen to learn, he built a pop star. I was putty in his hands. Jack's philosophy was that practice makes perfect and, that week, I learned a whole lot about how to be an entertainer.

He might not have liked my sideburns, or my primitive attempts to play guitar, but at least Jack approved of my stage gear. With my first decent cheque, I had gone to Soho and got a pink jacket made by a tailor in Dean Street. I accessorised it with a pink tie and pink socks. Of course, this was partly based on Elvis, who was also wearing cool jackets and ties with skinny trousers, sometimes in pink. I was pleased with the look: I had instinctively sussed that how a pop star looks is as important as how they sound. I still think that today.

My record label was still saying that 'Schoolboy Crush' was my debut single and 'Move It' was the B-side, but Jack was having none of that. He made it clear that if we were going on his show, it was 'Move It' or nothing, so that was what we played live, on TV, on 13 September 1958.

We were rehearsed to within an inch of our lives, Hackney Empire was packed and it was an incredibly exciting evening. The crowd got well into us, but I was also very aware of the cameras, and tried to act on Jack's tips about looking intently into them for dramatic effect.

I felt as if every eye not just in the venue but in the country was on me as I bopped and gyrated. It was a feeling that I liked very much. In fact, *it felt like my dream.*

Norrie Paramor was no fool and, after our appearance on *Oh Boy!*, he announced that 'Move It' was now the A-side of the single and 'Schoolboy Crush' was merely the B-side. Jack invited us back on the show to play that B-side the following week . . . and 'Move It' went into the Top 20 at Number 12!

Television is so powerful and going on *Oh Boy!* was the moment for me that everything changed. Suddenly, everybody knew who I was. Millions of people watched that show every week and, overnight, I became part of their lives.

At seventeen, I was public property! I was a pop star.

I quickly learned that being Cliff Richard was totally different from being Harry Webb, in every way. Immediately, everybody knew my (new) name, and my face, and wanted to talk to me. Whether I was in London or Cheshunt, it was impossible to walk down the street without people stopping me for a chat or to try to steal a kiss.

And everybody . . . everybody! . . . wanted autographs.

Luckily, I had been practising my autograph since I had got my new name. I worked hard at it and arrived at a version that was quick to write but still looked cool – a big 'Cliff' and then 'Richard' a little smaller across the bottom of the page.*

For some people, this new attention and celebrity might have been an ordeal. Not for me. I absolutely loved everything about it. My love for Elvis had always been based partly on his music, partly on his image . . . and a very big part on the fact that girls screamed at him!

I wanted the whole package. Although I was a shy teenager, my attitude to fame was: *bring it on!*

Cliff Richard & The Drifters kept going on *Oh Boy!* and 'Move It' kept creeping up the chart. There were a few other

---

* I still write my autograph the same way now (although nowadays, everybody wants selfies instead). I have done so many thousands in my life that I can write them with my eyes closed – but at least I do them all myself and don't have someone forging them for me, as I hear some artists do!

British rock and rollers emerging on the scene and I'd bump into people like Billy Fury, Dickie Pride and Vince Eager on the show. We'd share dressing rooms and chat in the make-up room.

It was all very friendly and we got on, but from the off, I thought of them as *my competitors*. Some people think it's odd to talk about other artists in this way, but I'm just being honest. From the off, I knew we were all chasing the same radio play, the same TV shows, the same chart positions . . . what is *that* if not competing?

My biggest early rival on *Oh Boy!* was Marty Wilde. Marty was a year older than me and a little bit ahead. He was already well known and he headlined our first show because he was having a big hit with 'Endless Sleep'.

After Cliff Richard & The Drifters had gone down well on that show, and as 'Move It' got bigger, Marty and I pretty much took it in turns over the next few weeks to headline *Oh Boy!* He was like my nemesis (even if I liked the guy) . . . but then, suddenly, my competition vanished.

Marty's manager was Larry Parnes, the music impresario, who was also looking after Tommy Steele and Billy Fury. Larry fell out with Jack Good. He told Jack he was lavishing too much attention on me and neglecting Marty, Jack told him he was talking rubbish and a furious Larry pulled Marty Wilde from the show.

It was a daft row, but it worked in my favour, as I got more top billings without my big rival around. After a few weeks, Larry backed down and Marty returned, but his absence had given us a real chance to establish ourselves and we seized it.

As I went on TV each week and became more used to the routine, it improved my confidence as a live performer. This was just as well – because Cliff Richard & The Drifters were about to go on tour.

Norrie Paramor had booked us as a support act for an autumn UK tour by The Kalin Twins. New York twin brothers named Hal and Herbie Kalin, they had just taken a sweet pop song, 'When', to Number 1 in Britain. It was to spend five weeks there.

We would be playing bigger venues than ever before, but we needed reinforcements. Ken Pavey, the guitarist who had filled in for us at Butlin's, didn't want to go on tour. With Ian Samwell now on bass full-time, it meant we were lacking a lead guitarist. So John Foster went back to where it had all started for us, the 2i's club, to try to recruit a replacement. It was to be a very successful mission.

John was originally planning to meet a guy called Tony Sheridan,* who had played with Gene Vincent and Conway Twitty on their British tours. For some reason, that meeting never happened. Instead, he got talking to a young guitarist named Hank Marvin.

Hank was a Geordie who had been in a Newcastle skiffle band with a school friend, Bruce Welch. They had moved to London and started hanging around the 2i's. Bruce began working at the club, on the orange juice machine, and had seen one or two of our summer shows there.

Hank played John a Buddy Holly tune on his guitar and he was clearly extremely good. John invited him to audition for us, to which Hank replied, 'Sure – as long as Bruce can come along.'

---

* Tony was to move to Hamburg two years later, where he would play with The Beatles.

So, Hank and Bruce turned up at my house in Cheshunt to meet me, Ian and Terry. I liked them straight away. They were my age, easy to talk to – and when they confessed that, when they had heard 'Move It', they had assumed I must be American, I liked them even more! They plugged in their guitars, we ran through a few songs, and it sounded great. We were a natural match from the start. So, that was decided: Hank would come on The Kalin Twins' tour as The Drifters' lead guitarist, and Bruce would play rhythm.

Right after that rehearsal, we went back into Abbey Road studio two to record a new single. Ian Samwell had written another song, 'High Class Baby', but although the recording went fine, I had misgivings about it. It just didn't seem to have the oomph and zing of 'Move It'. Still, for now we had other things on our minds – because The Kalin Twins' tour was about to swing into action.

Tours in 1958 were very different from today. The Kalin Twins' tour was a package. As well as them and us, there was a trumpeter called Eddie Calvert, a singing duo called The Most Brothers (featuring future record producer Mickie Most) and a jazz trio, The Londonaires. The cheapest tickets cost 4/6 (22p!).

We were scheduled to open up the second half of the bill, after the interval, and we threw ourselves into rehearsals as we got used to playing with Hank and Bruce. They were both super-talented and soon we were sounding terrific.

The acts all travelled from town to town on the same bus and when it first picked us all up from outside the newly opened Planetarium on Baker Street, I felt nervous but excited. The other artists were all friendly as we headed out of London, and we got on well, but I felt the same as I did towards Marty Wilde and Vince Eager on *Oh Boy!* These were *our competitors*, and I wanted us to outdo them.

The first date was at the start of October in Hanley, near Stoke-on-Trent (at least touring might improve my British geography!). It was easily the biggest live crowd we had ever played to and hundreds of girls were screaming: 'We love you, Cliff!' It was an incredible buzz and we went down really well.

Maybe a little *too* well. As the two-week tour progressed, it became clear there was a problem. We were getting such a great reaction every night that we were upstaging the headliners. They were finding us impossible to follow.

The Kalin Twins were quite sedate, Johnnie Ray-style crooners at heart, the sort of stuff your mum and dad would like. 'When' was by now falling down the chart and they didn't have anything to follow it up. By contrast, we were playing full-on rock and roll, with two brilliant new guitarists. *Oh Boy!* had made us famous, 'Move It' was up in the Top 10 by now and the kids were going crazy for us. The poor Kalin Twins felt like an anti-climax at the end of the night.

Their manager could see the problem and came to us with a proposed solution. Would we switch and come on in the first half of the show, so that the hysteria we generated could die down before The Kalin Twins appeared and not show them up so much? We said no – or, rather, *I* did. I felt sorry for the Kalins, because Hal and Herbie were lovely guys, but I wasn't about to give up our high place on the bill. The music papers were saying that we were blowing the headliners off the stage: it was great publicity for us. Why throw it all away?

As I said, I can be as tough as my career – *my dream* – needs me to be . . .

The dates rolled on and every night went better than the one before. I had never been to Glasgow or Manchester or Liverpool: now we were arriving in these great cities to find fans screaming their love for us. I kept having to pinch myself: *is this really happening?*

They were screaming partly because I was throwing some wild rock and roll shapes. Hank and Bruce joining the band meant I could mostly dispense with my guitar on stage, which suited me as it meant I could dance around and whip up the crowd frenzy even more. I'm no professional dancer but I found that I was good at moving around the stage. I worked at it: I would run to one side to sing to the people there, then to the other side, then gaze up and sing to the balcony. I tried to reach people and they appreciated it.

They also tried to reach *me*. One day, we got to the venue to find a crowd of girls waiting outside. As soon as they saw us, they ran towards me. It was lucky that John Foster was a big bloke: he put his arms around me, rushed us to the stage door, banged on it and shielded me until we got let in.

Fantastic!

We gained an important new member on that tour. Jet Harris was playing bass with The Most Brothers but didn't like the music they chose to perform. One afternoon, he visited our dressing room and said he loved what we were doing: could he play with us as well, for free?

Sure, we said. Jet was a cool character and we knew he'd bring an edge to the band. With his moody air, bleached blond quiff and a cigarette always glued to his lips, he looked like a rock and roll James Dean. He looked like a rebel.

I knew that *I* wasn't a rebel. Elvis had that image but that had never been what excited me about him. What I loved about early rock and roll was that it was *fun* and full of people singing about falling in love. There was a pure, innocent enjoyment to it and I loved that.

I simply wasn't an angry rebel without a cause. *It wasn't me and it never has been.* Jet was different – he liked a drink, and girls, and partying. If I'm honest, my only objection to him joining Cliff Richard & The Drifters was that he was too handsome! In those days, I had quite a round face, but he had the same chiselled cheekbones as Adam Faith: a face to die for. He looked incredible.

We weren't a bad-looking band on that tour. Hank looked like Buddy Holly in his big specs, Jet, Bruce and Terry were all handsome guys, and the girls were screaming that they loved me, so I can't have been *too* bad! I'd look around me on stage, and think, *Yeah – we look like a proper band.*

On my eighteenth birthday we played in Leicester. The crowd sang 'Happy Birthday' and threw presents on stage. The next night, we were at Birmingham's imposing town hall, with two thousand people awaiting us, and I was very nervous. But I needn't have been. The show was great, yet again.

The tour had one bum note. On the last night, at Bristol's Colston Hall, my guitar that Dad had bought me on hire purchase got nicked from the stage door where our equipment was being loaded onto our bus. I hated telling Dad – he hadn't even finished paying off all of the instalments. Luckily, by now I could pay the last few myself.

When The Kalin Twins' tour finished at the end of October, 'Move It' was Number 4 in the chart. The following week, it went up to Number 2. *Number 2! Unbelievable!* Only Connie Francis's 'Stupid Cupid' kept it from the very top – at least I was denied by a terrific singer and song.

'Move It'* was the record that made my dream come true. I recorded it as an unknown, and it made me a star. If a Martian came to Earth tomorrow and asked me, 'Cliff, how many iconic rock and roll songs have you made?' I would say, 'One – "Move It". And it made history.'

Who made the first rock and roll record? Some say it was 'Detroit City Blues' by Fats Domino. Others think that it was Ike Turner and 'Rocket 88', or that it all started with Chuck Berry. But nobody can ever take away the fact that I made the first rock and roll record outside America – the first *British* rock and roll record.

A few years later, John Lennon was kind enough to say: 'Before Cliff and "Move It", there was nothing worth listening to in British music' (*you have to admit – he has great taste!*). I was flattered by the comment – and I still am. Being called the first British rock and roller by such a legendary musician is an honour that I will take to my grave.

---

* Thirty-eight years after he wrote 'Move It', Ian Samwell wrote a second verse for the song. He sent it to me and I sang it on *Hank Plays Cliff*, a 1995 Hank Marvin album of my songs.

After the tour, I retreated to Cheshunt to reflect. What a time it had been! I had begun 1958 as a reluctant, inefficient credit-control clerk. As the end of the year neared, I was a pop star that magazines had started calling 'the future of rock and roll'. So, would the beautiful craziness that my life had become now recede a little?

Not a chance! It was about to get even crazier.

SIX
MAKING MOVES, MAKING MOVIES

As I reflected on all that had happened to me so quickly, Norrie Paramor sprang into action. The Columbia boss had realised that I might turn out to be big news for his company, and set out to tighten the team around me and eliminate what he saw as weak links.

The lorry-driving wide boy John Foster had done brilliantly to get me as far as he had, but he had no contacts or showbiz experience and was clearly never going to be my full-time professional manager. In his place, Norrie drafted in 'Schoolboy Crush' publisher Franklyn Boyd. John moved to being our on-the-road tour manager.

The other change was tougher, but necessary. Since he had joined at the 2i's, Ian Samwell had been excellent. He had penned our huge breakthrough hit, 'Move It', with its irresistible, insatiable riff, but his musicianship was not at the level of Hank, Bruce and Jet. Jet was a better bassist and the music had to come first. I didn't have the heart to tell him that he was out, so John Foster did it for me. Ian was hurt, but he understood and carried on writing songs for me.

Our new manager, Franklyn, now took over. Although we had just toured the UK, we had been playing scout huts only a few weeks ago and were still raw and unpolished. He decided we needed to tighten up as a live act and fixed us up some London dates.

As well as our usual *Oh Boy!* rehearsals and shows, we were to play two shows per night for three weeks at the end of 1958, at three venues – the Metropolitan on Edgware Road, Chiswick Empire and, finally, Finsbury Park Empire. To avoid me shuttling back and forth to Cheshunt, I would stay with Franklyn and his wife in west London.

This punishing schedule might have been just about doable – were I not also making a movie at the same time.

Norrie Paramor had been approached by a film company who were about to shoot a movie called *Serious Charge*, directed by Terence Young, who had made a few films with Victor Mature. It had a part perfect for an up-and-coming rock and roll singer: did Norrie have one?

Yes, he told them, he most certainly did. He phoned me up: did I want to be in a movie?

I was thrown. Ever since hearing Elvis, I had longed to be a rock and roll singer, but being in films wasn't part of my dream. I had no acting experience besides Jay Norris's drama group in school, and I doubted that playing Ratty in *Toad of Toad Hall* would count for much on a professional movie set! Did I *want* to get into this?

I wasn't sure, but Norrie and Franklyn both assured me that it was a great opportunity. *And, after all*, I thought, *Elvis makes movies! OK, I was in!*

Serious Charge was filmed in Borehamwood studios and Stevenage and it was pretty dark. It told the story of a small-town vicar ruined after being falsely accused of sexually molesting a young guy in the church youth club. Its homosexual connotations were pretty racy for 1959: unsurprisingly, the film was to have an X certificate.

It also had a stellar cast. Anthony Quayle was to star as the discredited priest and Winston Churchill's daughter, Sarah Churchill, played his bitter, rejected would-be love interest. Andrew Ray, the son of the radio comic Ted Ray, was Larry, the yob who wrecked the vicar's life.

I played Larry's younger brother, Curley Thompson, a confused and impressionable kid in danger of following his older sibling into degeneracy and delinquency. Although I didn't have too many lines to say, that didn't stop me turning up on the first day terrified.

On a rock and roll stage, by now I at least had some idea what I was doing. On a film set, surrounded by proper, experienced actors, I felt completely out of my depth. Luckily, Terence Young, Anthony Quayle and everybody else were kind. I think they found me a bit of a novelty: their own tame, teenage rock and roll star!

Weirdly, the make-up people had to perm my hair first thing every morning on set. It was a hassle for them and for me, but they said they had no choice as my character's name was Curley. I couldn't help thinking, *Well, I don't know much about movies, but why don't you just change my name?*

You wait around a lot on film sets, but it was all too new and exciting for me to get bored and I enjoyed watching the other actors do their scenes. On camera, I had to wear a leather jacket, mumble and sing a song or two to some other teenagers in the youth club/coffee bar.

I actually liked the fact that I only had a small part and was down on the bill as 'Introducing Cliff Richard'. It meant that if the film was a hit, I could say, 'Yes, I'm in that!' If it flopped, I wasn't the star, so I would get away with it. It was a win-win situation.

As it turned out, *Serious Charge* was a really good film. It did well, and there was one still from it that I particularly liked. I was being driven in the back of a car, pouting moodily through the window like a Cheshunt James Dean. Now, I'd never dare compare myself to *him*, but I had *a look in my eyes* . . . I saw that photo and thought, *Oh, OK, maybe I* can *act a bit.**

I would film during the day, then in the evening be driven back to London to play with Cliff Richard & The Drifters. The shows went well. The kids in the crowd were going crazy but some of the critics were not impressed. *NME* said my 'hip-swinging was revolting, and not the sort of performance any parent would want their child to witness'.

Well, excuse me! I thought I was just entertaining fans! Journalists are always eager for a story and they started talking about me as Britain's answer to Elvis. They had forgotten one thing: *Elvis was not a question.*

---

* I once said this to David Bryce, my tour manager for many years and the brother of the singer Dickie Valentine. David got hold of a copy of the photo and posted it to me. On the bottom, he'd written, 'Yes, you can.'

In any case, in America, the way that Elvis waggled his hips was seen as very sexual. Just look at how they only showed him from the waist up on US TV! But I wasn't like that: I knew I loved wiggling my hips on stage, and making the girls scream, but I never tried to be suggestive. That just wasn't me – and I'm not sure it was him, either.

I was far happier soon after, reading my favourite headline ever. We were releasing our second single, 'High Class Baby', and *Melody Maker* said:

ELVIS AND CLIFF BATTLE IT OUT IN THE CHARTS!

ELVIS AND CLIFF! In a newspaper! It was amazing for me, just to read my name next to his.

For a wide-eyed, 18-year-old lad, it was an exhilarating time. My life was crazy. I have a photo of me from 1959, with Jayne Mansfield at Wood Green Empire. *Jayne Mansfield!* I had just goggled at her movie, *The Girl Can't Help It*, and now we were on the same TV show.

I was taken to meet her, nervous that this fab movie star would brush me aside. Instead, Jayne was perfectly sweet and welcoming – and I bet she never knew how good she made me feel.

My schedule at this point was ridiculous. *Serious Charge* had some night shoots, so a few times I had to film all day, race to London to play two concerts, then head back to the movie set to film until the early hours. It was exhausting and it all got too much.

One night during the last week of shows, at Finsbury Park Empire, I walked on stage in front of an excited crowd, opened my mouth . . . and nothing came out. I had lost my voice and I had to croak my way painfully through the songs. Luckily, the screaming was so loud, nobody could tell.

I was done. When I came offstage, John Foster drove me home to Cheshunt and my dad stepped in. He was horrified to see the state I was in, packed me off to bed and cancelled all of my engagements for the next two weeks (I was still 'underage' so he signed all of my work contracts). It didn't even occur to me to argue. In fact, I was relieved.

Dad blamed Franklyn Boyd for overworking me until I had collapsed, and he was probably right. He didn't renew his contract. Norrie Paramor found us a replacement manager: a guy called Tito Burns, who also managed Cherry Wainer, one of my co-stars on *Oh Boy!*

Hank, Bruce, Jet and I also reluctantly decided we needed one final tweak to the band. Terry Smart's raw, primitive drumming worked on 'Move It', where it was exactly what the song required, but as a musician he was nowhere near the level of the rest of the group. We needed a better drummer.

I was sorry to see him go, because I had played with him since Dick Teague's skiffle group, but Terry was fine about it – he had always wanted to join the Merchant Navy when he turned eighteen. So, off he went for a life on the ocean waves and Tony Meehan, who had played with Hank and Bruce at the 2i's, took over. Tony was a great drummer, even though he was only sixteen.

We had to lick the band into fighting shape because we were set to go back on tour. Christmas came and went and we had a string of UK-wide dates lined up for early in the new year. I was fit and raring to go again and we knew things would run a lot smoother if I were based in London rather than Cheshunt. So Norrie, Tito and Dad hit on a plan: we rented a flat on Marylebone High Street, right in the heart of London. John Foster was to live with me – my parents knew and trusted him so it put their minds at rest.

The Kalin Twins' tour had been a package, but this time it was to be different. I met the promoter, Arthur Howes, who was certainly very persuasive. '*You* are going to be the star of the show, Cliff,' he told me. 'You can draw the crowds on your own. We don't *need* anybody else.'

This was a great confidence boost, although Arthur did stick two or three support acts on the bill each night. The compère was a very funny, upcoming comedian from Liverpool named Jimmy Tarbuck. He was eighteen, the same age as me.

With no luxury coach to ferry us about, John got hold of a Bedford van and we took off to towns whose whereabouts would have baffled me in my Atlas Lamps days: Wolverhampton. Dewsbury. Pontefract. Newark. In those pre-motorway days, the journeys were long and arduous. When we arrived, a bizarre ritual would ensue.

We never had accommodation booked in advance, so as soon as we got to a town, John, Hank, Jet, Bruce, Tony and I would jump out of the van and scatter in different directions. We would scope out the local B&Bs, then regroup to compare notes:

'I've found one for five shillings!'

'So? I've got one for four bob, with free coffee in the rooms!'

'I've found one that's three bob, *and* they give you breakfast!'

'Great, let's go there, then! Quick, where is it?'

Sometimes, three of us would take a room with only two beds, so two of us would have to share. But, who cared? We were young and on top of the world, the shows were fantastic and it was all a laugh and a great adventure.*

Interrupting the tour, we did a week of live *Oh Boy!* stage shows in Hammersmith with other acts from the programme. That was where we nicked – sorry, I mean *borrowed* – our nifty moves.

A group called The Dallas Boys did little dance steps as they sang and we liked the look of it. We started copying them and doing sideways steps, then took it a bit further and introduced more complex moves, where we crossed one foot in front of the other. Soon, Hank, Bruce and Jet were all doing it in a line behind me – *et voilà!* A move to last us sixty years.

We played more shows in London, but not all of them were enjoyable. I'd started to realise that some people had it in for me. Or, rather, some *blokes*. By now, there were a lot of girls screaming that they loved me at our live shows, and this meant there were a lot of boyfriends who didn't like that – or like *me*.

We appeared at the Trocadero in Elephant & Castle, south London, a theatre with a balcony. No sooner had we started playing than Teddy Boys began chucking missiles at us from on high. These included those hefty old pre-decimal-currency pennies. They were raining down like bullets. It was so dangerous – those coins could have taken somebody's eye out. But the worst that

---

* During one interview, years later, a journalist asked us how well we all got on. Hank told her, 'Oh, Cliff and I have slept together!' The poor girl looked shocked, and so did I!

Early photos of my
mum, my sisters and me
– in India and England.

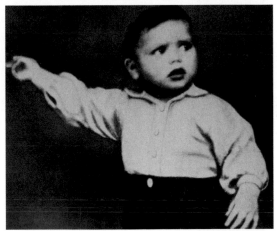

'*Ducks are a-dabbling/Up tails all!*'
Making my stage singing debut as
Ratty in *Toad of Toad Hall*, Cheshunt
Secondary Modern School, 1955.

Cheshunt's finest teenage a
cappella doo-wop band: me
(far left) in The Quintones, 1956.

'Hmm, that ceiling needs a dust!' The first ever band picture of The Drifters –
Terry Smart, me, Norman Mitham and Ian Samwell – at London's legendary
2i's coffee bar, April 1958.

More early shots of The Drifters, with
Ian Samwell on guitar and Terry Smart
on drums, 1958.

London, spring 1958: Ian
Samwell, Terry Smart,
my fan club organiser
Jan Vane and her sister,
me and John Foster,
The Drifters' manager.

'Me? Wear a red coat? You
must be joking!' Rocking
Butlin's holiday camp,
Clacton-on-Sea, with
The Drifters, July 1958.

A record deal and a new line-up: Columbia A&R chief Norrie Paramor, me, Jet Harris, Tony Meehan, Hank Marvin and Bruce Welch, summer 1958.

Ah, those short shorts! Performing on *Oh Boy!* with The Vernon Girls, 1958.

Hank with *that* famous Stratocaster, the first ever imported into Britain. Money well spent!

A Hollywood superstar with an overawed 18-year-old; meeting Jayne Mansfield at Wood Green Empire, 1959.

(Right and below): With Mum, Dad and my sisters in the house I bought them in Winchmore Hill, north London, 1959.

A kiss for the bride: being best man at Bruce Welch's marriage to Ann Findlay, August 1959.

With Donna at home: 'Listen, this is the B-side!'

With Mum, Jackie, Joan and Champs the dog outside our Rookswood house in Nazeing, Essex.

The Drifters become The Shadows:
rocking with Bruce and Hank,
January 1960.

You should *always* meet your heroes!
With Don (left) and Phil Everly,
January 1960.

A 1961 British TV
appearance.

With host Dick Clark
on famous US TV show
American Bandstand,
November 1962.

Intense mixing-desk
chats in Abbey Road
studio two, 1962. Back:
'Licorice' Locking, Brian
Bennett, Hank Marvin,
Bruce Welch and Norrie
Paramor. Front: Peter
Gormley (with me
bending his ear) and
engineer Malcolm Addey.

I hear it was a great night, but I'll never know: the 1963 Leicester Square movie premiere for *Summer Holiday* that I got turned away from.

What a welcome! Waving to my fans on my first trip to South Africa.

'Can you keep the noise down back there?' Asleep on the tour bus during our spring UK tour, 1963.

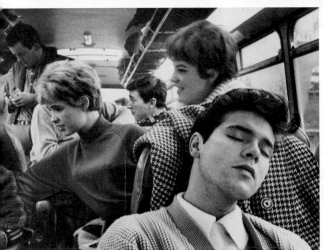

Wide awake, singing and on the way to Huddersfield ABC on the same tour, 13 March 1963.

With Norrie Paramor and a gold disc for Number 1 single 'The Next Time'/'Bachelor Boy', 1963.

Aladdin and Princess Badroulbadour, aka me and Una Stubbs in the London Palladium's Christmas pantomime, *Aladdin and his Wonderful Lamp*, 1964.

Cliff with a C meets Liza with a Z: with an 18-year-old Liza Minnelli on a 1964 British TV show.

happened was a penny knocked a chunk of wood out of Jet's bass, at which point we rapidly called it a night.

Still in London, in the first week of February we had shows lined up at the Lyceum on the Strand. Our first one brought more hooliganism. The theatre had a revolving stage and we stood on it behind the scenes and waited for it to rotate. As we started the intro to Elvis's '(You're So Square) Baby I Don't Care', it revolved around to face our audience . . . and a gang of Teddy Boys began throwing missiles at us.

They had everything: fruit, buns, eggs, tomatoes, cigarette packets, bits of lino ripped up from the Lyceum floor. They were pretty scary, but the bottles and glasses raining down were even more so. *Heck! What were we supposed to do?* Some of the Teddy Boys tried to rush past security and one of them clambered on stage and threw a punch at me. He missed and got bundled away. We stared, wide-eyed, at each other, stayed on the stage as it rotated back out of sight, and scarpered backstage. That show ended before it even began.

It was pathetic. I wanted to say to the Teds, 'If your girlfriends are so keen on *me*, *you* must be doing something wrong!' It was scary, though, and we cancelled the rest of the week at the Lyceum and hoped it wouldn't happen again. Thankfully, apart from a few minor flurries, it was the end of violence at our shows.

The next night, 3 February, was The Day the Music Died: the date of the terrible plane crash in America that killed Buddy Holly, Ritchie Valens and The Big Bopper. This was nearly half a century before the days of rolling news and the internet, so we didn't know it had happened until the next day. It was awful to find out. It's still amazing to me that Buddy's incredible recording career was over and done in less than three years.

A week later, we made our first album. It was simply titled *Cliff* and we recorded it live, over two nights, in front of an invited audience of fans at Abbey Road studio two, which was beginning to feel like home. Norrie Paramor produced us again. It felt like an intimate gig and, despite the pressure, I enjoyed it.

We just played our live set-list. So, as well as 'Move It', The Drifters played a couple of instrumentals and we did four Elvis tracks, plus songs by Little Richard, Ricky Nelson, Gene Vincent . . . and Buddy Holly and Ritchie Valens. It felt weird singing 'That'll Be the Day' and 'Donna' a week after they had both died. It was our tribute.

It was good to have an album out now, because our singles' fortunes had declined slightly. After 'Move It' reached Number 2, our two follow-ups, 'High Class Baby' and 'Mean Streak', only just squeezed into the Top 10. But that was all about to change.

Unknown to us, my contract for *Serious Charge* said that Cliff Richard & The Drifters had to release a song from the film as a single. They wanted us to put out 'Living Doll', a song written by Lionel Bart that I had sung in the youth club in the movie. It was a weak, pseudo-rock song and none of us liked it very much.

We had even tried releasing a different song with a similar name, 'Livin' Lovin' Doll', but it flopped and the film studio was insisting that we fulfil our contractual obligation. Which brought us to the City Hall, Sheffield, on Valentine's Day, 1959.

At the pre-show soundcheck, we were sitting on the stage steps, grumbling about having to release 'Living Doll'. Bruce was strumming his guitar. 'Look, none of us like it as it is,' he said. 'Why not do it another way?' He picked at a few chords. 'Why not do it as . . . a country song?'

Wow! We all exchanged glances and nods. *This might just work . . .*

So many things were happening. It felt like there was no let-up. The day after we reshaped 'Living Doll', we played the Regal in Edmonton, where I had seen Bill Haley just two years earlier. It felt crazy that kids were now screaming at me the same way I'd seen them scream at him.

We were still appearing on *Oh Boy!* One week, Jack Good had Marty Wilde, Dickie Pride and me harmonising on The Coasters' 'Three Cool Cats'. When I watched it back, I thought the other two were, indeed, cool cats, but I looked like a greasy slob. *Why have they let me on there?* I wondered. Yet, somehow or other, I *was* a star now, with my name in front of the band – Cliff Richard & The Drifters.

When we played a week of shows at Birmingham Hippodrome, John Foster told us that we had a press conference to do before the first night. 'OK, lads, let's go and do it!' I said to the band.

'We're not coming,' they told me. 'You go. *You're* the star!'

So, I talked to the press on my own. When I got back, the band had written a new song without me. That happened a lot, and it was probably the reason I was never a major songwriter in the group. Still, they wrote them, I sang them and they sold. Everybody was happy – and *I was the star! What a dream!*

Then, something happened that was to shape the sound of the band for years. Hank played an old Antoria that looked like a plank carved into a guitar, but he coveted a Stratocaster. He pored over a Fender catalogue like a kid with his nose pressed against a sweet-shop window.

Hank said it would make us sound so much better so I decided to buy one for him to play for me. I wrote off to Fender in California, not asking for any particular colour. When the Strat arrived, it was pink (Fender claim they have never made a pink Strat, but mine certainly was!) It matched my stage jacket, so we were very happy with it. We later learned that it was their first-ever export to Britain. Hank could not have been more excited – and, when we heard it, so were the rest of us. It just made us sound so much richer and stronger. Hank was always a great player, but now he went up another level.*

While we were on tour, girls were screaming at us every night and would often try to get close to us. I began to get very used to being chased down the street outside venues. I loved it – I mean, who wouldn't? I often talked to, and wrote autographs for, female fans, but I was totally focussed on my career – and in those early days, I knew that having a girlfriend would kill everything for me.

For a month or so, I saw a girl called Jean and I remember being driven out of Finsbury Park Empire after a show. Jean was sitting on my lap and we waved at fans out of the window. I saw a few of them scowl – and one girl threw her programme on the floor and stamped on it!

---

* Bruce has that Stratocaster today and I sometimes tell him that I want it back. He says I gave it to the band, and possession is nine-tenths of the law. He's wrong – I have no problem with him using it, but I bought it for Hank to play in MY band. So, it's mine, Brucie!

Wow! Did it really mean that much to them? I was loving being Cliff Richard so much, and the band and my career were all-important to me, that I didn't want to do anything that might jeopardise it. I told Jean that I was sorry but I couldn't see her again.

If I had ever met a girl I had fallen head-over-heels in love with, of course, it might have been a different story. But none of them ever blew me away remotely as much as that.

Until I met Carol Costa.

As I said before, I had always had a thing for Brigitte Bardot, and Carol just had that look. She was sixteen, from Hounslow, and I met her in April 1959, when we played a week of shows at Chiswick Empire.

There was one major problem: Jet Harris met her then as well and the two of them hooked up and quickly became an item. In fact, to all intents and purposes, they were effectively living together in the spare room of the Marylebone flat I shared with John Foster.

I knew I liked Carol – a lot – and she seemed to like me. We did a bit of holding hands and talking intensely when Jet wasn't around, but at the same time, she was his girlfriend and I knew exactly what our fans would have thought of me seeing anybody at all.

It was confusing, and frustrating, but the issue appeared to be settled when Jet and Carol got married only two months after they met. I tried to put her to the back of my mind, and move on.

Because I was always in the studio, or playing shows, or being chased down the street, it was hard to find time to do the normal teenage things. But when I met a guy called Ronnie Ernstone at a party at Abbey Road, he quickly became a mate.

Ronnie was a car mechanic and he helped me to buy a yellow-and-black Lambretta scooter. It became my pride and joy and was great for quick getaways from gigs, or for zooming down the A10 to see my parents as often as I could. But zooming down the A10 on a Lambretta in the rain is not a lot of fun and I really wanted a car. Ronnie taught me how to drive and when I passed my test first time, he knew where to go to buy my first motor: a grey Sunbeam Alpine sports car with red leather seats. I loved that car!

Ronnie also had a great suggestion when I had a rare two-week gap in my work schedule in June – that we should go on holiday. Because my family had always been so poor, we had never had a holiday, so I jumped at the idea. Ronnie suggested a driving trip to Italy. Tony Meehan from the band wanted to come along, a female friend of Ronnie's named Pam made up the numbers, and off we went.

It took us three days to drive down through Belgium, Germany and Switzerland to the Italian coast and I loved every minute of it. Apart from my early years in India, I had never left Britain and everything – the sights, the languages, the food, the rivers, the mountains – felt new, fresh and *different*.

This was even more the case when we got to the pretty coastal town of Viareggio. The warm air of Italy felt exotic, the people were cool and beautiful, Italian sounded impossibly poetic and I had to admit that, just for a change, I liked being able to walk around town without people staring at me or trying to grab me!

It was a wonderful break. The four of us ate, drank (a bit too much!), relaxed, sunbathed, swam . . . and, on the way home, we decided to go and meet Elvis Presley.

Elvis had famously been drafted into the US Army to do his military service in March 1958. Since that October, he had been stationed in Germany, most recently in a town called Bad Nauheim, and we decided to make a detour and pay him an impromptu visit. As we drove up through Italy and into Germany in Ronnie's Morris Oxford Estate, we were all laughing and joking at the prospect of seeing Elvis, but as we neared his town, a silence descended in the car. I could suddenly feel my heart beating hard inside my ribcage.

Elvis! Meeting Elvis!

What on EARTH could I SAY to him?

His house was not hard to find. We asked directions, somebody pointed us the way and we were clearly not the first people to have made the pilgrimage. The three-storey house we pulled up outside was covered in 'WE LOVE ELVIS!' and 'THE KING!' graffiti.

We nervously discussed which of us should go and ring the doorbell. The conversation didn't take long.

'It *has* to be you, mate! You love him!' said Ronnie.

'Yeah, go on, Cliff!' urged Tony.

Oh, OK, then! I walked through a wooden gate, up a short flight of steps and stood outside Elvis's door. *Elvis's door!* I felt as if I was moving in slow motion: as if I was dreaming. With my heart in my mouth, I pressed the bell.

DING-DONG!

A huge guy answered the door. I had no idea who he was, but he certainly wasn't Elvis Presley.

'Hello!' I began, awkwardly. 'My name is Cliff, I am a singer from England and I'd love to meet Elvis . . .'

The guy cut me off, politely but firmly. 'I'm sorry, but Elvis isn't here right now,' he told me. 'I will tell him you called.'

'Oh, OK,' I said. 'Thanks!' I added over my shoulder, as I scuttled back down the stairs.

As our car pulled away, I wasn't sure whether my primary feeling was one of disappointment or relief. I would have loved to meet Elvis, but had I been unable to speak, or made a fool of myself, I would not have been able to bear it. So, maybe it was for the best. *Maybe* . . . *

Soon after I got back from my Italian holiday, The Drifters and I experienced an incredible high – because 'Living Doll' finally came out as a single and went to Number 1.

We were delighted – but also amazed. Who would have thought it would work out like this? Who would have thought a rock and roll band would take a pseudo-rock song, turn it into a truly fantastic country record and go to Number 1? It all seemed so bizarre.

Bizarre – but great. There's no feeling like being on top of the chart (or the hit parade, as we used to call it). I remember Lionel Bart, a very sweet man, made a couple of comments about how much we had changed his song, but I'm sure he was happy when the royalty cheques began rolling in!

What really amazed us was that 'Living Doll' also went to Number 30 in America. *America!* Could we really do well there? It seemed too much to even hope for, but on the strength of this

---

* Ronnie filmed me knocking on the door. The video was lost for thirty years then, remarkably, his mum found it in her loft. So, should you want to watch me Not Meeting Elvis, it's up there on YouTube!

success, Tito Burns began to arrange a US tour for us for the start of the following year.

Not everything was perfect for us. We got a bit of flak. Because I had started out as an Elvis-like rock and roller, a few music critics had a go at me and said I had 'sold out' by recording this softer-edged song that mums and dads were as likely to buy as kids. They said I had gone mainstream.

Well, I *had* – and you know what? I was happy to! I might have loved Elvis but, once again, I was never a rock and roll rebel. I mean, what did I have to rebel against? I didn't hate my parents and family – I loved them! I loved being a singer and I loved my life. I wasn't horrified by the idea of becoming a clean, all-round family entertainer – I embraced it.

If some misguided people thought I had betrayed rock and roll, well, so what? I wanted to sell records and I didn't care how I sold them. In any case, we still rocked, loud and hard, on the B-sides and at our live shows. And the fact that I wanted to be an all-round showman, and not pigeonholed as 'just' a snarling rock and roller, was emphasised when the very next thing that I did was to make another movie.

Expresso Bongo was set in the Soho of the 2i's club and I took the part of Bongo Herbert, a naïve young singer who gets exploited by a fast-talking wide-boy manager and an unscrupulous record label. It was a far bigger part than Curley in *Serious Charge* and so I had a lot more lines to learn.

The film was directed by Val Guest, who had made movies with Arthur Askey and shot the Hammer horror classic *The Quatermass Xperiment*. The big-name star was Laurence Harvey, who had just had a massive hit playing the lead role of Joe Lampton in *Room at the Top*. Harvey was a full-on thespian and a formidable figure, and a couple of people warned me in advance to be careful of him as he could be a tough cookie with his co-stars. I was fairly wary . . . until I realised that he was a real team player.

Laurence played Johnny Jackson, my wise-guy manager. After I had said one line to him, in an early scene, he put his hand up, halted the filming and spoke to me.

'Wait a second,' he told me, 'if you don't mind, let me advise you. Don't say the line until you are ready. Line it up in your mind, pull it out and *then* say it.' He was right. When we tried the take again, it felt so much better and more natural. *Sweet guy!*

In the film, I was helped and then seduced by an ageing American star, Dixie Collins, played by Yolande Donlan (who was Val Guest's wife). Yolande was great, a likeable diva, wafting around the set with her long cigarette holder. My seduction scene was cool: she just looked down at me, drunk and passed out on her bed, arched an eyebrow, and removed her earrings. *Fade to black . . .*

For its time, *Expresso Bongo* was risqué. Some scenes were set in a Soho striptease club, with the female lead Sylvia Syms and other actresses dancing in nipple tassels.* I went to watch the scenes being filmed, as any teenage boy would, and like *Serious Charge*, *Expresso Bongo* was given an adults-only rating – my second X film!

---

* I believe the producers also shot a tassels-free, fully topless take and included it in what they called the 'continental' version of the film, to be only shown outside of the UK. I don't recall ever seeing it – honest!

When the film came out and I went to see it, I was really proud and glad I had agreed to do it. My only reservation was that I wished somebody had given me a lesson in how to play the bongos, because in the scene where I had to do that, I looked all wrong.

When we finished filming, the first thing we had to do was change The Drifters' name. Columbia had tried to put one of our records out in America, only to receive a legal letter. It turned out a band called The Drifters was already operating in the US – a good one, in fact. Clyde McPhatter was one of a number of lead singers they had.

We needed a new name. Hank and Jet went off to the pub on their scooters to think of one and Jet instantly came up with Cliff Richard & The Shadows, 'because we're always in Cliff's shadow!' I wasn't *entirely* sure what he meant by that, but it was a good name so we went with it.

The hysteria around us was even louder now that we'd had a Number 1. We sold out a week at the Glasgow Empire in September, and the fans were unbelievable. I think if they could have got hold of me, they would have torn me limb from limb (in a nice way – well, if that's possible!).

Before the first show, the MC, a local comedian, was walking up and down in front of the curtain, trying to tell a few jokes as we got ready to play. He had no chance. The screams were so loud, it was like a hurricane:

'We want Cliff! We want Cliff!'

The comic was getting some good old Glasgow heckling ('Gerroff! Ye're rubbish!'), but he was going nowhere. 'I've been told to do five minutes, so five minutes is what you're getting!' he told the crowd. He didn't say any more – just walked up and down the front of the stage, glancing down at his watch and giving time checks:

'Four minutes!'

Walk. Walk.

'Three minutes!'

Walk. Walk.

'Two minutes!'

Walk. Walk.

'One minute!'

Walk. Walk.

'Ladies and gentlemen, here are Cliff Richard and The Shadows!'

When the curtain finally went up, the wild screams sounded like a jet taking off.

* * *

While we were in London in-between shows, I was still living at the flat in Marylebone High Street with John Foster. It had turned into an unofficial Cliff Richard & The Shadows and mates HQ/hangout/late-night party place. I don't know if it was due to the way I was brought up, but I wasn't really into that.

One morning I woke up, after being kept awake for hours by a noisy all-night party, to find ten or twelve people sprawled asleep in chairs or on the floor. A penny dropped for me: *I don't want this! I don't want drunken bodies lying all over my home!*

So, I gave up the flat, moved back home to Cheshunt and plotted a house move. I was suddenly making absurdly good money for a lad of my age. In Carshalton, years ago, I'd offered to buy Mum a house 'when I had £100': now, I had it, and more, and could actually do it.

At first, Mum and Dad weren't sure about accepting my offer of a new home, but they soon realised that I was making so much money that it would be daft not to. We settled on a semi-detached corner house in Winchmore Hill, north London. I furnished it with all the mod cons: a TV, a telephone and, of course, a record player.

I also managed to persuade Mum to give up work now that I could afford to help look after them – but there was no way Dad would agree to do the same. He was a proud, independent man and I think it would have felt wrong for him to be financially dependent on his own son. So he carried on heading off every day to Atlas Lamps.

It was now time to make my next album. Where *Cliff* had been essentially a live album, recorded in front of an audience, *Cliff Sings* was to be a proper studio record. Norrie Paramor had a bit of a concept for it. 'Living Doll' going to Number 1 had shown him I could appeal to more than just teenagers, and so he was keen to push me as a family entertainer. He said I would record half of the album with The Shadows . . . and half with an orchestra.

I liked the idea: I trusted Norrie's judgement and I wanted what I've always wanted – to sell records to as many people as possible. So, in September 1959, I went into Abbey Road studio two and did eight tracks with The Shadows and eight more with the Norrie Paramor Orchestra.

It was fun. *Cliff Sings* was split into rock and roll on the first half of each side, and orchestra-backed ballads on the second. The

Shadows and I did Elvis's 'Blue Suede Shoes', Jerry Keller's 'Here Comes Summer' and Eddie Cochran's 'Twenty Flight Rock'. With the orchestra, I covered 'As Time Goes By', Nat King Cole's 'Somewhere Along the Way' and 'Embraceable You' by George Gershwin. I guess we were covering all bases!

There's a reason Norrie Paramor became a music industry legend. He sure knew how to sell records. For our follow-up to 'Living Doll' – our first post-Drifters single as Cliff Richard & The Shadows – he told us to sing another country-tinged song called 'Travellin' Light'.

'Travellin' Light' was a sweet, gentle lope of a song by two American songwriters I'd never heard of called Sid Tepper and Roy C. Bennett. It wasn't until decades later that I learned they had originally written it for Elvis, only for it to be cut from the soundtrack of his *King Creole* movie. It felt like I was forever destined to follow in his footsteps!

'Travellin' Light' certainly worked brilliantly for us – it followed 'Living Doll' to Number 1, knocking Bobby Darin's great 'Mack the Knife' off the top. Then *Cliff Sings* went to Number 2 in the albums chart. Suddenly, we really *were* hot property.

For months, I had been doing newspaper interviews. I routinely talked to music mags like *Melody Maker* and *NME* and teenage girls' publications such as *Boyfriend*, which usually put me on the cover. At first, I felt awkward doing them, but they usually asked very simple questions and by now I breezed through them.

A television interview was a very different matter. Late in 1959, I was asked to appear on an ATV show called *Celebrity*, which was a one-to-one interview with a very highbrow interviewer called Daniel Farson. I knew I wanted to do it, but it was an intimidating prospect.

Mr Farson grilled me on topics from my boyhood in India to current affairs. Watching it back now, I looked far more assured and confident than my 19-year-old self felt inside. I only dropped one howler. At one point, he asked me if I had ever acted any Shakespeare in school.

'We used to read his plays in drama group,' I told him. 'I was Oberon in *The Merchant of Venice*.'

'Oh,' said Daniel and we carried on talking. A little while later, he said, 'By the way, Oberon is in *A Midsummer Night's Dream*.'

'Yes, I know,' I agreed nonchalantly, trying to bluff it out. I'm not sure that I succeeded!

Farson was only the start. Our ascent into the higher altitudes of mainstream showbiz was about to get even more rarefied. Only a few weeks later, we were invited to appear on the pinnacle of British light entertainment shows: *Sunday Night at the London Palladium*.

Wow! Now we really *had* arrived! This was the show on which the crème de la crème of entertainers appeared, both British and visiting American superstars, from Gracie Fields to Bob Hope. As many as twenty million people watched when it was broadcast live every week.

No pressure, then!

The Shadows and I got suited and booted in tuxedos and nervously turned up at the cathedral of British showbusiness in Argyll Street. The Beverley Sisters were on the same show. We were to sing 'Living Doll' and then, later in the show, 'Travellin' Light'.

The pre-show run-throughs went fine; we were to perform 'Living Doll' and then take a bow as the curtain came down. We had some pretty serious nerves when the big moment came, but the song went OK and as the audience applauded, I waited for the curtain to fall.

And waited.

And waited.

Nothing was happening. What was going on?

Panicked, I looked behind me to see The Shadows grinning away as if they were having the best time in the world. I also caught sight of movement at the side of the stage. Bruce Forsyth, the show's wisecracking host, was walking towards me and appeared to be carrying something.

'Cliff, I want to present you with this,' he said, smiling as he handed me a framed record. 'It's a gold disc for a million sales of "Living Doll"!'

It was an unbelievable moment. I didn't even know our single had sold a million copies, let alone that *this* was going to happen. It turned out the show's producers had pre-warned The Shadows about the presentation but wanted to surprise me. On live TV. In front of twenty million people.

Thanks, guys!

The entertainment industry was very different at the end of the 1950s to how it is today. After The Shadows and I had had two Number 1 singles, selling a million copies of one of them, and headlined Britain's biggest TV show, we went to Stockton-on-Tees . . . to appear in a pantomime.

It was just something rock and rollers did in those days. Billy Fury had been in panto, as had Tommy Steele and Marty Wilde. I didn't think I was above it all: it was fun. We were in *Babes in the Wood* there for a month, I wore a natty pink jacket (*Oh yes, I did!*) and The Shadows and I belted out our hits at the end of the show.

What a year! Yet while movies, TV variety shows and pantos were all fine, now I was about to do something far more exciting. It was time to go off to the land that had invented rock and roll; the land that had spawned Elvis and was Mecca for not just me but all British rock and rollers.

It was time to go to America.

SEVEN
LOVE AND LOSS

You never forget your first sight of New York City. It's a view that you think you know so well, from countless movies and TV shows, yet nothing can truly prepare you for the shock of seeing it in real life. The Big Apple just looks so huge, so vast, so thrilling. As our tour party swept across Brooklyn Bridge into Manhattan on 18 January 1960, the towering skyline took my breath away.

It felt even more exciting as two limousines had met us at Idlewild airport (today known as JFK). We were a compact tour party. As well as my bandmates, myself and my manager, Tito Burns, Ian Samwell had come along to help out The Shadows – as had my dad, who longed to see just what the US was all about.

Here we were. In America. In New York City.

In my dream.

I felt like I was standing at the centre of the world.

We weren't actually starting our tour in New York – that was to get under way in Canada, a few days later. But we had two days to walk around NYC, craning our necks at the skyscrapers and soaking up the yellow taxis and the steam billowing up from the sidewalks, just like it does in the movies.

While we were there, I appeared on ABC TV on *The Pat Boone Chevy Showroom*, a variety show hosted by the easy-listening star. I had to do some cringy scripted banter with him. Pat was pretending to be frightfully English, saying, 'Top hole, whizzo, spiffing!' I looked baffled, then whipped out an English-American dictionary.

The tour was like a much bigger version of The Kalin Twins' package show I had done in the UK. It was called The Biggest Show of Stars for 1960 and the headline act was Frankie Avalon. Frankie's family-friendly rock and roll had made him a star in America, with Number 1s like 'Venus' and 'Why'. They had been minor hits in Britain but not as impactful.

There were ten acts altogether. Two teenage US rock and rollers, Bobby Rydell and Freddy Cannon, were on the bill, as were Johnny and the Hurricanes, soul/R&B acts The Isley Brothers and Sammy Turner, and doo-wop band The Crests, who had had a big hit with '16 Candles'. Also, there was Clyde McPhatter, the great former singer of The Drifters, the band who had made us change our name to Cliff Richard & The Shadows.

Across the poster advertising the tour ran a sash that contained the exciting, if flawed, words:

EXTRA ADDED ATTRACTION: CLIFF RICHARDS, ENGLAND'S NO. 1 SINGING SENSATION!

Cliff Richards! Maybe Ian Samwell's cunning plan about taking the 's' off the end of my name wasn't so foolproof, after all . . .

The tour travelled around on two Greyhound buses and we left New York on 21 January to make the long haul up to Montreal for the first gig. I felt a little overwhelmed by it all and was so nervous before the show that I puked up in the wings waiting to go on. But I didn't need to be. Because it was such a big bill, we were only playing five songs – Chuck Berry's 'Forty Days',* 'A Voice in the Wilderness' (from the *Expresso Bongo* soundtrack), 'My Babe', 'Living Doll' and 'A Whole Lotta Shakin' Goin' On'. Apart from 'Living Doll', it was a high-octane set and it went down brilliantly.

Every night, there were three acts that rocked the house and had the crowds baying for more: Clyde McPhatter, Bobby Rydell, who had a big US hit at the time with 'Wild One' . . . and us! We were getting an amazing reception, so much so that the artists who followed us on were having trouble getting going – it was The Kalin Twins all over again.

This is it! I thought. *We're going to make it here! America loves us!* It was such an incredible high.

Oddly enough, Frankie Avalon, the headliner, didn't go down all that well. He was a nice, good-looking guy and he came out and crooned *'Oh Veee-nus! Oh Veee-nus!'* every night, but the fans didn't go wild for him. It made me feel even more grateful for the dream reception that we were getting.

---

* Chuck's original version of the song was called '30 Days (To Come Back Home)'. But Ronnie Hawkins & The Hawks had changed it to 'Forty Days' when they had a US hit with it in 1959, and we stuck with that version.

We swung through the States for a month, mostly driving between shows by night. Racism and segregation were still rife in the US at the time, particularly in the South. We were not allowed to travel on the same bus as the Isleys or Clyde McPhatter, or to stay in the same hotels.

How stupid! I loved the Isleys' music, and Sammy Turner's 'Always', with its great brass section, is still one of my favourite songs of all time. When I first heard them, I had no idea what colour those artists were . . . and why should I care? We all hung out at the venues and were in and out of each other's dressing rooms all the time. Who on earth was to say that we could not travel on a tour bus together? Thank God those awful days are gone!

In Texas, we played Lubbock, Buddy Holly's birthplace and hometown. His widow and some of his family came to see us and were very moved because they said that Hank, on stage in his big glasses, was the absolute spitting image of Buddy. They were lovely people.

The only slight, nagging negative aspect of the trip was that nobody from our US record label bothered to come and see or meet us, even once. That felt odd but, looking back, it also set the tone for what was to always happen, or *not* happen, to my career in the States.

My father had a wonderful time on the tour. He fell in love with America and he was so happy and proud to see how well I was going down each night. Even so, he was always a robust critic: 'You are very good, Harry!' he would tell me. 'But why can't you sing *harder*, like Jerry Lee Lewis or Little Richard?'

'I sing like *me*, Dad,' I would tell him. I must admit, his criticism stung me and stayed with me – in any case, how could I sing 'harder'?*

Dad may have loved America at first sight, but our punishing tour schedule, with its late nights and overnight drives, was not good for his health. Combined with his non-stop smoking, it made him ill as The Biggest Show of Stars for 1960 wended across the US. He caught a bad flu and it stayed with him for the rest of the trip.

Dad was a prodigious smoker. He invariably had a cigarette on the go in India and, when we moved to England, he switched to Woodbines because we were poor and they were the cheapest brand. He was a twenty-a-day man, possibly even more (by contrast, I have never smoked, but not on health grounds – I hate the smell).

I'd love to say that my management had learned not to overwork me from the previous incident when I lost my voice and collapsed, but Tito soon repeated Franklyn's mistake of working me to death. Towards the end of the US tour, in mid-February, I did a ludicrous thing – I went back to England for one night.

NME had named me Best British Male Singer in their annual poll and so I flew back to get the award at their Poll Winners' Concert at the Wembley Empire Pool. Eddie Cochran, Gene Vincent and Billy Fury performed. I was well used to screaming by then, but the noise when I walked on stage nearly took the roof off.

---

* Actually, my singing did get a little harder, over the years. I think Dad would have been pleased.

Amazingly, after that, still jet-lagged and half-asleep, I was rushed to Oxford Street to headline *Sunday Night at the London Palladium*. It was a ridiculous schedule, The Shadows had wisely not made the trip and I knew that my performance on the TV show had been tired and underwhelming. I hated that.

The sole good thing about my daft one-day dash to England was that when I flew back, Mum came with me. She joined Dad and saw the last couple of dates of the tour; and then, back in New York, I had a very auspicious encounter.

Tito Burns had somehow arranged for us to meet Elvis's legendary manager, Colonel Tom Parker. We went to his office and chatted about whether he might be able to do anything to help me break America.

Colonel Parker was a quite tall, imposing man, and yet I was surprised at just how *normal* he seemed. There was no real indication that he managed the biggest music star on the planet, and he sat and chatted with us amiably.

Our meeting was during the late morning and, when it ended, the Colonel gave us an invitation: 'Would you guys like to have lunch with me?'

'Yeah, we'd love to!' we said, eagerly, picturing the best high-end restaurants that Manhattan had to offer. But, instead, Colonel Parker reached into his desk and handed each of us a pack of sandwiches!

* * *

It had been hard work but I had loved everything about the US. I hadn't made any huge breakthrough there yet commercially, but I was sure it was only a matter of time. Back home in England, I indulged my love of all things American by trading in my Sunbeam Alpine and buying a big red-and-white Ford Thunderbird.

My fame in England was reaching new heights. When word got out that my family and I had moved to Winchmore Hill, fans began flocking to the house in north London and hanging around outside. We had to add an extra two feet to the top of the garden fence to give us some privacy.

That spring of 1960, I had another Number 1 with 'Please Don't Tease'. I was particularly happy about this because the song was co-written by Bruce Welch, with Pete Chester. It was always great to have a big hit, but they felt even better when they were home-grown. And when it was knocked off Number 1, it was a bittersweet experience . . . because it was The Shadows that did it.

As well as being my backing band, The Shadows had their own contract with Columbia. A musician friend gave them an instrumental number called 'Apache'. It was a catchy tune, and a guy who worked as our publicist asked if I could play on it. He knew having a hit with an instrumental wasn't easy and thought my name might help. I tapped out the drum beat at the start of the song and the PR put out a press statement:

CLIFF RICHARD PLAYS ON HIS BAND'S NEW SINGLE!

As anybody who saw me trying to play the bongos in *Expresso Bongo* will know, I am no drummer (!) but the ploy worked. It got 'Apache' some attention, and because it was a great melody, it went to Number 1. Well, if anybody was going to knock me off the top, I was glad it was them.

In any case, The Shadows and I immediately had even more pressing business on our minds – because we had embarked on a massive six-month residency at the London Palladium. The deal was arranged by Tito Burns with Leslie Grade, one of the legendary family of British show business impresarios, who was then working as an agent. Leslie was famously driven, but when we went to his office, he was affability personified and seemed to care about us as artists and as people.

The Palladium show was called *Stars in Their Eyes* and was a typical variety package. It included Joan Regan, the singer, pianist Russ Conway and two comedians in Billy Dainty and Des O'Connor. We got very friendly with Des, who would also occasionally come on tour with us and be our compère.

The Shadows and I headlined *Stars in Their Eyes*, playing five songs at the end of each show, six nights per week. It was great fun, not at all demanding, and also gave us the opportunity for another interesting sideline.

Because I had listened to Radio Luxembourg since I was a boy, I was delighted when we were asked to make a weekly programme for the station. Once a week, we would pop along from the Palladium to their nearby studio in Hertford Street and record a fifteen-minute show.

The show's format was very easy-going: 'What's in the chart?' we would ask. 'Oh, Ray Charles has a new one out – let's play that!' We would play Elvis songs, or Ricky Nelson. The Luxembourg producers would record us and then broadcast the shows on the weekends.

I met a dancer at the Palladium shows called Delia Wicks. We did a little routine together where I sang her a song and then gave her a kiss. However, at the time I was more concerned with the fact that I was back in touch with Carol Costa.

It has been well documented that I had an inappropriate relationship with Carol. It's not a topic that I want to revisit here: should people wish to read about it, they can do so elsewhere. It was a mistake, the kind that people often make in life. All I will say now, sixty years on, is that I wish Carol well and I always will.

The Shadows and I were living in each other's pockets. We were not just playing Palladium shows six nights per week, but also making a new album. Our efforts came to fruition when *Me and My Shadows* was released in October 1960.

We once again made the record in Abbey Road studio two, produced by Norrie Paramor, and I was particularly proud of this album. We had written over half of the songs ourselves, which was still rare at this time. Jet and I wrote a song together called 'I Love You So' and Bruce and Hank wrote 'You and I'.

Yet my love for *Me and My Shadows* went beyond mere song-writing credits. Previously, we had just been aping the American art form of rock and roll. Now, it felt to me like, although still influenced by America, we sounded British – European, even. We had reached a musical maturity.

The slick new Stratocaster that I had given Hank helped, of course! Years later, Peter Green from Fleetwood Mac was to tell me that *Me and My Shadows* had helped to shape his band. 'We cut our teeth on that record,' he said. I felt so proud!*

Like *Cliff Sings* before it, *Me and My Shadows* peaked at Number 2 in the UK albums chart. It was kept off the top by the soundtrack from *South Pacific*, the screen version of the Rodgers and Hammerstein Broadway show, which, on and off, was unbelievably to spend well over a year at Number 1 in 1959–60. Now *there's* something you'd just never see happen nowadays!

It felt like everything we touched turned to gold. At the end of 1960, The Shadows and I released a song called 'I Love You' as a single. It followed 'Please Don't Tease' to Number 1 – and was top of the chart on Christmas Day. What a fantastic end to the year!

* * *

My music career could not have been in better shape at this point, but, sadly, there was a dark cloud gathering over my home life. Since we had come back from America, my dad had been ailing. His constant smoking and debilitating flu had left him finding it difficult to breathe and he had given up Atlas Lamps and was spending a lot of time lying on the sofa at home.

Dad was now officially working with me. Because I was still under twenty-one, he had to approve all of my contracts, so it made sense for him to focus on that full time. I was pleased he no longer had to trudge off to his office every day.

---

* Today, it's common knowledge that Hank and our groundbreaking Stratocaster went on to influence many now-famous guitarists, from Eric Clapton to Mark Knopfler and Chris Rea.

My relationship with Dad changed in these months. I always loved him, but the main emotions he triggered in me were often respect and a little fear. He was always in total control of our household and what he said went, regardless of any fame and success I may have had.

Now he was physically poorly, Dad had no choice but to let me take more of a lead role. As well as being the main breadwinner, I also took on the kind of DIY jobs around the house that he would *never* have let me do before. He became a little less of a disciplinarian.

Just after Christmas 1960, Dad's health grew worse and he had to go into hospital. It was a worrying time, but he picked up a little in there and after a few days the hospital sent him home. He was mostly bed-ridden and all we could do was hope that he would recuperate.

The Shadows and I went out on another UK mini-tour at the start of '61. It was a lot of fun and we enjoyed ourselves, both on stage and with a few little parties afterwards. I was always fairly moderate but some of the others – Jet especially – liked to go to town.

One night, we all had rooms along the same corridor in a hotel. We were in and out of each other's rooms, guests and fans were coming and going, and as I walked along the corridor late at night, I almost fell over Bruce. His room door was open and he was lying, half-asleep, with his body in his room and his head in the corridor, resting on a pillow.

'Bruce, what on earth are you doing?' I asked him.

'I don't want to miss anything!' he declared.

Like Hank, Bruce has always been a master of one-liners.

By now, the fans' hysteria around us was out of control. People would do anything to try to get to us. One girl posted her marriage banns in her local church, claiming she and I were going to get married. I had never even met her! Nor did I know the lady who wrote to me with the big news that I had fathered her child in Brighton.

In Edinburgh, a big, heavy box addressed to me was delivered to the venue before the show. It looked as if somebody had sent me a TV, or a stereo. When I opened it, out jumped a girl! I nearly had a heart attack!

'Can I have your autograph, please?' she asked, cheerily.

* * *

Back home, after the tour was over, Dad was still very ill but that didn't stop him being active in my career. He had been increasingly unsure that Tito Burns was the man to manage me, and was thrilled when he persuaded Peter Gormley to take over.

An amiable, bluff, middle-aged Australian, Peter was already managing yodelling country singer Frank Ifield. He had also recently taken on The Shadows and Dad felt that he could trust him to look after me. It was to be the last thing my father did for me. How prescient he was.

Peter came to one of our shows and then met me for a chat. He was smart, friendly, polite, quietly spoken and obviously shrewd. I took to him straight away and was really happy when he took over. He was to manage me for the next twenty-five years.

It felt like the world was opening up for me and The Shadows and, after America, we were about to investigate another exotic corner of it. In March 1961, we embarked on a short tour of South Africa.

It was mind-blowing. We knew that our singles had done well there but we had no idea of the ferocity of the reception that was awaiting us. When we landed in Johannesburg, the runway was packed with screaming fans and people waiting to greet us.

I had never met the South African golf star Gary Player, and I still haven't to this day, but he had loaned me his red sports car to drive me from the airport. When I climbed in with his driver and we set off for our hotel, the fans from the airport followed us in a convoy of motor scooters and bicycles.

All the way to Eloff Street in the city centre, where we were staying, crowds lined the roads and people hung out of windows, waving. I waved back to them the whole way. It was a small taste of what the Queen has to do! On the radio, the local station gave a running commentary on our progress: 'Cliff is turning into Eloff Street now . . .'

Now this really WAS like a dream!

As security shepherded me into the hotel, a fan caught hold of my woollen tie and yanked it. I managed to grab the top so I didn't get choked, but by the time I got inside, the tie was hanging down by my knees.

The crowd showed no sign of dispersing so the police asked if I would wave to them. My room had a tiny balcony and when I stepped out onto it, the people seemed to stretch as far as the eye could see. Even had I spoken Afrikaans, they wouldn't have heard me over the screams.

The shows in Johannesburg and Durban were amazing . . . but also disturbed me. I was not at all worldly in my teens and had no interest in politics, so the reality of the evil apartheid system in South Africa had passed me by. It came as a shock to realise that black people were not allowed to come to our gigs.

Playing to just white faces felt wrong, so we pulled out the stops and managed to arrange shows in black townships in Cape Town and Durban, with profits going to an African charity. I resolved that the Shadows and I would never again play to whites-only apartheid audiences in South Africa.

When we got home, it was evident to me at once that Dad was going downhill. We were all really worried about him and one day, in desperation, I phoned up Leslie Grade and told him how ill my father was. Leslie took control immediately.

'Stay where you are,' he told me. 'Don't do anything and don't say anything to your dad. I'm sending a doctor straight away.'

Leslie sent his own private physician around. The guy took one look at Dad and said, 'He should be in hospital.' He made a phone call, an ambulance arrived and my father was admitted to Highlands Hospital in Enfield.

Even in this parlous state, Dad remained his own worst enemy. He had to be puffing on a fag, whatever the cost. He had always been an inventive character, keen to understand how things work and great at making things – look how he had built our furniture when we couldn't afford to buy any – and in the hospital, he turned this talent to nefarious ends.

The doctors had put Dad inside an oxygen tent to help his breathing. It zipped up from the outside, but he still managed to hide a safety pin in his bed so that he could undo it from the inside and have a sneaky cigarette. He was totally incorrigible. The nurse caught him at it and zipped him up again.

Dad was so tough and resourceful that I always thought that he was indestructible. I was sure the medics would save him and he would pull through – but it was not to be. He died on 15 May 1961, aged just fifty-six.

He was a tough taskmaster, and he was not always easy on me, but my father had done so much for me and shown such faith in me. I was devastated by his death. My stiff-upper-lip upbringing has often made me loath to show public emotion, but I sobbed like a baby at Dad's funeral and I didn't care who saw me.

There are so many things in my life and my career that I would have loved my dad to see, but I'm so pleased that at least he saw me have hit records, and headline the London Palladium, and that he came to America with me. He saw the start of my success.

More than fifty years on, I still dream about Dad sometimes. In that dream, I know that he is dead but *there he is*, alive again, in front of me, the same as he always was. And every time I wake up from the dream contented, happy and pleased to have seen him again.

But back in 1961, I was only twenty and I had lost my dad. I knew I would miss him so much, even the memory of his little *jhaps*! My mum seemed lost without him and it was an incredibly sad and difficult time for our whole family. Whatever happened next, I knew that my life would be very different from now on.

EIGHT

'THAT LOVELY, CHUBBY CLIFF RICHARD!'

The death of my father had left an enormous hole at the heart of our family and I knew it was down to me as the only son to try and help fill it. Even though Dad had always been the head of the family, and that was how it should be, I suppose in some ways I had become the main breadwinner for a little while now. I was selling a lot of records and making a lot of money, and more than anything, I wanted to make sure Mum and my sisters were OK.

The first new duty fell to me very quickly. My eldest sister, Donna, was due to get married to her boyfriend, Paul, a few weeks later, and after Dad's death, she came to me in tears.

'I don't know who's going to give me away, now,' she sobbed. 'Would you do it, please?'

I was happy to, both because I wanted to help Donna and because I knew how proud Dad would have been to walk her down the aisle. They were married in Waltham Abbey, not too far from Cheshunt, and I tried to represent Dad as well as I possibly could.

It took weeks and months for our family to come to terms with the death of Dad, and I myself had to go on a long, spiritual journey to do so. At the time, I was at least grateful that my next major work project was to be fairly local, meaning that I could spend a lot more time at Winchmore Hill. I was going to make another movie.

It was a very different beast from *Serious Charge* or *Expresso Bongo*. Leslie Grade and his people were keen on filming a musical with me as the star and had been trying to talk me into signing up for quite a few months by this point. I wasn't sure, at first, partly because it seemed like another big step away from rock and roll, the thing I did best. However, I slowly came around to the idea – after all, hadn't Elvis made plenty of musical films? – and eventually I agreed to it on certain conditions.

'OK,' I told the film's producer, Kenneth Harper, 'I'll do it as long as The Shadows are in it, as well. And they have to be able to write some new, original Cliff and The Shadows songs for the soundtrack.' Which they were to do, alongside two film composers.

We had a deal, and the script that Harper came to me with was for a film called *The Young Ones*. It told the story of a young singer, Nicky, who united with his chums to stage a musical show to raise funds to save their Soho youth club, which was scheduled to be demolished to make way for an office block.

The architect of this scheme was a property developer, Hamilton Black, to be played by the redoubtable Robert Morley. And the sting in the tale was (spoiler alert: if you have never seen *The Young Ones*, look away now!) that Hamilton Black was Nicky's father.

It looked like a lot of fun, and so it proved when filming began in the early summer of '61 at Elstree Studios. But this didn't mean that I wasn't apprehensive. I had had decent parts in my previous two films, but this time around, it was very different: I was the star name.

The Young Ones was being trailed as a Cliff Richard vehicle, which meant that I would carry the can if it flopped. Neither had I ever filmed, or been in, a musical before. These thoughts were all playing on my mind on my first day on set, when I was introduced to the venerable Robert Morley.

'I'm nervous,' I confessed to him.

'Dear boy, we're *all* nervous! *I'm* nervous!' he replied in his inimitable style. And this was a giant who'd starred in classic films like *The African Queen*, with Humphrey Bogart and Katharine Hepburn! It helped set my mind at rest a little to realise that even huge stars like him could suffer the same butterflies as I was feeling.

With our age difference and everything, I never got all that close to Robert, but he was a real sweetheart. One day, we were all halfway through filming a big scene when the director, Sidney J. Furie, suddenly yelled, 'Cut!' The scene had been going well, but he didn't look at all pleased.

'Somebody has left a radio on somewhere!' he announced. 'The sound man is picking it up. Who the *hell* has done that?'

Oops! I remembered I had been listening to music in my dressing room before I was called to the set, and had forgotten to turn the wireless off. I was just about to confess my crime, when . . .

'I'm sorry, my dear fellow, I think I may have left the horse racing on in my room,' fibbed Robert Morley. 'I'll turn it off straight away!' And he nipped to my dressing room and turned my radio off. *That* was cool.

I made a whole load of amazing new friends as I filmed *The Young Ones*. The Shadows didn't have acting roles in the end, just played music, but I had a bunch of co-stars who were all about my age. We were not only to work together for years, but become great friends.

Melvyn Hayes, Teddy Green, Richard O'Sullivan and I were like a little gang, really tight on and off the set. We had such a good time that sometimes we would burst out laughing that we were actually being paid to have such fun. I think that camaraderie came across in the movie.

The film climaxed with a variety show in the youth club that saw us perform a specially written vaudeville number called 'What D'You Know, We've Got A Show'. We were in tears of laughter filming it, but it was later to come back to haunt me, thousands of miles away, a few months later . . .

* * *

While making *The Young Ones*, I was dating Delia Wicks, the dancer I had met during the Palladium residency the previous year. She was a great girl and we were close but, as ever, we had to keep a low profile so that the press wouldn't find out about us, spill the beans and dismay my fans. How things have changed!

We wrapped up the filming of the movie in the summer and I took off with The Shadows on a short, freezing tour of Scandinavia. I've been back a lot of times since and, believe me, summer is *definitely* the best time to go! I sent postcards to Delia in London from every town. However, I was about to meet a girl who would make an even bigger impression on me.

Peter Gormley, my new manager, had booked The Shadows and me in to do a summer season at the Opera House in Blackpool. We had done two shows in the same venue the year before, but this was to be a full six weeks in the northern capital of sea, sand and kiss-me-quick hats.

We were to headline the kind of old-school variety show that had jugglers, comedians and dancers. One of the dance troupe members was a girl called Jackie Irving. She was nineteen and extremely beautiful, and soon she and I were virtually inseparable.

Jackie was a local girl and her parents ran a B&B in Blackpool. That summer, she and I pretty much became an item and hung out all of the time at the shows and in our spare time. Jackie was such a good laugh and, of course, a great person to go dancing with!

Delia, by this time, was dropping out of my life and we had never been 'committed' anyway, so I didn't feel I was doing anything wrong in seeing Jackie. In any case, my attention was about to be distracted by a very pressing band personnel problem.

The Shadows contained two individuals who had extremely different, irreconcilable personality traits. Bruce Welch was a perfectionist and a stickler for punctuality. He was invariably the first person in the studio, or on the tour bus, and he believed lateness to be a crime bordering on a sin.*

Tony Meehan was the exact opposite. It's funny that the secret of great drumming is timing because, offstage, our drummer had no notion of time whatsoever. I lost count of how often we had kicked our heels in soundchecks or hotel foyers waiting for him.

Once, we were due to leave a boarding house at ten to drive to our next show. The rest of the band got up at eight, had breakfast and were packed and ready. When Tony wandered down at five to ten and began ordering scrambled eggs, we had had enough and left him behind to find his own way to the next town.

It all came to a head in October '61. I hate confrontation and so I am pleased I wasn't there when Bruce and Tony had a huge bust-up over something or other (I'm not a gambling man, but I would have a big bet that it was time-keeping!). Tony had had enough and walked out, informing Hank and Bruce as he went that they could stick their band.

In fairness, Tony later said that he had just had his first kid, he was never home and our schedule wasn't fair on his family. I can see that – we worked non-stop in those years. In any case, our

---

* Bruce is still the same today. If you dare to get to the studio even five minutes late, you will be greeted by a cold glare and one accusatory, barked word: 'Waiting!' It became Bruce's catchphrase nearly sixty years ago, and it still is – only now it's a joke!

manager sprang into action and recruited a new drummer: Brian Bennett, who used to play in Marty Wilde's band, The Wildcats.

Peter had no choice but to move quickly because we had another exciting jaunt coming up: we were making our first trip Down Under, to play dates in Australia and New Zealand. We were to fly to Oz, via shows in Singapore and the Philippines, on my twenty-first birthday – 14 October 1961. Norrie Paramor had decided to mark this special occasion by releasing a new LP on the same day, so we had gone into the studio to record the album, *21 Today*.

The record opened with Hank's distinctive echoed Strat sound leading The Shadows in an instrumental version of 'Happy Birthday' and had our covers of both Chuck Berry's 'Forty Days' and the old Broadway number 'Tea for Two'. There were a few self-written songs, including 'Without You', which I wrote with Hank and Bruce.

By now, my fame was at its most extreme yet. Jan Vane, who was still running the fan club, told me that I had received more than thirty thousand birthday cards – you would need a very long shelf to put all *those* up! And, while I was out in Australia, *21 Today* became my first UK Number 1 album.

The shows were all sold out, the Australian fans were screaming and I enjoyed lapping up the bonus sunshine as Cliff Richard & The Shadows toured the Antipodes. The experience gave me a taste for spending winters away from cold old Blighty that persists to this day.

Australia is a tremendous country and we all loved the people, the amazing nature and landscapes, and performing there.

And when we flew back at the end of the year, 1962 got off to an even better start.

The Young Ones' premiere in Leicester Square was a glamorous and glitzy affair and the film was a big hit. The reviews were mostly very positive about the film *and* my performance, and so many people flocked to see it that it ended up being the second most popular film of 1962, behind *The Guns of Navarone* (which, in fairness, is a great movie!). Better still, the soundtrack went to Number 1 in the albums chart – and when we put out 'The Young Ones' as a single, it went straight to the top of the chart in its week of release, something that hardly ever happened. Suddenly, we felt as if we had the Midas touch.

There was only one minor drawback to the success of *The Young Ones* (although I found it very upsetting at the time!). I used to be a big *Coronation Street* fan and was watching the soap one night when one of the characters mentioned me.*

Ena Sharples, the show's hairnet-wearing battleaxe played by Violet Carson, was sat in the snug in the Rovers Return with two friends talking about musical films. They mentioned *Annie Get Your Gun* and *West Side Story* before sweet little Minnie Caldwell brought things up to date with *The Young Ones*.

'Isn't Cliff Richard a lovely, chubby lad?' she added.

---

* I used to love *Coronation Street* and watched it every week – until a few years ago, when I went on tour and asked my sister, Joan, to tape it for me. When I got back, there was a mountain of VHS tapes waiting in my home and I thought, *I can't watch all those!* Last time I saw it, about a year ago, it was full of new, young people and I didn't recognise anyone – except Ken Barlow! He has been around as long as I have!

Chubby? Chubby?! I was horrified – yet, when I went back to *The Young Ones* and watched it again, she was right. The Shadows and I had made the movie not long after our first trip to America, where we had made some very questionable eating decisions. We had pigged out in the States, putting half-milk, half-cream on our morning cornflakes and stopping the tour bus at two in the morning to wolf down steaks and burgers. I'd come back to the UK weighing twelve-and-a-half stones, the heaviest I'd ever been.

The fat-shaming Minnie goaded me into action and I went straight on a diet. I slimmed down to eleven stone, and nearly sixty years later, on the eve of my eightieth birthday, I am almost the same weight today. So, well done, Minnie!

By now, Jackie Irving had moved down from Blackpool to live in London and I was still seeing a lot of her. My career was going great guns, I was dating a fantastic girl, I should have felt on top of the world. And yet, increasingly, I was realising that I didn't.

Sure, I still loved having Number 1 records, being on the front of magazines and having thousands of girls screaming at me – who wouldn't? I wasn't crazy! I was still living the dream.

Yet at the same time, on another level, it was all starting to feel a little hollow and unsatisfying. I couldn't have articulated my doubts at this point even if anybody had noticed and asked me, which nobody did, but deep in my subconscious, a thought was stirring:

This can't be it.
This can't be everything.
There must be more to life than this.

I knew how lucky I was, and I was grateful, and yet, in some ways, it almost seemed success had come too easily. My first ever single had been a hit, I had been a pop star by seventeen and my first major movie was a runaway success. But when you have success after success after success as young as I was – well – great as it is, after a time it becomes routine. It doesn't fulfil your deeper needs. So why was I feeling so empty, so lost?

I was still a long way from getting over Dad's death. If I compared my life to his, and how he had always worked so hard, and raised four kids in what was, for years, grinding poverty, it made me feel oddly guilty. It even made what I was doing seem empty. Almost futile.

Every day, I missed Dad so much. While in Australia, I had seen an advert for a medium who claimed to put people in touch with the dead. He was probably a con artist – such people often are – but I gave serious thought to going to see him, or someone like him in England.

It would be wrong to exaggerate the depth of my angst at this time, because so much in my life was going well, but I was casting around for extra meaning and direction. And my first guidance was to come from an unexpected source: a voice within The Shadows.

Since Jet Harris and Carol Costa had split a few months earlier, Jet's drinking had been getting worse and he was starting to be a bit of a liability in the band. He would turn up to studios late, or drunk, and get into fights in bars. Peter Gormley could see the problem and began scouting around for a possible replacement.

Our new drummer, Brian Bennett, had a good lead to follow. He recommended a young bassist named Brian 'Licorice' Locking, with whom he had played in Vince Taylor's band. We all liked Licorice when we met up with him, so that was it: he was in and Jet was out.

Jet took the news of his firing reasonably stoically when Bruce broke it to him, but maybe he had seen it coming. He quickly got a solo record deal and had a hit that summer with 'The Man with the Golden Arm', which took us all by surprise.

Jet then teamed up with Tony Meehan and they had a few hits as a duo the following year, including a Number 1 with 'Diamonds'. Sadly, drinking then took over his life and he ended up working manual jobs before finally getting sober, nearly thirty years later.

We all wished Jet well when he left, but we knew he couldn't have gone on in the band the way he was and I suspect, in his heart, *he* knew it, too. At the time, I wasn't very involved in his departure because I was busy getting ready to leave for Athens. I had another movie to make.

* * *

The Young Ones had been such a huge success that Leslie Grade was very keen to make a follow-up musical. Working on the sound basis that if it ain't broke, don't fix it, producer Kenneth Harper recast as many stars of the first movie as possible.

The film was to be called *Summer Holiday* and I liked the sound of it immediately. It took the gang from the first film – me, Melvyn Hayes and Teddy Green, and new boy Jeremy Bulloch – and transplanted us to Greece on holiday. And how were we to get there? On a double-decker London bus!

The idea was so simple that it was brilliant. We played three young mechanics in a bus depot, unable to afford expensive plane tickets to Athens, who persuade our boss to lend us a double-decker to drive down through Europe. On the way, we hook up with three girls – and I met one of the best friends I've ever had.

Una Stubbs and I hit it off from the start. Three years older than me, she had been working as a dancer in London, including in Lionel Blair's dance troupe. She was sweet, funny, ditzy and great company, and we just clicked as soon as we met.

There was no question of any romance between us, although I loved her and still do to this day. Una quickly slotted in with me, Melvyn, Teddy and Jeremy to become a much-loved member of our little gang.

The producers considered casting a very young Barbra Streisand as my love interest, and even went to see her in the chorus line of a New York show but, in the end, they went with Lauri Peters, a teenage American dancer who had been in *The Sound of Music* on Broadway. Lauri was dating the soon-to-be-legendary US actor Jon Voight and, to our amazement, flew back to New York every weekend to see him. Now *that* is love!

The Shadows had minor, comic parts in the film and also wrote songs for the soundtrack. Bruce Welch and Brian Bennett came up with a stunner. Sometimes you know a song is a hit the second you hear it, and that was certainly true of the insanely catchy theme tune:

We're all going on a summer holiday . . .

Bruce and I also wrote a song that some people say has become my theme tune (!): 'Bachelor Boy'. It wasn't going to be in the film until the producers decided the movie was a little too short after the edit and so we filmed an extra scene (with a slightly camp little dance) of us singing 'Bachelor Boy'. *Summer Holiday* was not to be released until the beginning of the following year, but we had plenty to occupy us in the meantime – because we were making a return trip to America.

Although our previous visit had yielded no commercial breakthrough, Norrie Paramor was keen for us to have another crack and so he and Peter Gormley arranged a month-long States tour. These shows had an odd format: the first half of the evening was a showing of *The Young Ones* (which was just coming out in America and had been re-titled *Wonderful to be Young* – don't ask me why!) and the second half was a gig.

America has never worked out for me and this trip was no exception. Our timing was terrible. We arrived in the US in October 1962 to find its citizens understandably somewhat distracted: the nation appeared to be on the verge of nuclear war with the Soviet Union.

The Soviet premier, Nikita Khrushchev, had parked his nuclear missiles in Cuba, pointing at the States, and there was a deadly stand-off between him and the US president, John F. Kennedy. No one wanted to back down and it really did look for a few days as if the outcome would be nuclear Armageddon. In Miami, we saw a tank trundling down the road.

In the circumstances, no one was too bothered about going out to see a rock and roll band from England. They were too busy digging fallout shelters in their gardens! It was the tour where we emptied every venue. In Memphis, we went on stage to find two hundred people in a theatre meant for at least five times that: 'Shall we play for you?' I asked. 'Or would you just like to come backstage and have a cup of tea?'

I made the most of our time in Memphis, though. I was excited to be there because it was the birthplace of my all-time hero, Elvis, and I wasn't going to let the occasion pass without making a pilgrimage to Graceland.

Elvis was not in town at the time – honestly, that guy! He was *never* home when I called! – but Peter Gormley spoke to somebody and even managed to arrange for Elvis's dad, Vernon, to show me around the house. *Wow!*

Vernon Presley was a man of very few words but he walked me around Graceland. It was a really imposing mansion, with colonnades out the front, and I was in awe: *This is where Elvis lives! His bed! His guitars!* One room had a lavish hearth rug with Elvis's face on it. I walked around it carefully.

'I'm not going to tread on his face,' I told his father.

Vernon didn't say anything.

Oh, while I think of it: on another visit to Memphis, years later, my then tour manager, David Bryce, took me to a local restaurant that Elvis went to all the time. I asked the waiter where my hero normally sat and I parked myself in the exact same corner seat.

'What does Elvis usually eat?' I asked him.

'He always orders frogs' legs,' he told me. 'Shall I get you half a dozen?'

I pictured the dainty little nibbles that I had occasionally had when I had been in Paris. 'No, let's get a dozen,' I suggested. The waiter looked surprised but took the order.

When they arrived, they were absolutely massive! They must have very different frogs in Tennessee to Paris, because these legs were like turkey drumsticks. I only managed to eat two, David ate three and we had to send the rest back. I can certainly see why Elvis had weight problems in his later life!

* * *

Memphis was a gas but, on the whole, my 1962 US visit was a troubled tour. The half-empty houses every night were depressing and *The Young Ones* (sorry, I mean *Wonderful to be Young!*) wasn't doing nearly as well as it had in Britain. American producers did their own edit on it and didn't do a very good job. Well, that's my excuse, anyway!

Back in New York, I appeared on *The Ed Sullivan Show*. It was a huge deal – or, rather, it should have been. The programme was the holy grail of American show-business TV. Twenty or thirty million people watched it every week and, of course, it was the show that was later to help The Beatles to break America.

Lucky them! My experience was hugely disappointing. I wanted to play two rock and roll songs but, because my appearance was linked to the film, Sullivan insisted that I had to sing the corny 'What D'You Know, We've Got a Show' from the climax of the movie. He let me do thirty seconds of 'Living Doll', a Top 30 US hit, but then I had to put on a bowler hat and tie-and-tails for this music hall number.

It was so frustrating! Here I was, live on American TV, chirping the kind of vaudeville number that rock and roll had just killed off in England. But Ed Sullivan was never going to budge, so I had no choice.

I heard a theory, many years later, that Colonel Tom Parker, Elvis's manager, was worried about me becoming a rival to Elvis in the US and had sabotaged my chances by leaning on Sullivan to make me sing that cheesy ditty. It may be true, but I really don't want to believe it ... because, when I met the Colonel, he had been a lovely man.

However, this jinxed American tour did yield one of the most crucial conversations of my life. I was still pining for Dad and still dreaming about him. It made me think again about maybe seeing a medium to try to contact him.

One day, in an anonymous hotel room, I was talking about this to our new bass player, Licorice Locking. Unlike Jet Harris, Licorice was a quiet, studious guy who kept himself to himself and I didn't really yet know much about him or what made him tick. I was about to find out.

Casually, I mentioned that I was thinking of finding a medium to try to talk to Dad in the afterlife, if there was one. Licorice was horrified. 'That's a *terrible* idea!' he told me. 'Do you *realise* how dangerous it is? In any case, it is expressly forbidden in the Bible! You must never do that!'

I was shocked by the strength and vehemence of his answer. 'Oh, yeah? Where does it say *that* in the Bible?' I asked him. Licorice at once picked up a copy of the holy book and opened it to Deuteronomy 18:10. He read it aloud:

There should not be found among you any one that makes his son or daughter to pass through the fire, anyone who uses divination, anyone practising magic, anyone who looks for omens or a sorcerer, anyone binding others with a spell, anyone who consults a spirit medium or a fortune-teller, or anyone who inquires of the dead. For whoever does these things is detestable to Jehovah.

Wow! I was amazed that somebody in the band was able to just pick up a Bible and quote from it with such authority and passion. It certainly wasn't something Jet would ever have done! I asked him how he was so well versed in the Scriptures.

It turned out that Licorice was a Jehovah's Witness. He had first got into it via our drummer, Brian Bennett, when they were both in Marty Wilde's band, The Wildcats. Brian had been brought up in a Witness family. He wasn't one himself but his descriptions had piqued Licorice's interest and he had studied the faith before converting to it in 1961.

It was all new to me but I found it fascinating and, after this, Licorice and I had frequent talks about belief and religion in general as we wended our way across the US. Hank was also intrigued by this new conversational angle and often sat, listened and joined in.

In Miami, Licorice took Hank and me to a Jehovah's Witness meeting. It was nothing like a Church of England service: all the congregation introduced themselves, hugged us and were so friendly and the sermons were powerful and dynamic. It was different, and strange, but it spoke to me on an intense level.

OK, I had failed to break America again, but the trip had definitely awoken something in me – something very important. I flew home from the States with a thousand questions in my head. As soon as I got back, I sought out my mum.

'Hey, Mum, I'm getting interested in the Jehovah's Witnesses!' I told her.

'That's strange,' she said. 'So am I!'

What a coincidence! It turned out that an aunty and uncle of Mum's, who had moved back from India a little after us, had converted to the faith and had been talking to her about it. In fact, all of the signs seemed to be that I was about to embark on a spiritual journey . . . the kind that can transform your life for ever.

NINE

'SECRET CONCERT! TEN ESCUDOS!'

It might sound strange to some people that I had any desire at all
to transform my life at the beginning of 1963 – because, if I'm
honest, my life at that time was really pretty brilliant.

Right at the start of the year, there was a star-studded premiere
for *Summer Holiday* at the Warner Theatre in Leicester Square. At
least, I have always been told that it was star-studded. I guess I will
just have to take people's word for it, because I couldn't get in!

The movie's producers had sent a limousine to pick me up
from my home, so Mum, my sisters and I were driven into the
West End with Peter Gormley. As we approached the cinema, we
saw scenes of pandemonium. Thousands of screaming girls
were filling Leicester Square and the police looked to be having
trouble controlling them.

The fans spotted our limo and surged towards it. At which
point, a burly copper opened one of the doors and barked instructions at the driver:

'You can't stop here! Drive on! Now!' he told him.

'But I'm Cliff Richard,' I said. 'It's my movie!'

'I don't care!' said the policeman. 'On your way! *Go!*'

There was no arguing about it, so we inched our way through the girls banging on the limo's windows and went to watch coverage of the night on TV at Peter's apartment in Maida Vale, by Abbey Road studios. I must still be the only star in history to be turned away from his own movie premiere!

Right after this non-event (for me, anyway), I made a return trip to South Africa. This was another great experience. There were crowds waiting for me again, Jackie Irving came with me – she was one of my group of dancers – and we made sure we could play to blacks as well as whites. Unfortunately, there were not many black faces in the audiences, but we would have welcomed them.

The fans went wild for our cover of Chuck Berry's 'Forty Days' from my *21 Today* album. I had no idea why, until somebody explained that young South African guys had to do forty days' national service in places like Mozambique. So they had adopted it as their unofficial anthem.

By the start of 1963, The Beatles were emerging in Britain. They had had a hit with 'Love Me Do', and then 'Please Please Me' was heading up the singles chart. On my South African tour, I was a bit of an unofficial PR man for them.

On my previous trip to the country, I had done many radio interviews and the DJs had all asked if they could play my favourite record by another artist. I hadn't known what to say, so this time I decided to be better prepared and I took a copy of 'Love

Me Do' with me. I told the DJs, 'I wish The Shadows and I had this song, because it's great!' They would play it, and after they had finished, I would ask for the single back so I could take it on to the next station. I even had a little joke about the brand-new hopefuls.

'Do you think they'll be huge?' one presenter asked me.

'I shouldn't think so,' I replied. 'Their name just sounds like something that you tread on!' This was not my finest prediction . . .

Then again, The Shadows and I didn't think The Beatles were anything special at first. Around the time of 'Apache' we had heard them covering some old track or other and they hadn't sounded very good at all. *That* was before they had gone off to Hamburg. Something big must have happened there, because when they came back, they blew everybody away.

Paul McCartney has said in interviews that the main reason the band went to Germany was that 'Cliff and The Shadows had got everything sewn up in Britain'. I knew we were doing well, but I didn't know we were forcing our competition to emigrate! Well, for whatever reason, it worked for them.

When they came back from Hamburg, they were tremendous. In my idle moments, I occasionally wonder: what would have happened had it been the other way round, and The Shadows and I had gone to Germany, rather than The Beatles? Well, it's all speculation. We'll never know.

I was always so busy that I had not met The Beatles in their early days, but that soon changed. After we played a short UK tour when we returned from South Africa, Bruce Welch told me that he was throwing a party in his home, and The Beatles were coming, after their gig at Lewisham Odeon.

It sounded fun, so I headed over. The Beatles were friendly, and smart, and we sat in Bruce's kitchen and chatted away like mad. John Lennon was very funny and asked me to delay releasing my next single to give their follow-up to 'Please Please Me' a chance.

'Oh, what's that going to be?' I asked.

'We dunno yet,' said John. 'But we've got one song we quite like.'

'Here you go,' said Bruce, handing him a guitar that was lying around his kitchen. 'Play it for us!'

The Beatles glanced at each other and shrugged, then John took the guitar, started strumming, and he, Paul and George began singing in perfect harmony:

If there's anything that you want . . .

Wow! The first few bars of 'From Me to You' blew my head off! What a song! But The Beatles seemed totally blasé about it. When they had finished, John put Bruce's guitar down and looked at us.

'We're not quite sure about it,' he said.

'Are you kidding me?' I said. 'That's fantastic! That's your first Number One, right there!'

And I was absolutely right.

* * *

There was so much going on for me at this time. Shortly after we had met The Beatles, the BBC asked if I would host a one-off TV variety programme: *The Cliff Richard Show*. My response was the same as it was to pretty much all of the new, exciting things I was being offered: 'Sure! Why not?'

It all happened so quickly that I didn't have time to be nervous. The Shadows and I played a few songs and I had some great guests – Sid James, the *Carry On* star, and Millicent Martin, with whom I duetted on a Broadway number, 'Happy Hunting'.*

Playing my concerts and doing lots of TV shows, I met so many great stars in the early sixties, even though I was still shy of meeting people I admired. Sadly, I have never been great at keeping photographs, but the few I have trigger wonderful memories. I have a picture of me looking very serious as Liza Minnelli gazes at me at a TV rehearsal – she was just eighteen!

Eartha Kitt was a more formidable proposition. I sang a song on a TV show at the old BBC studio at Wood Green. She was a huge star at the time, and was top of the bill. I thought I was far too lowly for her to bother with, so I was surprised to be given a message: 'Miss Kitt would like to meet you.'

'Really?' *Gulp.* 'OK!'

I was ushered into her regal presence. Eartha was reclining on a chaise longue in her dressing room, like Yolande Donlan in *Expresso Bongo*. She looked me up and down as I tiptoed in nervously.

---

* I became friends with Millie. Today, I still love watching her on TV as the maid's mum, Gertrude Moon, when they show repeats of the American sitcom *Frasier*.

'Er, nice to meet you, Miss Kitt,' I said.

She frowned at me.

'Young men like you,' she drawled, imperiously, 'are making it *very* difficult for people like me!'

'But, Miss Kitt,' I replied, 'young men like me can do *nothing* that would make things difficult for people like you!'

My answer must have pleased her, because she beamed and did her world-famous, trademark purr, like a sexy big cat: *'Grrrrrrrr!'*

I was relieved to re-emerge from the lioness's den unscathed.

* * *

Norrie Paramor was always coming up with innovative new plans to further my career and his next idea was certainly an interesting one. He wanted to make inroads into Europe and decided that I should do an album in Spanish.

My reaction, again? 'Sure! Why not?'

So, Norrie, The Shadows and I decamped to Spain for a fortnight. We recorded in Barcelona and stayed in a one-horse town called Sitges. John Lennon happened to be staying in the same hotel with Brian Epstein, The Beatles' manager. We dined together one night, but we didn't see a lot of them.

Making *When in Spain* was fun. Obviously, I couldn't speak a word of Spanish, but I was given phonetic transcriptions of the lyrics to songs like *'Perfidia'* ('Perfidy') and *'Vaya Con Dios'* ('Go with God'). Norrie would say, 'This is a happy song!' or 'It's a sad one, Cliff!' and off I'd go. Amazingly, this quirky, Spanish-language album was a Top 10 hit . . . in Britain!

Back in England, my path crossed with The Beatles again in that summer of '63. In those days, pop stars still did summer residencies and after our previous successful visits to Blackpool, Peter Gormley booked me and The Shadows in for three months at the ABC Theatre.

It was a fantastic summer. The Shadows and I started off sharing a bungalow in the town, but our fans soon got wind of where we were staying and besieged the place. So, I left the band to it and took off to stay with friends down the road in Lytham St Annes, a posh town just south of Blackpool.

During the summer, The Beatles came to town to play a few one-off ABC shows. We were doing Mondays to Saturdays, and they did one or two Sunday nights. By now, we were experienced in escaping the fans who mobbed the theatre each night, but The Fab Four were not yet so well versed.

When we met up with them in Blackpool, they said that they were planning to walk back to their hotel after the shows. 'You have *no* chance!' I told them. I explained that we sped away from the theatre in a van every night: would they like to borrow it? They did, and they were very grateful for it.

While all of this was going on around me, I was still thinking hard about religion. On tour, Licorice and I would sit up late into the night talking about his faith and what it all meant. There were aspects of it that troubled me, but I found the intensity of his belief seductive.

So, I thought it was a shame when Licorice quit The Shadows, after just eighteen months, that October. He wanted to devote his life to the Witnesses and decided he couldn't do that if he was on tour all the time. His replacement on bass was John Rostill, a nice guy we met in Blackpool.

Still very aware of my new responsibilities to my family since Dad had passed, I was worried the house in Winchmore Hill was no longer the right place for them, or *me*, to live. Scores of fans were beating a path to our door, which had become very intrusive. I was lucky enough to be earning seriously good money by now, so I took a deep breath . . . and bought a mansion.

Rookswood was a very grand house that stood in eleven acres of land in a little village called Nazeing, in the west of Essex. It cost me £11,000, a small fortune in those days. But it had a swimming pool, a tennis court and, most importantly, six bedrooms, which meant Mum, Jacqui, Joan and I could all have our own corner of the house and share the rest. And no one could peer over the fence at us.

That house certainly cost a vast amount more than the one that Peter Gormley bought for me at around the same time. I had not asked him to do anything of the sort and it came as a total surprise. My manager broke the news to me one day while we were having a catch-up meeting: 'Hey, Cliff, guess what? I've just bought you a house!' he told me. 'It's in Portugal!'

I could not have been more flabbergasted if he had told me that he had bought me an igloo in the Arctic. 'What . . . *why*?' I asked. 'I have never been to Portugal, or even thought of going there. I might not like it! Why have you done *that*?'

Peter's reply was sheer, bluff Aussie common sense. He had just been on holiday to Albufeira, a small fishing town in the

Algarve, and had fallen in love with the place. He said houses there were so cheap that he had bought six in one go – one for himself, one for me, one for Bruce Welch, one for Frank Ifield and two for Leslie Grade.

'It's a beautiful place, Cliff – you will love it!' he told me. 'There, you can get away from everything. And if you don't like it, you can just sell it again, right?'

'Hmm . . . I suppose so,' I conceded. But, for now, I had no chance to examine this surprise addition to my suddenly growing property portfolio. I had to go back to Spain. After the success of *The Young Ones* and *Summer Holiday*, producer Kenneth Harper and his team were determined to make another film musical vehicle for me. So, at the start of December 1963, I headed off to the Canary Islands to begin filming *Wonderful Life*.

Summer Holiday director Sid Furie was in place again and a lot of the old gang reconvened for this latest adventure – Richard O'Sullivan, Melvyn Hayes and the lovely Una Stubbs – but *Wonderful Life* was ill fated from the off. Originally, we were going to film it in Mexico, but that would have cost too much, hence downsizing to the Canaries.

Film and TV critics say a series that has lost its way has 'jumped the shark' and, if I'm honest, that's what I think *Wonderful Life* did. It was supposed to be about a bunch of kids, on a movie set, secretly making their own film behind the director's back, but the plot ended up being a little convoluted and not very believable either.

Even the landscape sabotaged us. The sand in that part of the Canaries was volcanic. We would film scenes on lovely golden sand dunes, a little way inland, then return the next day to find overnight rain had turned the dunes black! It made continuity impossible. At times, we had to rewrite the plot as we went along.

There were some fun moments. I loved it when I got to impersonate Charlie Chaplin, Groucho Marx, James Bond and Rudolph Valentino. Being Valentino even allowed me to put on moody kohl eye make-up, like Elvis sometimes did.

The leading lady, Susan Hampshire, was impressive. Where I still sometimes felt I was messing around making movies, Susan was a pukka actress. She thought her face looked too gaunt, so she put cotton wool in her mouth to push out her cheeks and *still* delivered every line immaculately. Classy!

Overall, though, *Wonderful Life* was probably a film too far in that movie-musical series. When it came out, it got worse reviews than *The Young Ones* and *Summer Holiday* had and, thinking back, I'm afraid that it probably deserved them.

Two major things happened while I was in the Canaries. One was that Jackie Irving and I broke up. We had been seeing each other for two-and-a-half years by now, but the truth was that I still found myself thinking more about my career than romance.

I remembered the fan outside the Finsbury Park Empire who had screwed up her programme and thrown it on the ground when she saw Jean sitting on my lap, and I didn't want to throw away all that I had built up. So, I went to talk to Peter Gormley.

'If I were to get married, what effect would it have on my career?' I asked my manager.

'You might lose between ten and twenty-five per cent of your fans,' Peter told me. 'But you would still have enough to be successful.'

Wow! I didn't like *that* estimate at all! It sounded like it would be a major issue for me and I knew instantly I didn't want that to happen. I also realised it wouldn't be fair to mislead Jackie and so I ended it with her.

Ultimately, I think marriage is just not for me. Well, at nearly eighty, I don't suppose it's likely to happen now! *But who knows?*

When two people break up, it is usually one person's fault. In my life, it has always been mine. I guess it's just how I am. Jackie was upset at the time, but she went on to marry Adam Faith and they had a daughter together, Katya. I wished them nothing but happiness.

If I were ever to have had a romance with Una Stubbs, it would have been as we were filming *Wonderful Life*. Her own marriage to Peter Gilmore, who went on to star as Captain James Onedin in the BBC drama *The Onedin Line*, had hit a rough patch and we were both in a strange place. We flirted a little more than usual in the Canaries, but, ultimately, I have always loved Una as a dear friend and, thankfully, that is what we stayed. I am so glad we did.

The other major event while I was in the Canaries concerned my new musical arch-rivals, The Beatles. While I had had two singles – 'It's All in the Game' and 'Don't Talk to Him' – stall at Number 2 in Britain in '63, they had enjoyed three consecutive Number 1s with 'From Me To You', 'She Loves You' and 'I Want To Hold Your Hand' and were about to try to export their success to America.

Where my US record company had always been somewhat lackadaisical and hardly tried to support me in breaking the States, The Beatles' label bosses were far more proactive. Their record label, Parlophone, was owned by my US company, Columbia, but their executives were much cannier. When the band flew into JFK airport at the start of '64, Brian Epstein – it is rumoured – paid thousands of girls to scream at them. It really announced their arrival.

After that, when The Beatles went on *The Ed Sullivan Show*, they took America by storm. It could not have been more different from when I was forced to do a daft music hall turn on the same programme. The wind was behind them, and this was their moment.

I didn't begrudge The Beatles anything. They were a fantastic band who wrote amazing songs and they deserved all they got. At the same time, I got so fed up of their ubiquity at this point that I went to talk to Peter Gormley again.

'Peter, every time I open a paper, all I read about is The Beatles,' I complained. 'It's ridiculous! Has everyone forgotten *me*? What's going on?'

'Cliff, are you still doing concerts?' my manager asked me.

'Yes,' I said. 'You know I am, all the time.'

'And do your concerts still sell out?'

'Yes, every one of them.'

'And was your last record a hit?'

'Yes, they all are.'

(I had just had my twentieth consecutive Top 10 single.)

'So, what the bloody hell are you worrying for then, mate? There's room for everyone!'

He was absolutely right, of course. I was still doing incredibly well and The Beatles' success was a daft thing for me to get het up about. I think, maybe, I just needed a holiday . . . and luckily, thanks to Peter, I now had an exotic new holiday home to escape to.

* * *

The first time ever I went to Albufeira, I thought I had discovered paradise. It was quite hard to get to, in those days. We had to fly into Lisbon and then do a three- or four-hour drive over rough and bumpy roads down to the Algarve.

The Algarve then was nothing like the busy, developed tourist centre it is now. Albufeira was little more than a fishing village nestling on the bottom of a hill. From my neat house, above the beach, it was a five-minute walk to some truly glorious sand.

My house was next door to the one owned by Frank Ifield, another of Peter Gormley's charges. Frank was a nice guy and we hung out now and then. I had always liked the way he yodelled during his songs, although I'd never dared try it myself – yodelling had never been big in Cheshunt!

Now, I could see that Peter's idea had been genius. I could relax in Albufeira, away from the pressures of fame, celebrity and competing for chart places. With Peter, Bruce or whoever was around, I would spend the day sunbathing, either on the beach or else on my roof, listening to my record player. I would put an umbrella over the Dansette so the burning sun didn't melt the vinyl. In the evening, we'd go to the village's one club – *Clube Sete e Meio* (Club Seven-and-a-Half).

We got to know one or two of the local fishermen, who often invited us to join them in one of their houses. There was always a crowd and we'd eat sardines and melons and local bread. Some afternoons, a guitar would come out and we'd have a bit of a sing-song. It was all very laid-back and informal, which is why I was surprised when a girl on holiday from England approached me on the beach one morning.

'I'm coming to see your show today!' she told me, excitedly.

'What show?' I asked. 'I'm on holiday!'

'Your fishermen friends invited me to lunch and said you would sing. It's ten escudos!'

Ha! It seemed the cheeky devils had been pulling a fast one and cashing in on my lunches with them. But it was so funny, and they were so charming, that I really couldn't be cross.

At the *Clube Sete e Meio*, I got very into Fado. For me, it was – and still is – Portugal's soul music. The locals got up and sang, the men with their hands in their pockets and the women wrapped in shawls, and they always sounded so dramatic and passionate and melancholy. The hairs on my arms would stand up.

Norrie Paramor knew everybody, and that included Portugal's most famous Fado singer, Amália Rodrigues. When Norrie came to stay with me in Albufeira, we went to Lisbon and dined at her house. Then Amália stood by her piano, with a guitarist and viola player, and sang. I will never forget it: it was an incredible experience.

So, I came home from my first trip to Albufeira, and my subsequent ones, revitalised, refreshed and ready to face the world once more. Portugal was to become more than a mere holiday home: it was my spiritual second home, bolthole, and special place for more than fifty years. I will always love it.

On my return to Britain in early 1964, it was back to the grind of a London Palladium TV show, a British tour and dates in Europe. It was back to my life . . . but I still had a sense of unease, and of confusion, and a voice that was eating away at me inside my head, becoming increasingly insistent and impossible to ignore.

I really wasn't sure if I wanted to be a pop singer anymore.

TEN
A BIG-HEARTED HELPING HAND

The Shadows and I had always put the world to rights. For years, we had spent hours at a time cooped up together in tour buses, dressing rooms and planes, chatting freely about big topics like religion, politics and sex (though not necessarily in that order!).

In his time with the band, Licorice Locking hugely increased my interest in religion, a subject I had never had much time for prior to my dad's death. I took to taking a Bible on tour with me and perusing it in our downtime. I didn't particularly read the Old Testament, but the New Testament fascinated me – I was amazed how little I knew about it.

Even after Licorice had gone, I carried on thinking seriously about the Jehovah's Witnesses. My mum was close to converting by now, and I liked the strength and security her new faith brought to her life, as it had to Licorice's. Could it also give *me* the peace and the sense of purpose that I craved?

I had my doubts about some elements of the Witnesses' creed. I didn't like their insistence on abstaining from all blood transfusions: from my reading of the Bible, it seemed to be cautioning against drinking the blood of sacrificed animals (which I tend not to do!), not eschewing blood donations. I didn't agree with their interpretation.

But I figured no faith is perfect and I was still considering setting my reservations aside and joining the Jehovah's Witnesses. I had stayed in touch with my old secondary modern teacher, Jay Norris, and the next time that she contacted me, I confided in her.

Jay was calling to invite me to an event she was organising. Every year, on her birthday in July, she would pair her friends up into teams and send them off in their cars, armed with her cryptic rhyming clues, to find landmarks around the local Hertfordshire countryside. It was a lot of fun and I was keen to go along.

Jay was dismayed when I told her that I intended to join the Jehovah's Witnesses. She didn't say much to me on the phone. Instead, she introduced me to a man who was to become one of the most important influences in my life.

A couple of years older than me, Bill Latham was the new religious education teacher at Cheshunt Secondary Modern School. He was also a leader in the Crusaders, an evangelical Christian youth organisation he had belonged to since he was a kid, which ran Bible study classes and outdoor camps for teenagers.

Jay paired me up with Bill for her mystery car rally, and I was later to learn that she had placed him under strict instructions to instigate a religious discussion with me. He was certainly successful with that, as it turned into a heated discussion.

I liked Bill, and we got on well, but as we whizzed around the country lanes looking for Jay's clues and prizes, he certainly made it clear that he didn't agree with what the Jehovah's Witnesses preached and favoured a more open-minded, less judgemental style of Christianity. I found our talk invigorating and wanted to meet up with him again. Over the next few weeks and months, whenever I had time off from my work, we had far-ranging and deep-rooted conversations about spirituality, both at Rookswood and at his home in Finchley, where he lived with his mother, Mamie.

I had so many questions for Bill. Licorice had spurred me to read the Bible closely, yet it threw up so many points I didn't fully understand. Was Jesus truly the son of God, and the only route to God? The Witnesses didn't think so. Another question in my mind was about the Holy Trinity of the Father, the Son and the Holy Ghost – how did *that* work, exactly?

Bill was great to talk to about these things – and, ironically, he was most persuasive because he didn't pretend to have all the answers. 'I'm a Christian, Cliff, and I know a lot of Christian people,' he would tell me. 'I can't answer that particular question, but I know a man who can.'

As we became not just debating partners but also good friends, Bill introduced me to some of his Christian circle. Graham Disbrey, one of his colleagues from Crusaders, came to Rookswood and talked long into the night to Mum and me about God.

Another friend, David Winter, told me: ' "God" isn't His name – it's His occupation.' *Yes, of course!* I thought. That made sense to me, as the Jehovah's Witnesses had said He was called

'Yahweh', or 'Jehovah'. I increasingly found myself moving closer to orthodox Christianity.

Bill also invited me to attend his Crusaders' meetings for teenagers in Finchley. I went along and sat quietly at the back. At first, the kids were surprised to see Cliff Richard in the classes – to say the least! – but they all welcomed and accepted me, and I became engrossed in what was taught there.

* * *

While my spiritual awakening was going on, of course, I still had the little matter of being a pop star. The Shadows may have been slightly nonplussed by my new lifestyle and social circle, but as far as my career was concerned, it was still business as usual.

A big part of my business from 1964 onwards involved going on a new BBC TV show: *Top of the Pops*. I was still having a lot of chart hits in those days, so midweek trips to film the programme – in Manchester initially, then at TV Centre in London – became a regular event.

The whole pop world would be there. I have always kept myself to myself and in those days, I never used to run in and out of other artists' dressing rooms all that much if I didn't know them, but I met so many amazing stars as I hung around waiting to do my turn.

Britain had some great female stars in the mid-sixties. *Top of the Pops* may have been the first place that I met Cilla Black, who had two wonderful Number 1s in '64 with 'Anyone Who Had A Heart' and 'You're My World'. I was also hugely impressed at just how soulful Dusty Springfield and Lulu were.

I got to know the presenter DJs a little. I'd met Pete Murray on TV shows before and Alan 'Fluff' Freeman on his radio show. They were both nice and friendly. Jimmy Savile was a different matter entirely.

Savile was always a very weird man. You could talk to him and never feel as if you had had a conversation. He would just repeat his catchphrases – *'Now then, now then, goodness gracious!'* – and make that bizarre yodelling noise that he used to do. I used to think, *Yes, I know that's your act – but where's the person inside it?*

Over the decades that followed, I was to appear on *Top of the Pops* more times than any other artist (probably because I'm older than everyone!). They used to like you to mime. I always preferred singing live, although the studio acoustics were not great. You wouldn't always sound like your record – but the show certainly sold them!

There was a real camaraderie between the acts on the show – but I once had a weird experience on it. I was on with The Who, and when it came to my turn, they raided a BBC props cupboard for a load of wigs, which they threw at me as I was singing. I have no idea why: maybe because Pete Townshend was losing his hair?!

Having previously seemed indifferent about me, my American label, Epic Records, began to show some interest in trying to break me over there in '64. A senior executive, Bob Morgan, presented Norrie Paramor and me with songs he thought might work in the US and arranged for me to record in Nashville, Chicago and New York.

I went over to the States that summer. Being in Studio B in Columbia Studios, Nashville, was a dream come true because of all of the great music that had been made there by people like The Everly Brothers and, of course, Elvis. Just the thought of it gave me goose bumps.

It took me a little while to get used to Nashville sensibilities, though. Slightly nervous on my first day in the studio, I turned terribly English and enquired of a passing engineer, 'Excuse me, please, how close to the microphone would you like me to stand?'

The gum-chewing guy looked me up and down and smiled. 'Heck, you're the singer! You stand where you darn well want, and we'll do the rest!' he advised me.

Bob Morgan oversaw the sessions. Nashville is famous for country music, of course, and Morgan linked me up with a renowned country producer, Billy Sherrill, and chose a killer C&W-tinged track called 'The Minute You're Gone' for me to sing. We also recorded 'Wind Me Up (Let Me Go)' and 'On My Word'.

Up in New York, Morgan produced the sessions himself and gave me two gorgeous Burt Bacharach and Hal David songs to sing: 'Everyone Needs Someone to Love' and 'Through the Eye of a Needle'. People who know about these things tell me I'm one of only two people ever to have committed the latter song to vinyl. This amazes me. Bacharach and David were geniuses and I can't believe that every single one of their songs hasn't been covered to death. In an ideal world, they certainly would be.

After the excitement of my solo American recording trip, I was back with The Shadows in Britain that autumn. We played a UK tour and then began preparing for another staple of our existence back then: a Christmas pantomime.

The London Palladium asked the band and me to appear in their panto, *Aladdin and his Wonderful Lamp*. I knew this was quite an honour as the Palladium's was the most prestigious panto in the country . . . but I had a few requests before I would agree.

In British pantomimes, a girl traditionally plays the lead role while a man is the dame, but I wanted to play Aladdin. The theatre agreed, so I had a fine time running around stage, singing and summoning up genies. The Shadows became Wishee, Washee, Noshee and Poshee (I'll leave you to work out which one was which!).

Una Stubbs played Princess Badroulbadour and it was lovely to work with her again, while the all-important role of Widow Twankey went to Arthur Askey. Arthur had by then been a comedian, actor and music hall icon for thirty years and was one of the biggest stars in Britain.

It was fierce competition to be in a pantomime with Arthur, who was right at the top of his game. Night after night, he had the audience in stitches with a routine in which he (or rather, his stunt double) dived in and out of a window so fast that he became a blur. Yet he lived up to his stage name of 'Big-Hearted' Arthur Askey by helping me out when one of my jokes was falling flat. I had a line that wasn't working at all, until he took me to one side and gave me the benefit of his three decades of stagecraft.

'Look, son, I'm standing in the middle of the stage and you're at the front, and that's why your line's not getting a laugh,' he said. 'Try walking up to me, going just behind me and *then* saying the line.'

I had no idea why this should make any difference, but the next night I did exactly what Arthur suggested and heard appreciative chuckles from the audience. I was grateful that such a comedy living legend had been kind enough to share his precious know-how.

Early in 1965, Norrie Paramor put out 'The Minute You're Gone' from my Nashville sessions as a single in Britain (the B-side was 'Just Another Guy' by some unknown US songwriter called Neil Diamond). To my delight, it went to Number 1 – the first chart-topping single I had had since 'Summer Holiday', nearly two years earlier.

It was great news. Bob Morgan's strategy was clearly working. If 'The Minute You're Gone' was a big hit in Britain, just *think* how well it would do in country-music-loving America! I eagerly awaited the single's imminent release in the States – only to be dumbfounded by some news from Norrie.

Epic Records in the US had phoned Norrie and told him that they had decided not to put out 'The Minute You're Gone' in America as it was 'not right for their market'. The news absolutely flabbergasted me. I ran it through my head, trying to make sense of it.

So, let me get this straight . . . A country-and-western song, that the US label had asked me to sing, and I had recorded in Nashville with a top C&W producer . . . *was not right for their market? Excuse me?* I didn't know whether to laugh or cry – and it seemed to confirm that my American career was destined to be jinxed.

Yet, disappointing as this news was, it didn't devastate me in the way that it would have done a year or two earlier. It was beginning to feel as if my career, once all-important to me, was now mere background noise to the crucial quest taking place in my head: my need to make sense of religion and my life.

I was still going to Bill Latham's Bible study classes and talking long, hard and passionately with Bill and his fellow Christians as I tried to find my way forward. I was looking to balance the arguments of the Jehovah's Witnesses with those of orthodox Christians, and coming down more and more on the side of the latter.

To me, it all seemed to hinge on the role of Jesus. By now, there was no doubt in my mind that Jesus had lived on Earth. There was as much documentary and anecdotal evidence of His existence as there was of, say, Julius Caesar – and nobody has ever doubted that he existed!

So, as Jesus existed, what excuse did I have for not embracing Him and welcoming Him into my life? I had tried hard to think of one and I had failed to do so. Now, it finally felt like time to make that ultimate leap of faith.

When I met Bill and his friends at his home in Finchley for Bible study and discussion, I was in the habit of crashing out in his mum's spare room to avoid the long journey back to Essex. And so that was where I was on the fateful night that changed my life for ever.

One of Bill's Crusader friends had advised me to read a specific piece of scripture, Revelation 3:20, as it might answer any final questions or doubts that I had remaining. Lying in bed, I flicked open the Bible that I always had with me and read:

> *Behold, I stand at the door and knock. If any man hears my voice and opens the door, I will come in to him, and will sup with him, and he with me.*

I closed the book, and closed my eyes. 'OK, Jesus, I believe in you and I want you to come in,' I said. 'I want you in my life.'

I can't pretend anything spectacular or dramatic happened at that moment. I wasn't serenaded by angels, or bathed in light. I simply fell asleep and woke up the next morning feeling exactly the same as usual. But I had taken the step and I knew that I was now a Christian.

Initially, accepting Jesus into my life was a very private conversion. On the surface, nothing changed. My music career just carried on rolling along. I interrupted a welcome holiday break in Albufeira to travel up to Lisbon with Norrie Paramor to record *When in Rome*, an album of songs in Italian.

Norrie seemed to be pulling me in a more orchestral direction, away from making albums with The Shadows, and, if I'm honest, I just went along with it. My *Love is Forever* album in summer '65 featured two Bacharach/David recordings from my New York sessions, plus easy-listening standards like 'Fly Me to the Moon' and 'Have I Told You Lately That I Love You' – it was certainly a long way from Elvis!

That autumn, The Shadows and I toured a lot, both in the UK and Europe. Nobody who attended those shows would have known that I had become a Christian, or seen any difference in me whatsoever – but people who knew me better could see that I had changed.

While we were in Paris on that tour, I went down to a little bistro next to our hotel to treat myself to a coffee and my favourite French dessert, Mont Blanc. I was sitting happily scoffing puréed chestnuts and whipped cream, and watching the world go by, when I heard someone call my name.

It was a mate from the British music industry whom I had known for years and he joined me for a coffee. We had been chatting away happily about this and that for ten minutes when he went quiet and fixed me with a quizzical look.

'You've changed!' he told me.

'Have I?' I asked, surprised. 'How?'

'Well, for one thing you haven't said "f***!" once!'

'Oh!' I said, taken aback. But he was totally right. When I was a teenager, like any young guy keen to impress, I used the 'f' word left, right and centre. As I'd got older, I'd tried to say it less and for a while I'd asked The Shadows to help me by telling me off if I said it. It hadn't worked. Now, it seemed that without trying, or even thinking about it, I had stopped swearing completely.

Wow! Maybe there was more to this Christian conversion than I had imagined, after all!*

One band that I imagined *did* swear rather more than me were The Rolling Stones. Unlike with The Beatles, I never had any relationship at all with the Stones. Our paths simply never crossed . . . until I had a hit with one of their songs by mistake.

Norrie Paramor, Peter Gormley and I used to have meetings where we'd go through Norrie's piles of song demos and choose what might be good for me to sing. We'd always have three piles of tapes: 'Yes', 'No' and 'Maybe'. Towards the end of '65, we had a session where a song called 'Blue Turns to Grey' turned up.

---

* Today, people occasionally ask me if I ever swear. I tell them the truth: 'No, but I sometimes *think* swear words!'

The tape didn't have any songwriters' names on it but we thought it was a nice song, and would suit me and The Shadows, so we shifted it from the 'Maybe' to the 'Yes' pile. It wasn't until after we recorded it that we knew it had been written by Mick Jagger and Keith Richards. Well, we'd have done it anyway – we had our own sound and our own approach to songs.

Around this same time, I started my own charity – The Cliff Richard Charitable Trust. I was earning very good money by now and knew I was in a very lucky position and, particularly as a Christian, I wanted to give something back to people less fortunate than me. Bill Latham helped me to run the trust and it was Bill who had the brainwave of making lots of donations to smaller charities rather than big lump sums to the most successful ones. For many years, I gave 10 per cent of all my earnings from live concerts to the Trust.

As England won the World Cup in '66, The Shadows and I were busy making another musical movie with the promising tagline 'The beat is the wildest! The blast is the craziest! . . . and the fun is where you find it!' *Finders Keepers* was set in Spain (although we never got any nearer to the Med than Pinewood Studios).

The film had a few major stars, such as Peggy Mount, John Le Mesurier and good old Robert Morley again, and a bizarre plot that had The Shadows and me running around and singing songs while looking for an unexploded bomb. It was fun to make but, like *Wonderful Life*, never quite fulfilled its potential.

So, in the middle of '66, I was still doing all the things I had always done – recording albums, playing tours, making movies – while also privately working out, in my heart and mind, what changes I had to make to my life now I was a Christian.

For a little while, that dual existence suited me, but it came to an end the day I was given a bombshell message. Bill Latham was by now working in my office and called me with some extraordinary news.

'We have had a letter from Billy Graham,' he told me. 'He wants you to speak at one of his rallies.'

ELEVEN
A POP STAR OR A CHRISTIAN?

I knew all about Billy Graham, of course. The Reverend Graham was the world-famous American evangelist preacher who held vast rallies, or 'Crusades', in the US and around the globe. His weekly radio sermons attracted millions of listeners and he had preached with Martin Luther King. His life's mission was, in his own words, to bring people 'to accept Jesus Christ as their personal saviour'. I even had an aunty who bought all of his magazines.

Yes, I knew a whole lot about Billy Graham and I admired him even more. What I *didn't* know was whether I was ready to align myself with him.

I guess I was still taking my baby steps as a Christian. I had accepted Jesus Christ as my personal saviour, that was true, but I hadn't told many people about it. My Christianity was not public knowledge. I instinctively knew if I accepted the invitation, I had a lot to gain . . . but also a lot to lose. Did I *really* want to do this?

I went back and forth for a few days. I asked close friends for their advice. Some people told me to go for it: 'He's a fantastic preacher and a very good man,' they said. 'What harm could this possibly do?' Others were more cautious. Peter Gormley warned there was a danger of me being exploited and cautioned that if I came out as a Christian, I would inevitably lose some fans. Yet he didn't advise me *not* to do it, nor did Norrie Paramor: they both stressed that, ultimately, it was entirely my decision.

I had one or two angst-ridden nights as I mulled it over: *I don't know about this . . . My music career is going along great guns and now I'm going to get up on stage and start talking about Jesus?* I decided that I would do it, as many times as I decided not to!

Then, I had an idea. Reverend Graham had asked me to appear at a youth rally at Earls Court on 16 June 1966, but he was also preaching at the same vast venue for a couple of nights beforehand. I decided to go along on one of those nights, incognito, and watch him first hand before giving him an answer.

When I did, I was very impressed. Billy didn't do what press reports had accused him of, which was playing on people's emotions to pressurise them into sharing his faith. I saw no flaw in him. He spoke articulately, and passionately, about his belief and his love for Jesus, then invited anybody who wanted to 'accept Jesus Christ as their personal saviour' to stand up and walk to the stage.

'If you want to make a change in your life, you're welcome to step forward,' he said. 'Somebody will be beside you and you can ask them questions. If you *don't* want to make a change, then please stay seated.'

Well, you can't say fairer than that, I figured. By the time I got home to Rookswood, my mind was made up. I was in.

This didn't mean I wasn't nervous. The Greater London Crusade of 16 June 1966 was the most terrified I have ever been on a stage in my whole life. There were twenty-five thousand people in the arena, with another five thousand in the Earls Court car park listening to a broadcast of what was going on inside. On the stage, my mind was a whirl: *Am I doing the right thing? Well, it's too late to change my mind now!*

The England cricketer Colin Cowdrey gave a reading, then Billy Graham called me forward to speak. I walked to the lectern, gripped it tight and said a few words. I thanked my parents for raising me in the Church – then told the world that I had given myself to Jesus.

'I can only say to people who are not Christians that until you have taken the step of asking Christ into your life, you are missing out on so much,' I said at the end. 'It changed me for the better. It works . . . It works for me.'

The Reverend Graham's organist then struck up and I sang 'It Is No Secret (What God Can Do)', a Southern gospel song that Elvis had interpreted in 1957.

The chimes of time ring out the news, another day is through

I didn't realise it at the time, but when I finished singing, I found that I had been gripping that lectern so hard, I had lost all circulation in my arms. My blood had congealed and I couldn't even move my arms properly! I had to gently rub and flex them until I could finally bend them again. *That* was how scared I had been.

The next day, the newspapers went to town with the news of my shock appearance at Billy Graham's rally. As I had expected, and was braced for, the headlines were a mix of surprise and mockery:

CLIFF FINDS GOD!

CLIFF GETS RELIGION!

WHAT *IS* CLIFF DOING?

I knew this was just a taster of the kind of media treatment I could expect in the future, but for now, I didn't have much time to dwell on it . . . because another, very different kind of bombshell was about to explode in my life.

After my dad had died, my mum had doubtless been quite lonely. She had been with him since she was sixteen years old, raised four children with him and then, suddenly, became a widow while still quite young, having only just turned forty.

My sisters and I had all taken care of her and, initially, I had taken her with me to a lot of shows, premieres and showbiz events. But being on tour meant I was inevitably away a lot, as well as spending time with Bill Latham and his Christian friends in Finchley.

I had bought my mum a Chevrolet and also hired a chauffeur, Derek Bodkin, who moved in to the gatehouse at the end of the long drive at Rookswood so that he could be available whenever Mum wanted driving around. What I *never* imagined in a million years was that the two of them would begin a romantic relationship.

The first that I knew about it was when I received a call, just two days after I had spoken at the Billy Graham rally, telling me that Mum and Derek were literally just about to get married! The news blindsided me and I was reeling as I raced to Rookswood to throw rose petals over the bride and groom.

What to make of this? As an employee, Derek was a nice enough guy, but I wasn't about to call him 'Dad': for one thing, he was the same age as me! My sisters felt the same way, and Joan, who was still in school, was particularly upset. Even today, she hates to talk about it.

Yet, ultimately, all that Donna, Jacqui, Joan and I could conclude was that Derek was Mum's choice. *It is what it is*, as they say, and we had to make the best of it. But it gave the press, who were still making hay with me becoming a Christian, another thing to write about.

With Mum married and moved out, it was clear to me that holding on to Rookswood made no sense. Donna had gone, Jacqui was also about to get married and I was hardly there. Even when I was, that old pile was far too big for just Joan and me to be rattling around in. Within a month of Mum's marriage, I had sold it.

With money thankfully no object, I bought a new place for Mum and Derek to live in, and helped to buy houses for Jacqui and Joan. It also meant I was temporarily homeless, so I carried on crashing in Mamie and Bill's Finchley spare room pretty much full time. It was kind of them to let me stay but the place was quite small, and it wasn't ideal, so I hit on a solution. I had no wish to live on my own and I liked sharing a place with them, so would they allow me to buy a bigger place for all three of us to live in?

Bill and Mamie were open to the idea so we started looking around for a suitable place in the nearby vicinity. Surprisingly quickly, we managed to find a decent-size Georgian house three miles farther out of London, in Totteridge. I could buy the place outright, which made the move very straightforward.

While all of this upheaval was going on, I was also thinking very hard about exactly what I wanted to do with my life . . . and reaching a very surprising conclusion. For the first time since I had first heard Elvis when I was sixteen, I didn't want to be a pop star anymore.

I had found another dream.

I felt like I had changed when I became a Christian, and now it was time for my life to change with me. The circle of friends that Bill and I were now hanging out with were nearly all schoolteachers, or vicars, or youth leaders – so what was *I* doing singing pop songs?

Some evangelicals at the time felt that showbiz was not an appropriate calling for a Christian: wasn't it all based on the sins of pride, and ego, and vanity? I wasn't sure about *that*, but I knew I was hankering to do something different.

My career had probably hit a bit of a plateau at that point, with the rise of psychedelia and hippy culture, which I wasn't involved in, but more to the point, I had become distracted, if not detached, from it. My newfound focus was my Christianity. I wanted to stop focussing on *me* and help others. But how could I do that?

Well, how about if I became a teacher?

As soon as I had the idea, it grew on me. *Yes! Why not?* Friends like Jay Norris were hugely encouraging. She told me to contact the head of Trent Park Training College in Cockfosters and I went to see him and enthused about my new ambition.

'Do you think I could be a teacher?' I asked him.

'Well, the most important thing is that you clearly *want* to be one,' he replied. 'If you can get another O-level or two, I'll accept you on our course.' *Fantastic!* Through a Christian friend, John Davey, I arranged to sit a religious education O-level at a school where he taught in Lewes, Sussex.

I told Peter Gormley and Norrie Paramor what I intended to do. I don't suppose it was what either of them wanted to hear, but they didn't try to talk me out of it. My accountant also assured me that I was solvent enough to make this unexpected career change without hitting the skids.

My plan was coming together! Now, I just had to tell the world.

In July 1966, I called a press conference to announce my plans for my new life. I explained to the gobsmacked journalists that I would honour all of my outstanding contractual obligations but I would not be taking on any more showbiz commitments. I was going to eschew music for the classroom.

The resulting press coverage was the same mix of surprise and ridicule I had got when I spoke at Billy Graham's rally, but, by now, I had come to expect it. I knew this mockery was part of the deal. The decision I had made to come out as a Christian would inevitably expose me to some derision.

I can't pretend it didn't hurt. Ever since I had emerged and been called an English Elvis, I had got used to being feted, admired and screamed at. Everyone loves to be loved and it was tough suddenly to be viewed as a figure of fun, a wimpy, Bible-bashing Goody Two-Shoes.

Well, so what? I didn't have the slightest doubt about the new life I had chosen. It had been nice being 'cool', but if I was now 'uncool' in journalists' eyes, that was their lookout. If they thought rockers who swore were cool, well, that just wasn't me. Not anymore, anyway. In any case, I remained determined to fulfil my showbiz obligations . . . and the first of those was another Palladium panto.

The Palladium's offering for Christmas '66 was *Cinderella* and I played Buttons. It was a blast! The Shadows wrote all of the music, including our new big hit, 'In the Country', and Hugh Lloyd and Terry Scott from the BBC's *Hugh and I* were the Ugly Sisters. Although I never met her, a 14-year-old Sharon Osbourne was apparently in the chorus line.

My fondest memory is that every Saturday, between the matinee and the evening show, I would get the theatre managers to rig up a projector and us cast members would all sit, eat popcorn and watch a movie together. I've done something like that in all of the theatrical productions I've done ever since.

After a few weeks' intensive cramming, I sat my religious education O-level in the school in Lewes. Teachers took it in turns to invigilate and make sure I hadn't smuggled in any crib notes. I thought that was so funny: *Imagine! Cliff Richard cheating to pass an RE exam!* Happily, unlike my teenage tests at Cheshunt Secondary, I sailed through.

Yet my teaching career – full time, at least – was not to be. In life, you make some decisions too hastily and come to realise you have got things wrong. I quickly realised my pop career didn't have to be at odds with my faith. In fact, it could be a huge asset.

No sooner had I announced my 'retirement' than interesting offers began coming in. Norrie Paramor called me up: 'OK, Cliff, you're a Christian now,' he said. 'So why don't you record a gospel album?' Next, Billy Graham's people got in touch again. They were looking to make a Christian film: would I consider starring in it? I also received offers to present religious shows on TV and to go to schools, universities and churches to talk about my conversion and my new life.

Of course, I was being offered all of these things *because* I was a pop singer, not despite it. It made me realise that I could turn my fame and celebrity as a singer into a force for good, to help communicate my faith. I could continue my career *and* be a valuable, hardworking Christian.

'We don't have your fame, so we can't do what you can do,' some of Bill Latham's friends told me. 'But as long as you are well known, you will be given a platform from which to spread the word.'

It all made sense to me – and, of course, I felt quietly relieved that I didn't have to sacrifice my rock and roll dream, and give up everything I'd worked so hard to achieve. I accepted most of the offers, called another press conference and explained that I wasn't, after all, about to retire: I was going to be a pop star who was also a Christian.

In one of the religious books that I later wrote, I compared this process to a Bible story, The Binding of Isaac. It tells how God ordered Abraham to sacrifice his son, Isaac, for Him. Abraham took Isaac to Mount Mariah, laid him on a stone and was about to strike him dead when God intervened, saying, 'Now I know that you believe and trust in me.'

It had been a test, and in the same way I had shown I was willing to sacrifice the most important thing in my life – my career – for God, before learning that I did not have to. I call this incident 'my little Isaac'. It may sound dramatic, but it makes sense to me – even if my sacrifice was not as great as Abraham's would have been.

Now I had resolved on a course of action, I recorded two albums in 1967. Norrie Paramor was still pulling me away from rock and roll and towards orchestral music and drafted in Mike Leander, who had produced Marianne Faithfull and Joe Cocker, for *Don't Stop Me Now!* It was an interesting mix of material, from the Isley Brothers' (and Lulu's) 'Shout' to Buddy Holly's 'Heartbeat', 'Homeward Bound' by Simon & Garfunkel and The Beatles' 'I Saw Her Standing There', plus a new, brassy arrangement of 'Move It'.

Yet I was more excited to record my first gospel album. Norrie and Mike were again on hand when I went back into Abbey Road studio two to make *Good News*, a record of spiritual reflections. It had some hymns and traditional songs, such as 'What a Friend We

Have in Jesus' and my take on Psalm 23: '*The Lord is my shepherd, I shall not want.*'

However, I felt it was important that the album also rocked out – as they say, why should the Devil have all the best tunes? So, I gave songs like 'Get on Board, Little Children' plenty of welly. We also included 'It Is No Secret (What God Can Do)', the song I had sung at Billy Graham's Earls Court rally.

As I was making *Good News*, The Beatles were recording the *Magical Mystery Tour* EP in the next studio. They are forever associated with Abbey Road studio two and yet, amusingly, Paul McCartney told me they felt always that *I* was EMI's favourite, and they could only use it if I wasn't there.

'Every time we phone up to book it, we get told, "No, you can't have it – Cliff is using it!"' he said.

'That's funny!' I replied. 'Every time I ask to use it, they always say that *you* are in there!'

* * *

I threw myself into religious projects as '67 progressed. As well as appearing on the BBC's Light Programme to talk about my faith, and beginning work on a Christian book, *New Singer, New Song*, I talked about my new beliefs on a TV show with fellow guest Billy Graham and presenter Cathy McGowan, and debated with the then atheistic Manfred Mann singer, Paul Jones.

Yet my biggest project was *Two a Penny*. Financed by Billy Graham's organisation, this film cast me as Jamie Hopkins, a young hustler, ne'er-do-well and would-be drug dealer who reacts badly when his girlfriend finds God at one of the Reverend Graham's Earls Court Crusades.

I loved making the movie – it had a great message, and where the musicals such as *Summer Holiday* and *Wonderful Life* had required The Shadows and I merely to play wacky versions of ourselves, this was proper acting, with a meaty role for me to get my teeth into. I enjoyed being taken seriously as an actor.

The director, James F. Collier, was fantastic to work with and directed me with real depth and imagination. He reminded me a little of how Jack Good had moulded me at *Oh Boy!* Before one scene, he asked me to share with him a deep emotional moment from my past that had always stayed with me. I told him of my shame at having to tell my dad I had failed my school exams, and of feeling our coal fire burning the backs of my legs as I did so.

We had a big scene set at one of Billy Graham's Earls Court rallies. My character had snuck onto the platform behind him while he was preaching and the camera was in close focus on my face to capture my reaction. Before the scene, James gave me six or seven cards to put into my top jacket pocket. He instructed me to pull out one of the cards and do what it told me: 'When the cameraman sees you pull it out, he'll start rolling,' he said.

So, I did. The first card read, 'Look at Billy Graham and think, "What a load of crap!"' so I gave a sardonic sneer. The next one said, 'Look at the audience and look cynical,' so I rolled my eyes. I must have done OK, because some of my fans, who were also at the rally but didn't know I was making a movie, wrote to me and asked, 'How could you *behave* like that when the Reverend Graham was on stage?!'

In the movie, I was up against brilliant actors and actresses such as Dora Bryan, who played my mother, Geoffrey Bayldon, Peter Barkworth, Ann Holloway and Avril Angers. As a Christian film, *Two a Penny* was never going to be a box-office smash, but I found it hugely fulfilling to make.

* * *

Yet I knew my career would not all be spiritual ventures from this point on. I would be balancing them with the usual business of being a pop star – and one of the more exciting aspects of this came late in '67 with my first trip to Japan.

I toured with an orchestra conducted by Norrie Paramor and it was a tremendous experience. Japan is the opposite of New York, where you go for the first time and feel like you already know the city. Going to Tokyo felt more like arriving on an alien planet.

It was so exciting. Everything was different: the language, the food, the people and how they behaved. I went down well, yet the crowds were so polite it was as if they thought it was rude to applaud! It made a change from non-stop screaming, but it was disconcerting.

We recorded our last night in Tokyo and released it as an album, *Cliff in Japan*. My future trips to Japan were different as fans got more used to Western pop-music culture and became less reserved. Soon, they were screaming loudly, not to mention throwing cuddly toys!

I found in Japan that the confusion between the letters 'l' and 'r' that comedians laugh at is a real thing. Japanese people *can* say both letters, but they mix them up. I once bought a cassette machine in Tokyo and, on the box, it said not 'tape player' but 'tape prayer'. Which I guess quite suited me!

Another tour had my name behind me on stage in big poly-styrene letters. On the last night, for a joke, the promoter switched the 'l' and 'r' around so it read:

C·R·I·F·F   L·I·C·H·A·R·D.

I'm sure that was the only night some of the Japanese fans ever said my name properly!

The following year, back in London, I appeared at a charity show for the St John Ambulance Brigade at the Palladium. It was a special event because the headline act was true Hollywood royalty – Judy Garland. When Miss Garland went on, the stage wings were packed as all of us other, lesser performers crowded together and craned our necks to try and get a glimpse of this living legend.

Sadly, Judy was not in the best of shape at the time and her performance was a bit ropey. She certainly wasn't good enough to impress Bruce Welch, who is no respecter of reputations, however mighty they may be. He quickly made an exit, rolling his eyes. 'Let me know when she starts singing in tune,' he muttered to me as he passed.

Yet my focus remained firmly on the spiritual side of my work. As well as religious media appearances, I was speaking regularly in youth organisation meetings and churches, and at St Paul's church in Barnet, north London, I met a lady named Cindy Kent.

Cindy was also an evangelical Christian and sang in a folk-rock band called The Settlers. She and I became friends, and when I went with Bill Latham to see her band play the Royal Festival Hall, I asked them to be involved in a major venture I was planning.

Having made the *Good News* album, the obvious logical next move for me was to take it on the road on a gospel tour. To that end, I met up with a guy called Dave Foster, who worked for a Christian charity for European nationals called Eurovangelism.

We seemed a natural fit and decided to put a gospel tour together, with me singing with Cindy and The Settlers and all of the proceeds going to the charity. Peter Gormley was wary of launching it in Britain, in case fans began seeing me as *just* a Christian artist, so Dave fixed up dates in Sweden, the Netherlands and Yugoslavia.

But before that, I had another, extremely different European venture to concern myself with – because I had entered the Eurovision Song Contest.

I realise that many, many artists would not have done this. Even fifty years ago, a lot of people saw Eurovision as cheesy. In many ways, I agreed with them, but I just saw it as a great chance to play my new song to millions and millions of people – and if I won the contest, so much the better!

Becoming a Christian wasn't 'hip', doing Eurovision wasn't 'hip', but, again, *so what*? Doing those things never really damaged me. I guess my old friend and rival Adam Faith summed it up once, when he said, 'The amazing thing about Cliff is he has done everything that would appear to be wrong, and it seems to have worked!'

Because Sandie Shaw had won the previous year with 'Puppet on a String', the Eurovision final was to be live from the Royal

Albert Hall in London. I was to sing a song called 'Congratulations', written by Irish folk musician Phil Coulter with Bill Martin. It is a jaunty little ditty but I can't claim that it's my favourite song I have ever sung. However, people have always loved it and even today you hear them singing it in restaurants, along with 'Happy Birthday'.

In fact, if I had ever been offered 'Happy Birthday' to sing, I think I would have done it! I just like selling records. I'm naturally competitive and I will always like to be Number 1 in the charts, rather than Number 27.* I make no apologies for it – it's just the way I am.

'Congratulations' was riding high in the British singles chart on the night of the Eurovision final and in fact was to go to Number 1 the day after the contest – my first chart-topper for three years. Norrie Paramor was conducting the orchestra at the Albert Hall and it's fair to say that I was the strong favourite.

I knew that I was performing live on TV to a European audience of millions, but I didn't feel too nervous, my performance went well and I enjoyed it. When it came to the voting, it seemed to be going our way, and I was in the lead as the presenter, Katie Boyle, prepared to call in the last few votes.

As the national juries were awarding their points, one by one, the TV networks had their cameras pointing at the artists' faces. I wasn't enjoying that. Why should all of Europe watch us writhing as we waited to learn our fates? I went to my dressing room for some privacy and locked myself in the toilet with my guitar. I'd

---

* Of course, I learned a hard lesson over the years that not every song I recorded would be Number 1!

been in there for maybe twenty minutes when Peter Gormley came in and knocked on the bathroom door.

'It's OK, you can come out now, Cliff,' he told me. 'But I'm afraid you didn't win. You came second.'

I was obviously disappointed but I thought to myself, *Oh well, I guess second is not too bad*. Peter told me that I had lost by one point to the Spanish entry, 'La, La, La', sung by a charming lady called Massiel. I went out, rushed up to Massiel and shook her warmly by the throat . . .

I'm joking, of course (and I've used that line many times, over the years!). I congratulated her and wished her well, and I assumed I had been beaten fair and square. However, when I was told about the marks that the last few national juries had doled out, it all began to smell rather fishy.

I had always been big in Ireland, 'Congratulations' was Number 1 there and yet they had given me the dreaded *'nul points'*! Similarly, Yugoslavia, where standing ovations meant I was often unable to begin my concerts for five minutes, had awarded me nothing at all. *Huh?* A solitary point from each of those countries would have won me the contest. *What was going on?*

Forty years later, a Spanish television documentary producer said she had 'irrefutable evidence' that the contest had been rigged by General Franco, who had bribed and nobbled two or three of the juries. That was news to me, and yet as soon as I learned it, it made perfect sense. Apparently, Franco was keen to make Spain a big tourist destination. Well, I guess it worked!

I semi-jokingly went to the Eurovision organisers and asked if I could have the award after all, as I seemed to have been cheated out of it! But nothing came of it and the truth was that I really wasn't all that bothered. In my very long career, I've learned that you can't control everything in life and you have to roll with the bad things as well as the good.

The good thing was that 'Congratulations' went to Number 1 in a host of European countries, including Sweden and the Netherlands, and, would you believe it, in Spain, where it became the fastest-selling single ever! I wonder if General Franco bought it?

'Congratulations' being a big hit in Europe would have been excellent news for my imminent Eurovangelism gospel tour . . . except that I had decided that I wouldn't be playing the song. I didn't want to cheat any of my fans, so I made it very clear before the tour that I would be singing only gospel songs; there would be no 'Move It' or 'Living Doll' or 'Congratulations'. This inevitably put some people off, and while my handful of European gospel dates went well, they weren't sold out, as my shows usually were.

I had a fantastic time doing them, though. They were different from my usual gigs: I would be welcomed to the stage with a cheer, but there was no screaming after that. People wanted to listen to me. We were all there for the same purpose, to affirm our faith, and I believed fervently in every word I spoke or sang.

Soon afterwards, The Settlers and I did our first UK gospel concert, in London. I had a strange encounter after the show. Cindy Kent told me she wanted to introduce me to a guy she'd met and I shook hands with a young man with frizzy hair who told me his name was David Bowie.

David told me he wanted to break into the music business. When some people say that, you think *No chance!* but I didn't with him: he had an *edge* about him. Someone took a photograph of us that night. Bowie was smiling, and I was glancing away with a look on my face as if I was thinking, *Who is THIS?!*

Bill Latham was by now involved in Tearfund, a Christian charity providing help for the world's disaster areas, and we gave them the takings from that first UK gospel show. They used them to buy a Land Rover for relief work in Argentina. I didn't know it then, but Tearfund was to play a very big role in my life in years to come.

My new plan was working out. I seemed to be finding the balance to carry on with my pop career *and* be a good Christian. But I had no time to feel pleased with myself – because I was about to get another major shock.

TWELVE

'MUM, THIS IS LIBERACE . . .'

In September 1968, The Shadows and I marked our tenth anniversary with an album called *Established 1958*. It was a light-hearted record – I sang tracks like 'Don't Forget to Catch Me' and The Shadows did instrumentals with fun titles like 'Voyage to the Bottom of the Bath' and 'The Magical Mrs Clamps' – and it felt like a milestone.

Ten years! So much had happened in the decade since 'Move It' that I felt dizzy even thinking about it! Yet I realised our first competitors, the other early British rock and rollers like Billy Fury and Marty Wilde and Vince Eager, had all fallen by the wayside and here we were, still rocking on, still living the dream.

It was the first time I felt confident that my career might have proper longevity. So, it was bitterly ironic that I woke up one morning a few weeks later to find that I didn't have a band anymore.

Like any group, The Shadows always had their tensions. Even after Jet had gone, there were occasional intra-band rows. Normally, they involved Bruce, whose musical perfectionism and absolute insistence on punctuality could verge on the obsessional.

I remember one gig in Blackpool when Bruce was having trouble tuning his guitar beforehand and got so frustrated that he stormed off and left us to play the show without him. He got in his car and drove all the way to London, where he turned up at Peter Gormley's apartment.

'What are *you* doing here?' our manager asked him, amazed.

'I couldn't tune my bloody guitar!' grumbled Bruce.

'Get back in that car and get back on tour!' ordered Peter.

And Bruce did. He just turned up on the road again as if nothing had happened.

If I am honest, Bruce's obsessive nature could at times be wearing on the rest of the band – but his perfectionism also frequently lifted us to greater heights. We all respected his drive, and he was eventually to grow a lot happier and more relaxed and positive. It was great for him, and for everybody. In any case, The Shadows' rows were really few and far between. Other bands had them far worse.

The Shadows and I had maybe not been so tight over the last couple of years. They weren't involved in my gospel career and I had made a lot of albums with Norrie Paramor's orchestra. Yet they were still my band, so it was a shock when Hank phoned me to tell me they had split.

The good thing was that our parting was not acrimonious – in fact, The Shadows did a farewell tour of the UK and Japan with me the following year, after they had announced they were going to part. Hank also wrote a couple of very good songs for the 1969 *Sincerely* album that I recorded with Norrie Paramor.

'Throw Down a Line' was great and was a Top 10 hit for me. I also love a song that Hank wrote for me on that album called 'London's Not Too Far'. It's about a girl saying she is leaving home, to go to London, and it's not until the last line that you find out she's only five years old. I think it's lovely, and very underrated.

Although I was sad that The Shadows had split, I have to admit I would have been far more upset had it happened five years earlier. Then, my music career was my whole life. Now, I also had my Christian and spiritual activities to focus on, and I was finding them very fulfilling.

In 1969, I made a six-part religious series for Tyne Tees TV, *Life with Johnny*, with Cindy Kent, The Settlers and Una Stubbs. Each of the episodes was based on one of Jesus' parables, with a cast of actors and singers acting them out. It was yet more confirmation that I could use my fame and position to do good.

In a lesser, different way, I certainly used it to do good for my mum the same year, when I introduced her to one of her all-time heroes. Mum used to love watching Liberace when he was on TV. She adored his style and the flamboyance with which he used to play the piano.

When I appeared on one of his TV specials, she came along to watch the recording and afterwards, I took her backstage. I'd cleared it with his management first and so I took her to his dressing room. Liberace was charm itself – he certainly had it turned up full. 'Oh, *Ma'am*, how lovely to meet you!' he cooed, leaping from his chair to shake Mum's hand (I think he may even have kissed it). 'You look *gorgeous* tonight!'

I thought Mum was going to faint. Or melt.

Now that I wasn't so tied to the routine of making one or two albums a year, then touring them, I began doing more TV. Right at the end of the sixties, I went to Israel and made *His Land*, a documentary about the Holy Land and its history, for Billy Graham. It was very moving – but then, I guess it was always going to be.

Far more high profile was a BBC series that I made in 1970 called *It's Cliff Richard*. It was basically a family variety show that aired on BBC1 on Saturday teatimes at 6.15. Hank and Una were on it every week with me, and we would do songs and sketches and have special guests.

One thing I was surprised, and pleased, to learn making that show was that I was a decent dancer.* I had to do a few routines with professional dancers and I felt nervous beforehand: *I'm a singer, I'll never keep up!* But after a few sessions with a choreographer, I turned out to be a bit of a natural.

Who'd have thought it, huh?

Our special guest in the last show of the series was Cilla Black. I had been bumping into her for years by then, at shows like *Top of the Pops*, and she had become a great friend. In later years, in a land far away, we would get very close.

Before doing Eurovision, I had sung 'Congratulations' on her TV programme, *Cilla*. On my show, Welsh folk singer Mary Hopkin sang the contenders for this year's British entry. The viewers voted for their favourite song and it was quite a big deal. The winner was the last song she sang: 'Knock, Knock, Who's There?'

---

* I still don't think that I'm a 'dancer', as such – but I can move OK!

It was fantastic fun making *It's Cliff Richard* and the shows got really popular. We would record them on Thursdays, then go out to eat, and people would come up to us in restaurants, asking, 'Who's on this week's show, then?' One or two famous actors did it and I could not believe that *they* watched us. The viewing figures were great: some weeks, it was twenty million people.

Because the show was doing so well, I went to the BBC and asked if we could be moved to 8pm on Saturdays – the grown-ups' time. They said no, because people tuned in to our show at tea-time, and once we'd reeled them in, they'd carry on watching BBC1 for the rest of the evening. I was disappointed, but I *suppose* it was a compliment of sorts!

We did one very special episode of the show where the guest star was Aretha Franklin. It was wonderful to meet her because, whatever kind of music you like, Aretha had the voice of voices: unbelievable. As I say, I'm very bad at keeping souvenirs, but I treasure my photo of the two of us together.

After I had finished on Saturday night BBC TV, I switched to Sundays! We made a short series called *Sing a New Song* and I went on every week to sing hymns or gospel songs with Cindy Kent and The Settlers. As a Christian show, it didn't get the same ratings as *It's Cliff Richard* – but it meant as much to me, if not more.

Around this same time, I went to Lisburn in Northern Ireland to play a gospel concert in a church at the height of the Troubles. After I had finished the show, the vicar passed on a request from a friend of his, a local BBC Radio Ulster journalist, for an interview with me.

'She's lovely!' he assured me.

'OK, sure, why not?'

He made a phone call, and an hour later, a very pregnant lady turned up at his manse, where I was staying the night, and asked me lots of smart and interesting questions. I liked her immediately – but I had no way of knowing that Gloria Hunniford was later to become one of my very closest friends.

* * *

Looking back, I can see that the public perception of me changed in these days. Even in my own eyes, I think I was probably: 1) a Christian, 2) a TV entertainer and 3) a pop singer. My music had slipped down my list of priorities, and it showed when it came to making my albums.

With Cliff Richard & The Shadows, I used to be intensely involved in song selection for our records. Now, I was taking far more of a back seat. When Peter Gormley called to say it was time to make another album, I'd go into the studio, where Norrie Paramor would play me a load of songs.

'Yeah, that one's OK,' I'd say. 'That one's not bad.' Or, 'No, I don't like that one.' I'd go away again so Norrie could record the music track, and then I'd come back to the studio at the end and stick my voice on top. That was how I made an album like 1970's *Tracks 'n Grooves*.

That album had a Mike Leander song called 'Early in the Morning', which got to Number 1 in Japan and yet was not even released as a single in Britain! That makes no sense to me now, yet back then I don't even remember being that bothered.

If somebody had told me at that time that I had lost my way in my music career, I'm sure I would have been offended and denied it indignantly, but the truth is that I think I had. My band had split, and I was preoccupied with my faith and doing TV.

After *Tracks 'n Grooves*, I didn't make another album for four years. I was still recording and putting out singles, but they bumped around the charts in the twenties and thirties rather than going to the top, as they used to do. In the early sixties, that would have *killed* me. Now, I was just preoccupied with other things.

* * *

After The Shadows broke up, Hank and Bruce formed a trio called Marvin, Welch & Farrar with an Australian singer and guitarist called John Farrar. They made a couple of fantastic, classy albums – not only were they three great guitarists, but they had classic harmonies. If you've never heard them, check them out!

Hank and Bruce met John when Bruce's then girlfriend, an English girl who had grown up in Australia, recommended him to them. That girlfriend was called . . . Olivia Newton-John.

I first met Olivia right at the start of the seventies, when Peter Gormley started managing her. We hit it off straight away. She was just a lovely person, really easy to talk to, who was starting to make her way in music. She was the sort of soulmate that you meet and you know is a friend for life.

Olivia and her friend, Pat Carroll, who was, and still is, married to John Farrar, came on tour with me as backing vocalists.

They were fantastic singers and a lot of fun to be around. We did one show in Germany in 1971 and I noticed they had put their microphones near to mine at the front of the stage – *my area!*

We'll see about that!

I had a word with the tour manager and the next night, Olivia and Pat's mics were behind the piano. I came on and opened the piano lid – and you couldn't see them! They still remind me of this joke occasionally.

Olivia also came on my next series of *It's Cliff Richard* and sang a Bob Dylan cover, 'If Not for You', which became her first big hit. The camera loved her, the viewers loved her – everybody loved her! She quickly became a regular part of the show, appearing in the sketches with me, Hank and Una.

It was clear from our on-screen chemistry that Olivia and I got on well, and the papers began to speculate that we might be an item. We never were – she was by then engaged to Bruce, although they split up and never married. But we were as close as it's possible for two just-good-friends to be.

* * *

I loved still having my Portuguese haven but I also thought I'd like to have a bolthole nearer to home – and, in 1972, I found one. It came about by a rather circuitous route.

I met a Christian conservationist who said that, if we wanted to save the planet, we had to plant more trees. This galvanised me into action and I bought 180 acres of land in North Wales and forested it with pine trees. It felt good to do something so altruistic and positive.

I also purchased a smaller plot of land with a cottage called Bryn Moel near the beautiful town of Betws-y-Coed in Snowdonia. A truly idyllic spot, this was perfect for weekend retreats and longer breaks, whenever I got a chance. I had such good times there over the years – just me, my guitar and my faithful dog, Kelly.

Ever since I had released 'Move It' back in '58, Norrie Paramor had shaped my music career as my record label boss, album producer and all-round guiding figure. However, in 1972, he asked to see me and told me that he thought it was time for us to go our separate ways.

Norrie was frank with me. He was nearing his sixties by now, and he felt that I needed someone younger and less old-fashioned to work with. Even so, I felt nervous at the news: he'd always watched over me, the father figure I hadn't had since Dad passed.

Always a reassuring figure in times of trouble, Peter Gormley sprang into action and began looking for more cutting-edge producers for me to work with. His first choice was a guy named David Mackay, who had worked for EMI Music Australia before moving to London.

David had a very high-profile first single by me to produce, because I was about to repeat an earlier adventure (well, some might say I was about to return to the scene of a crime!). I was to represent Britain in the Eurovision Song Contest once again.

The 1973 final was in Luxembourg and this time I was singing a great, upbeat number called 'Power to All Our Friends'. I gave it my best shot, but I ended up coming third (the host country won with 'Tu Te Reconnaîtras' – 'You Will Recognise Yourself' – sung by Anne-Marie David). But at least my entry became a big hit across Europe – and I don't think the competition's votes were rigged this time!

Some people sneered at me for doing Eurovision, as they had when I had done it previously, but I cared even less what they thought this time than I had before. In any case, the best way to stop people laughing at you . . . is to laugh at yourself.

I have never taken myself as seriously as people think, as was evidenced in a sketch when I appeared on *The Morecambe and Wise Show* in 1973. Eric and Ernie were in their flat and I arrived and started chatting away to Eric. The joke was that he hadn't recognised me. Ernie put 'Living Doll' on the stereo.

'Turn that rubbish off!' said Eric, horrified. 'I can't stand that fella!'

The three of us then did a turn to 'The Fleet's In', as sailors dancing on the deck of a ship. We invented two new dance disciplines on that show: tap-dancing with a bucket on one foot, and dancing on your knees in a lift. I'm afraid neither became a national craze.

Recording with Morecambe and Wise was hilarious. The script changed so many times. Eric would always ad lib, and because he was so funny, his ad libs would be written in. We'd do it again and he'd have even more ad libs, which would also go in. I don't know if I ever met a funnier man than Eric Morecambe.

With my music career in a lull, I made another musical movie. Set in Birmingham, *Take Me High* saw me play opposite Anthony Andrews as a businessman who gets involved in a new restaurant. George Cole, Debbie Watling and Hugh Griffith were also in it. It was an interesting film and I thought the soundtrack was tremendous.

Yet *Take Me High* was to be the last film I ever made – well, to date, anyway. The screenplays that I was being sent weren't that good, and when mega-movies like *Star Wars* came along, I decided to take a step back and focus on music again.

While all this was going on, I was still living with Bill and Mamie in Totteridge. This was to change in 1973, when we moved south of London to Surrey and got ourselves a bigger house in St George's Hill, just outside Weybridge.

The press got wind of this move and it enabled them to return to one of their favourite topics when it came to me. In fact, now I come to think of it, I've been putting up with this particular tabloid-media obsession for more than fifty years.

The papers looked at the fact of two single guys, in their thirties, sharing a house, and put two and two together to make five. By then I had had romantic flings with many girlfriends, all chronicled in those same prurient newspapers. Bill had dated my sister, Jacqui, when we first met. Plus, Bill's mum, Mamie, was also living with us!

So, it was ridiculous, and, most of all, *it was none of their business*. Bill and I lived together because it suited us. It worked for me, he was a Christian, and we appreciated each other's company. I knew I would far rather come home to Bill and Mamie, who was like a second mum to me, than an empty house on my own.

I am naturally a sociable, gregarious person. I like to talk and I like having people around me. Being solitary for more than a very short time has never suited me. I have never lived on my own and, as far advanced in life as I am now, I hope I never will.

When I first became a Christian, I think that I was quite hard-line and judgemental until I realised that God tells us in the Bible, *judge not, lest you be judged.* Now that I'm a lot older – and, I hope (!), wiser – I'm a lot more tolerant and understanding. It's about time the media also became more understanding and less intrusive and judgemental.

I meet with a lot of fans, I have lots of friends, and only the press ask me about my sexuality . . . and, as I say, it's none of their business. Are they just doing their job? Well, it must be a pretty rotten job if they are! I'm quite a stiff-upper-lip person, I grew up in a different era, and I simply think my private life is nobody's business. And if that makes me an enigma, great! I'm happy to be one!

As it happened, Bill and I sharing a place around '73 made sense on even more levels, because we were about to start working together. He had just left his teaching job to become the deputy director of Tearfund, the evangelical charity I had played my first gospel concert for.

Bill was deputy to Reverend George Hoffman, a young vicar who had founded the charity. George said he thought that my celebrity could help to raise awareness of Tearfund, so we agreed that I would go on some of their relief missions to disaster areas. Which, in November 1973, brought me to Bangladesh.

Ever since partition, which I had witnessed as a child in India in 1947, India and Pakistan had largely been at loggerheads. This had erupted into outright war in 1971, when hundreds of thousands of people fled for their lives to the new state of Bangladesh. These refugees were now crammed like animals into desperate, disgusting, disease-ridden camps. People were dying from starvation and malnutrition. It was a full-blown humanitarian crisis, and the most devastating thing I had ever seen in my lucky life.

I didn't know how, or *if*, I would cope with it. I'm naturally quite squeamish and on the day that I arrived at the camp, I was told I would have to wear thigh-length boots to see the refugees: there was no sanitation and we would be wading through human waste.

As it happened, they took me to a marginally less filthy part of the camp, but what I saw was heart-rending. Sobbing women were trying to give their desperately sick babies to nurses in the hope that they could save them. With limited resources, the nurses had to be tough, and take only those with a realistic chance of survival.

Watching these noble, selfless men and women risk sickness and infection themselves to help these suffering people, I felt helpless and worthless. I said so to one of the nurses one night as we were having dinner.

'I couldn't do what you do,' I admitted. 'I'm not brave enough to be out there giving injections like you do.'

'You don't *need* to be,' she replied. 'Just go home, talk about us and raise money for us – and then you will be saving lives, too.'

George, the director of Tearfund, said a similar thing to me: 'You are only one man, and one man cannot change the world – but you can change the world for one man.' *Wow*, I thought, *that is so true!* And I applied myself to fund-raising for them with a vengeance.

Since that first trip to Bangladesh, I have travelled all over the world for Tearfund – to Kenya, to Haiti, to India – and I must have raised hundreds of thousands of pounds for the charity. I have absolutely no doubt that it is the most important thing that I have done in my entire life.

* * *

Back in England, my new producer, David Mackay, had thoughts on how to resuscitate my music career. Hearing my last few albums, he had detected – correctly, I think – that I had been drifting and a little bit rudderless, and he had ideas on how to correct that.

David introduced me to some very talented Australian musicians now based in London, including guitarists Terry Britten and Kevin Peek, bassist Alan Tarney and drummer Trevor Spencer. We hit it off – and two of them were to become major figures in my career.

David said that I needed to work with the band in the studio, as a unit, as I had with the early Shadows, rather than just turning up at the end of the sessions to add my vocals when they had all finished. That made sense to me, as did his suggestion that I should start writing songs again.

I had always liked songwriting and had never stopped deliberately. In the early days of Cliff Richard & The Shadows, I had ceased being so involved as Hank and Bruce would often write together while I was off doing my media duties. Now, I welcomed the idea of writing again.

The album that came out of our first sessions was 1974's *The 31st of February Street*. The title came to me on a short holiday in Madeira. I saw a street named 23rd of February Street and thought to myself, *Hmm . . . what if there was a similar name, with a date that doesn't exist?*

The album came together well, and Terry, Alan, Kevin, Trevor and I worked songs into shape in the studio together just as Cliff Richard & The Shadows used to do. I wrote four of the songs and I suppose it was a bit of a conceptual album, to an extent. The opening track, which I wrote, found me musing gently on a strange, almost mystical place.

I was proud of *The 31st of February Street*. I thought it was a sweet, sensitive album, and after getting immersed in writing and recording it, I felt closer to it than I had to any album in years. That didn't mean that my fans felt the same.

The public always let you know what is right and what is wrong, and they didn't take to *The 31st of February Street*. It hardly charted at all and EMI didn't even release any singles off it. And yet, I credit that album, and David Mackay, with rekindling my interest in music. It really felt like a rebirth.

After that record, Peter Gormley then said that any producer who was able to source great songs could work with me next – which brought an old, familiar face back into my orbit. Bruce Welch had been doing more and more work as a producer, including producing singles and albums for Olivia Newton-John. He knew lots of good young songwriters, and said that he was up for a go at producing me.

The first track that he worked on came the next year when he produced a single for me, 'Honky Tonk Angel', that had recently been a US hit for Conway Twitty. Elvis also sang it on his *Promised Land* album at the start of '75. It was a great song, I liked it a lot and my record plugger, Eric 'send a limo' Hall (because 'I'll send a limo!' was always his answer if I asked how I was going to get somewhere to do promo), said it was going to be a hit. It was all looking extremely promising.

Then, a week before the single was due to come out, Bill Latham and I were speaking at a Christian youth event. A teenage girl in the audience raised her hand to ask a question.

'Why are you singing a song about a prostitute?' she asked me.

What? Dumbfounded, I promised to investigate. I made a call to Peter Gormley, who asked around and came back to tell me that, no, it wasn't about a prostitute, but, yes, it *was* about a lady of ill repute. After that, I didn't feel able to support the record, so it died. I think now I may have overreacted: it was a great song.

Despite that false start, I had enjoyed recording with Bruce, and we agreed that he would produce my next album. He set about looking for songs . . . and then early one evening, in the summer of 1975, he turned up at my house in Weybridge, looking very excited and brandishing a cassette tape.

'Cliff!' he said, as soon as I opened the door, 'you've just *got* to hear this . . .'

THIRTEEN
'JUST CALL ME SYLVIA. SYLVIA DISC.'

In that house in Weybridge, I had a big music room that I used for listening to records and strumming my guitar and trying to come up with ideas myself. We went straight there, Bruce virtually sprinting up the stairs in his eagerness to show me what he'd found.

He clicked the cassette into the deck in my hi-fi and pressed play. It was a warm summer's evening and as he and I stood on my narrow balcony, leaning on the railings and facing into the room, I heard gentle strings and a hushed vocal lap out of the speakers. Hooked from the first notes, I craned my head to hear as the music swelled and the first verse build to its aching climax:

But these miss you nights, are the longest . . .

Wow! What a song! I felt a familiar prickling, triggered by emotion, on my forearms and showed them to Bruce: 'Look, I've got goose

bumps!' Bruce grinned, and held out his own a
'So have I!'

'Miss You Nights' was an amazingly pow
I loved it from the off. Bruce said he had foun
leased album recorded by a singer-songwri
Townsend, who had written it about pining for h i
had gone away on holiday. It was ours to use if
please!

That wasn't the end of our listening party. B
song called 'I Can't Ask for Anymore Than You'-
up from two young songwriters and I loved that
put on a song called 'Devil Woman'.

One of the co-authors of 'Devil Woman' was
home: Terry Britten, the guitarist in my band
instantly, and I'd had it for weeks while not being
that it was right for me. But Bruce thought it w
second that he heard it.

It was all a hugely promising launch pad for
and a few days later, I reconvened with Bruce
Abbey Road studio two. Before we began work,
some ground rules: 'If we're going to do this albu
do it *properly*,' he said. 'And that means we don't
sound anything at all like "Congratulations",
"Summer Holiday".'

We shook hands. We had a deal.

I knew from past experience with The Sha
would be a challenging producer to work with,
was. He sets himself the most demanding standa

himself up – or beats up anyone in the vicinity – if he doesn't achieve them.

There's an old music industry term that somebody has got 'good ears'. It means that they are able instantly to spot a smash hit song that might pass others by. I'm not too bad at this, but Bruce is just fantastic. He can hear things that nobody else can.

This can be both a blessing and a curse. I was well used to Bruce's perfectionism in the studio. He would be standing by huge state-of-the-art speakers, with the volume cranked up, listening to one track over and over, again and again. It would sound flawless to me.

'Now take the guitar out,' he'd instruct the engineer, and scrutinise it yet again. 'Now take the drums out.' Another play-back. 'A-ha, I've got it!' he'd declare triumphantly. And there it would be: one single cymbal tap, a microsecond off the beat.

'Bruce, nobody on the entire planet will hear that!' I would protest. And he would fix me with his gimlet glare: 'I don't care. *I* can hear it!'

Bruce brought his usual exacting standards to this new album, but he also brought fantastic songs that he garnered from his many contacts in the music business. He produced such a wealth of material that the hardest thing was deciding which tracks *not* to record.

To his credit, he made the sessions fun while also organising them with military precision. I guarantee you will never hear a bum note on any of my records produced by Bruce Welch because, if I ever sang one, he made darn sure that I went back and did it again.

He drafted in a backing vocal group for the record, led by a guy called Tony Rivers, the former singer from Tony Rivers and The Castaways. Tony was one of the best session men in the business. He used to *think* in harmonies. We might all be sitting in a pub, having a break, and Tony would suddenly dish out the vocal parts: 'Right, yours is de-de-de-DE! Yours is de-de-DE-de!' He would count us in, we would all sing our notes, *et voilà!* – a fabulous harmony. He was always spot on.

'Miss You Nights' was one of the first songs we got down. I sang it live with an orchestra and then Tony guided us into the backing vocals. Bruce made it sound even better than it had on the demo. His production brilliantly amplified the ache and the sense of yearning at the song's heart. Then we turned our attention to 'Devil Woman'.

My misgivings about this song were nothing to do with its quality. I knew it was great as soon as Terry Britten came up with it. In fact, I had the same internal reaction as *any* singer, when a member of their band comes up with fabulous material: '*Uh-oh!* I won't be able to hang on to *him* much longer!'

When he first played it to me, Terry told me that 'Devil Woman' was influenced by Marvin Gaye's 'I Heard It Through the Grapevine'. *Really?* I couldn't hear the link, at first. 'I just turned the intro guitar riff upside-down,' Terry explained. Then, yeah, I could kind of hear it.

No, my apprehensions were not to do with the tune, which was fantastic, but the lyric, telling a tale of a guy being seduced by a fortune teller:

She's just a devil woman, with evil on her mind . . .

The song had a real edge. I knew a lot of my audience preferred me crooning jaunty, family-friendly ditties such as 'Summer Holiday' or 'Congratulations' – would this be a step too far for them? And should a Christian believer *really* be singing a song about a fortune teller?

I added a couple of admonishments – 'Stay away!' and 'Look out!' – to warn people against messing with the occult. But it was just a great song, a potentially huge hit, written by one of my own band: what was not to like? Reassured, I stepped up to the mic and gave it my all. I looked over at Bruce, expecting a thumbs-up.

'Cliff, can you sing it through again, and this time can you *try* to sing it in the same key as the track?' he said.

Charming! 'Bruce, I'll keep doing it until I get it wrong!' I replied.

Bruce really pushed me all the way through making the album, but that was great: it was what I needed. Then he cracked the whip again when we turned to the other song that he had played at my house, 'I Can't Ask for Anymore Than You'.

My problem was that half of the song had to be sung falsetto. 'I've never used falsetto on a record, Bruce!' I protested. 'Well, start now!' he snapped. 'Just do it!' I just did it, and he was right. It sounded fine.

We had so many great songs to work with. There was one sad, string-driven ballad called 'Lovers', about the end of a passionate love affair. I have never sung it live, but I'm thinking I might do it on my next tour.

When it came to choosing a title for the album, I went with the name of another track on the record: 'I'm Nearly Famous'. It was a song about a wannabe trying to make it in the music business, but never quite getting there. Peter Gormley was decidedly puzzled when I told him of my plan.

'But you *are* famous!' my straight-talking Aussie manager said.

'Yes, I know, Peter,' I said. 'It's a sort-of joke!'

It *was* a sort-of joke, but there was more to it than that. I *had* been super-famous, ever since my teens, but my music career had been in slow decline in recent years. Maybe, just maybe, this might be the album that pulled me back to where I had been? Where I wanted to be?

The record that reignited my dream?

I developed the theme on the sleeve. One thing I loved about vinyl albums was that the covers were large enough to carry a big, evocative image. We used a picture of me lying on a bed, with my guitar, as if searching for inspiration. On the back of the sleeve, photos of my first influences – Elvis, Little Richard, Ricky Nelson, Chuck Berry – gazed down from the bedroom walls.

The initial signs for the album were good. Radio 1 loved 'Miss You Nights' when we released it at the end of '75, although it was a tough sell – we worked it for three months and it only got to Number 15. The following spring, 'Devil Woman' got into the Top 10.

When *I'm Nearly Famous* came out, in May 1976, critics gave it easily the most positive reviews I had had in years. 'It is the best collection of new songs ever!' raved *Melody Maker*, declaring that it deserved to reboot my flagging career. And, more importantly, music-lovers appeared to agree.

On its release, *I'm Nearly Famous* went into the chart at Number 24. Two weeks later, it stood at Number 5 – amazingly, my highest placing for an album since right back in 1962! It was a comeback beyond my wildest dreams.

In Britain, anyway. America, as ever, was a different story. After my last few albums had fallen flat in the States, my US label decided not even to release *I'm Nearly Famous*. That opened the door for a British superstar who has definitely always had *very* good ears.

Elton John is famous for keeping up with new music, and the very first time he heard my keening falsetto on 'I Can't Ask for Anymore Than You' on the radio, he was intrigued.

'Who's that?' he asked his manager, John Reid.

'Cliff Richard.'

'That's *Cliff*?' said Elton, amazed. 'I want to release it!'

Elton had his own record label, Rocket Records. With EMI America so lukewarm towards me, we were more than happy to go along with his plans when he got in touch. So, he put out *I'm Nearly Famous* on Rocket in America.

I did a month-long promo tour of the US, doing interviews in almost every major city. Some journalists knew all about my long backstory, while others didn't have a clue about what I had done before. In California, Olivia Newton-John, who had recently moved to the States, threw a party for me.

One journalist knew Elvis well and offered to introduce me. My mind at once flew back to standing on the great man's porch steps in Germany, in 1959, with my heart beating fast, and to visiting Graceland to find him not at home. Was this finally to be my opportunity?

Yet I said no. The guy wanted to bring a photographer along. Elvis was in Las Vegas and had put on a lot of weight and was not looking great then. I didn't want me and a Fat Elvis on my fridge magnet! *I'll wait until he's back in shape*, I thought to myself, *and THEN we'll do it!* Little was I to know that, just over a year later, Elvis Presley would be dead.

I'm Nearly Famous did well in America. It was my first album ever to sneak into the *Billboard* 100. Even better was the performance of 'Devil Woman'. The single went up, and up, and up the US singles chart, climbing every week, until it came to rest at . . . Number 6.

What an amazing performance! It was wonderful, beyond my wildest hopes – and, I must confess, I enjoyed a little sneaky *schadenfreude* wondering how the executives at EMI America must be feeling about its success.

The UK record label got some button badges made. They said:

I'M NEARLY FAMOUS

Elton was photographed wearing one, as apparently was Jimmy Page from Led Zeppelin, and then there was a picture of *Elizabeth Taylor*, of all people, sporting a badge on one of her fabulous bosoms! I think Peter Gormley had definitely come around to the album title by now!

Elton was a laugh to deal with. He loves to give his male friends and colleagues female nicknames. He has always called his old mate Rod Stewart 'Phyllis' (nope, I have no idea why). His chauffeur was known as 'Betty', after Betty Driver, who played Betty Turpin on *Coronation Street*.

Elton began addressing me as 'Sylvia'. I didn't particularly mind, but one day I asked him why he had chosen that.

'It's because John Reid says you're always phoning our office, asking if your record has gone silver yet,' he explained. 'So, I call you Sylvia Disc. But I don't *always* call you that. Sometimes, you're the Bionic Christian!'

I got used to being Sylvia Disc and I grew to like it. Apparently, Neil Sedaka was always ringing Rocket asking if his album had gone gold, so he was nicknamed 'Golda Disca'. I have no idea how Neil felt about that, or if he even knew.

* * *

Sometimes, releasing records and playing the same venues all of the time can feel like a bit of a treadmill, but my next adventure in 1976 took me very much off the beaten track. I went to Russia – or, rather, the Soviet Union, as it still was in those days.

This was a very big deal. The Cold War was at its height and very few artists ventured behind the Iron Curtain. In fact, I was the first internationally known Western pop star ever to tour Russia. Well, *tour* might be pushing it – I played two dates, in Moscow and in Leningrad, as St Petersburg was still called then. The trip was a real culture shock and it was certainly one of the most fascinating places I had ever been.

First, a lot of the clichés that you read in newspapers and saw in spy movies were true. The Russian authorities were obsessed with security and our gear was locked down with chains and bolts all of the time. A helpful local warned that my hotel room would almost certainly be bugged with microphones: '*Take care what you say, my friend!*'

At both shows that we played, I looked out to see the first ten rows of the audience filled by middle-aged men in bow-ties: the local Communist Party officials and councillors. Meanwhile, hundreds of Russians milled around outside the venues, unable to buy tickets.

The Russians were friendly and desperate to get their hands on anything from the West. They gave us beautiful samovars in exchange for pairs of blue jeans. Westerners had to pay more in shops and to stay in hotels – the Soviets had at least picked up on *that* side of capitalism!

In Leningrad, I met a group of Christians who had come all the way from Tallinn in Estonia, nearly four hundred kilometres away in the far west of the Soviet Union, to see me. They told me that because of the attitude of the authorities to Christianity, they had to go into the forests to pray and worship in secret. I talked long and hard with them – my first, and only, encounter with the underground Church.

One memorable moment from that Russian trip stays with me. After our Moscow show, some of our tour party went to Red Square. It's so dramatic at midnight, under the beautiful St Basil's Cathedral, and we watched two soldiers guarding Lenin's tomb outside the Kremlin.

Suddenly, we heard the unmistakable sound of marching boots: *CRUNCH! CRUNCH! CRUNCH!* Two more soldiers loomed into view and high-stepped up to the tomb. They did a spectacular choreographed turnaround, and the guys who

Going back to Cheshunt Secondary Modern School to catch up with my inspirational English teacher, Jay Norris, December 1965.

Nice cardie, eh? Performing with The Shadows on ITV show *Thank Your Lucky Stars*, Birmingham, 1966.

A Christian, out and proud: the day that changed my life. Outside the Reverend Billy Graham's Greater London Crusade rally, 16 June 1966.

'I think we've missed one, Cilla! Better start again…' Cilla Black and me counting her TV show *Cilla*'s viewers' votes for the Song for Europe contest, 1968.

Singing 'Congratulations' in the Eurovision Song Contest, Royal Albert Hall, London, April 1968. I was pipped by Massiel… and General Franco.

Still, never mind! The Shadows and I celebrate 'Congratulations' selling one million copies worldwide, June 1968.

Meeting some young hopeful called David Bowie after I played a gospel show in south London, 1968. I look as though I'm thinking 'Who is this guy?' Little did I know…

All bow before the Queen of Soul: with the great Aretha Franklin on my *It's Cliff Richard* TV show, 1970.

I went on *Top of the Pops* more times than anybody else (or is that just because I'm so old?): one of my many appearances on the BBC's prime pop show, 1971.

Lifelong friends from the day we met: with Olivia Newton-John on my BBC show, 1971.

Promoting *The 31st of February Street* album on TV, 1975.

'*We'll meet again…*' – and we did, now and then! At a Variety Club tribute to (pre-Dame) Vera Lynn with (pre-Sir) Harry Secombe, July 1975.

A souvenir of a special day: meeting Mother Teresa at her hospice in Calcutta, 1976.

Love only Jesus
and others as He loves you
God-bless you Teresa

Getting nearly famous: promoting the album that re-kickstarted my pop career, April 1976.

In rehearsals with the classic Shadows line-up of Brian, Bruce and Hank, 1978.

Mr Nice (or so they say!) meets Mr Nasty: playing tennis with Romanian legend Ilie Nastase.

Marking my 21st anniversary in show business (and I was just getting started!) in July 1979. Back: Christopher Timothy, Joan Collins, Hank, Brian and Bruce. Front: Anita Harris, Lionel Blair, Patti Boulaye, Elaine Paige, me and Kenny Everett.

I enjoyed spraying the press with Champagne! Celebrating 'We Don't Talk Anymore' hitting Number 1, August 1979.

No, it *doesn't* stand for Old Big 'Ed: collecting my OBE at Buckingham Palace, July 1980.

The Queen and I: at a Royal Variety Show at the Theatre Royal, Drury Lane, November 1981.

Pop star or time traveller? In rehearsal for *Time – The Musical* with Dawn Hope, Jodie Wilson and Maria Ventua at the Dominion Theatre, London, March 1986.

It's a kind of magic! The great Freddie Mercury drops in to see the show.

With *Time* director Dave Clarke (to my left) and the full cast of the musical.

Getting the Ivor Novello Award for the best-selling single of 1988 for my Christmas Number 1, 'Mistletoe and Wine'.

The eighties was the decade of big glasses! At a London party to mark my thirtieth year in show business with Mum and my sister Joan, 1988.

The Event? You can say that again! With Bruce and Hank at my massive two-night spectacular at Wembley Stadium, June 1989.

had been on duty marched off into the night, their footsteps echoing and fading as they rounded the corner of the Kremlin. It was a truly unforgettable moment and the Russia trip felt very special.

When we got home, Terry Britten wrote a song – 'Free My Soul' – about the lot of the oppressed Russian people. It ended up on my *Green Light* album, a few years later.

* * *

After the success of *I'm Nearly Famous*, I felt I was back in the game as a singer, and my record company shared my positivity. Nothing excites a label like a hit and before the end of '76, EMI had rushed me back into the studio to record a follow-up.

Bruce Welch was the producer again for *Every Face Tells a Story* and, this time around, we had a mountain of songs to wade through as every new and experienced songwriter going beat a path to our door. I went into the album feeling really confident . . . but it didn't quite scale the heights of its predecessor.

It's hard to say exactly why. Maybe we had rushed into it a little too quickly, and our song choices weren't as good? It was no disaster – it went Top 10 in Britain and spawned a Top 20 hit in 'My Kinda Life' – but when Elton put it out in America on Rocket, it didn't chart.

Every Face Tells a Story was released into a difficult environment in Britain because it came out at the height of punk rock. Punk's whole ethos was confrontational, of course, with bands sneering that more established performers such as Elvis, Rod, Elton and me were boring old rubbish.

So, I guess it's hardly surprising that I couldn't stand it! But my main objection wasn't the attitude; it was that the music itself wasn't very good. The Sex Pistols couldn't play, and Johnny Rotten was certainly well-named when it came to his singing! It came as no surprise to me when punk didn't last very long.

By contrast, my favourite band of all time were huge in the mid-seventies. I *loved* the Bee Gees! They had an amazing wealth of songs and their harmonies were impeccable. People talk about how The Beatles revolutionised pop, and they *did*, but the Bee Gees were not far behind them and, in truth, many times were a step ahead.

Life was good at this time. I was loving my pop comeback and being back in the charts, but there was no way I was going to neglect the spiritual side of my life. It remained all-important to me and at the start of 1977, I went back into the studio to record another gospel album.

Bruce Welch was not religious. He had never joined in the intense discussions between me, Hank and Licorice in Cliff Richard & The Shadows, and nor did he want to be involved in producing gospel music. That was fair enough, I respected his decision and so I produced the *Small Corners* album myself.

It was always harder to find material for my religious records – there are simply far fewer decent Christian songwriters out there. But I sang a couple of songs by an American 'Jesus rocker' that I had always liked, Larry Norman, and Terry Britten wrote two songs, including a single, 'Yes He Lives'.

When I took this album out on tour, I stuck to my normal policy of only playing spiritual songs and none of my pop hits – with one very surprising exception. For obvious reasons, 'Devil

Woman' was the last song I ever expected to play on a gospel tour. At least, that was until I received a letter.

A fan in Australia wrote to me and said that she had been about to get involved with the occult when a friend had given her a copy of 'Devil Woman' to warn her against it. She had listened to the lyric and taken heed, and now she was running the youth group in her local church. *God moves in mysterious ways!* How great that a pop song had such a profound effect for good on that lady's life, and that was a strong enough reason for me to add it to the gospel tours set list and tell that story at the shows.

Also, in 1977, I returned to South Africa on tour. I insisted in advance that I would only go if I could play to mixed audiences, white *and* black, and I was assured that when I arrived in the country, I would be given paperwork to that effect.

When I got to Johannesburg airport, that paperwork was notable by its absence, but I wasn't about to be tricked into playing to whites-only crowds again: 'Right, I'm not leaving here until I have it!' I said. I sat in an airport lounge for six hours until an official finally arrived with the signed permission.

Albufeira was still my special place, my bolthole to reflect, repair and recharge my batteries. I vanished to Portugal for a holiday as my tour dates ended, but I returned to the UK to truly horrible news. I was watching the TV news programme about 10.30 one night, in the days when the newsreaders still had phones on their desks. The guy's phone rang and he picked it up, listened, put it down and looked serious.

'I'm afraid I have bad news,' he said. 'Elvis Presley has been rushed to hospital.'

Oh no!

I listened to what he said closely, but I was none too concerned. Elvis was in the right place and receiving treatment; surely, he would be OK? He was only forty-two, after all. I went to bed not too worried.

At four in the morning, I was woken by my phone ringing. A journalist was on the other end. 'Cliff, can you give us a comment on the death of Elvis Presley?' he asked me.

What? I was sure the guy had got it wrong. 'C'mon, I saw the news, he's not dead!' I told him. 'He's just been taken to hospital.'

'I'm afraid he just died there.'

'I don't believe you!' I told him. 'But if you *are* telling the truth, we have lost somebody truly fantastic, who meant everything to me.'

I hung up and fell back into a sound sleep, still convinced my caller must be mistaken. When I woke up the next morning, of course, the death of Elvis was all over the TV, radio and newspapers. I was in shock. Obviously, he had declined in his later years and wasn't the force of nature that he had been, *but he was still Elvis Presley.*

I think it's fair to say that Elvis had probably lost his way a little bit in life. During his Vegas residency, he would get a private jet to Chicago because he thought that they had better hamburgers there – *what a waste of money*, I thought! But I was prepared to forgive him a lot. *Anything*, really.

We lost him far too early. Even today, I still miss him and wish he were still around. But then I listen to those great songs like

'All Shook Up' and 'Blue Suede Shoes' and he is very much alive to me. His rock and roll lives on and it always will.

When we lost Elvis, we lost the man who gave us our American soul. We related to America through people like Buddy Holly and Little Richard and The Everly Brothers, and Elvis was the pinnacle of that. I still feel as if I owe him *everything*. My whole career was because of him.

Elvis Presley was the main reason why Harry Webb had turned into Cliff Richard . . . and, a month after his death, I was to get a reminder of just how far I had come in the years since. EMI put out a compilation record, *40 Golden Greats*. It was a double album that collected all of my biggest hits, both with The Shadows and solo, from 'Move It' right through to 'My Kinda Life', almost two decades later. It was a great summary of my career to that point.

It's always hard to know how that kind of greatest hits album will do, but *40 Golden Greats* was a phenomenon. It was incredibly gratifying for me to see it shoot up the charts until it hit Number 1. In time, it became the first of my albums to go platinum.

In another nostalgia-fest, The Shadows and I hooked up again in 1978 and played a twentieth anniversary tour. Well, maybe *tour* is not quite the right word. We didn't go anywhere – we did sixteen sold-out nights at the London Palladium, a record for the venue. It's always great to be told you've set a new landmark.

Greatest hits albums and nostalgia shows are OK, but one thing about me is that I've always been about the current moment and what's coming next. I don't like living in the past, and I was just as excited to get back in the studio and make my next LP.

Green Light was the third album that I made with Bruce Welch, but just as important was the fact that Terry Britten had by now become my main songwriter. Terry wrote and co-wrote half of the songs on the record, and with Alan Tarney and Trevor Spencer also chipping in, it was very much a homegrown affair.

I loved *Green Light*, and I still do. I thought it was a classic pop-rock album with great songs on there, such as 'She's A Gypsy' and 'Never Even Thought'. While we were recording it, we were all looking at each other and speculating that it could even be a smash in America.

For that reason, it was disappointing to me that *Green Light* did less well in Britain than *I'm Nearly Famous* or *Every Face Tells a Story*. My thing with Elton and Rocket had run its course by now, and Columbia put it out in the US, but radio didn't play the album and it sank without trace.

I began to worry: was my comeback starting to stall? More to the point, it confirmed a valuable lesson I have learned *many* times in my career: you can't second-guess the public. You can never be sure what your fans will like, and what they won't. You can only try your hardest, then hope for the best. Sometimes, you just don't know what will be a hit and what won't – a dictum that was made clearer to me than ever as the seventies wound to a close.

When I came to make my next album, *Rock 'n' Roll Juvenile*, I had decided on a change of producer. Bruce Welch had helped me to get my career firmly back on track, and I will be forever grateful, but I like to work with different people. I didn't want to get into the rut of using the same producer every time, as I had for years with Norrie.

Also, I had enjoyed producing the *Small Corners* gospel record and wanted to have a go at co-producing my next mainstream album. With all due respect to him, there was no way that Bruce would want to share his space behind the production console! So, I arranged to make the record in Paris, with Terry Britten as the main producer.

I've always hated confrontation and I was putting off telling Bruce the news – until, unfortunately, he heard about it on the grapevine before I had done so. I may dislike confrontation but Bruce certainly doesn't, and he let me have both barrels! I was apologetic about not telling him, but not about my decision – because ultimately, as an artist, I had to follow what my gut instincts were telling me.

Terry and I worked well on the record in Paris. I wrote the title track, but other than that, he wrote virtually the whole album. He penned a lot of the songs in collaboration with B.A. Robert-son, a lanky Scottish lyricist and singer who was later to have a few hits himself, such as 'Bang Bang' and 'Knocked It Off'.

Terry and B.A. came up with a song called 'Carrie' that I liked a lot. It had a real sense of mystery about it: who was Carrie and who was searching for her – was it a lover? A detective? Why had she left her room on the second floor, and where had she gone? The ambiguity was a tease and I loved it.

Terry and I had nearly wrapped up the album when Bruce and Alan Tarney arrived in the studio one day. They had a tape of a song that Alan had written for Tarney-Spencer, his recording side-project with Trevor Spencer – but they thought I should record it instead. It was a song about the end of a love affair and it was called 'We Don't Talk Anymore'.

Now, I'm not daft, I could tell straight away that it was a cracking song. Even so, I didn't think it suited the feel and mood of what Terry and I were doing on *Rock 'n' Roll Juvenile*.

'It's fantastic!' I said, after I had listened to it. 'Can you save it for me?'

'Eh?' said Bruce. 'What do you mean, save it? You should record it right now!'

Peter Gormley and EMI agreed, so I recorded 'We Don't Talk Anymore' with Bruce producing. It was slightly out of my normal key, but we did it very quickly: three or four takes, no more than that. EMI immediately released it as a single in July 1979.

I'd love to say that I knew from the second that I heard it that 'We Don't Talk Anymore' was a sure-fire Number 1 . . . but I didn't. As I say, you never do. I could tell it had a good chance of being a hit – Top 20, Top 10? I wouldn't have dared to say. So, it was a welcome fillip when it inched into the chart, then climbed high. It hovered around the middle, then leapt to Number 2, where it spent two weeks stuck behind The Boomtown Rats' 'I Don't Like Mondays'.

Darn! So close, and yet so . . .

The following week, on 19 August, 'We Don't Talk Anymore' went to Number 1.

Number 1! It was my first UK chart-topper since 'Congratulations' in 1968 and it felt just as sweet – probably more so, because I liked this song rather more! In all of my career, one thing that has never palled is the thrill of having a Number 1 single. I always think: *This is the most bought piece of music in the country! With my voice! Wow!*

'We Don't Talk Anymore' was to spend four weeks at Number 1 and become my biggest-selling single of all time. It even took off in America, where it went into the Top 10. Thanks to that, it has since sold well over two million copies. It was unbelievable, really.

Oddly enough, 'We Don't Talk Anymore' is another song that I later began playing at my gospel shows, the same as 'Devil Woman'. The trigger for that came when I was speaking at a Christian meeting and a woman in the audience put her hand up:

' "We Don't Talk Anymore" is a gospel song,' she said.

'No, it's just a pop song,' I corrected her.

'Well, it's a gospel song for *me*.'

'How do you mean?' I asked, intrigued.

The woman explained that she was from a Christian family but had lapsed in her faith recently. One day, she had heard 'We Don't Talk Anymore' on the radio and realised that she had stopped praying: 'Goodness, I don't talk to God anymore!' The song had brought her back to her prayers and her faith.

A-ha, that's good enough for me! I thought. I began singing the song, and telling the story, at my Christian shows. After it became a phenomenon, obviously 'We Don't Talk Anymore' also found its way onto the *Rock 'n' Roll Juvenile* album. A Number 1 single has never harmed an LP, so it made Number 3 in the UK – higher even than *I'm Nearly Famous*. It squeezed into the *Billboard* 100, too, leading to ambitious talk of me having another crack at America.

I was happy simply to know one thing: my music career was in a lot better shape at the end of the seventies than it had been at the beginning.

FOURTEEN
POP SINGER SAVES THE WORLD!

The new decade began with such an amazing surprise for me. It was a real shock to get a call from Peter Gormley early in 1980, telling me that Buckingham Palace had been in touch and would like to offer me an OBE. Now here *was* the stuff of dreams!

The Order of the British Empire ... I had been born in the far-flung reaches of the Empire, in the last days of the Raj, and now dear old Blighty, which I had never even seen until the age of eight, was honouring me. How did I feel? *Grateful.* And humbled.

It was a gloriously sunny day and I took Mum with me. She loved the palace and, while I'd been there before, I was touched by its history and style, as I have been every time. The Queen was as gracious as you would expect and it was an exciting day – I knew that my dad would have loved it.

Another special, regal lady also summoned me early in 1980. Olivia Newton-John phoned from America, where she was still living, and sounded pretty excited at the news that she had to impart.

'I'm making a movie, Cliff!' she said.

'That's great!' I told her.

'We want to make a single to promote it,' she continued. 'There's only one problem. My co-star can't sing!'

Excellent! I thought, knowing what was probably coming next. But, of course, I couldn't say it out loud, so I said, 'Oh no!'

'Will *you* do it, Cliff?' asked Olivia.

Of course! The movie was an American musical fantasy called *Xanadu*. A few days later, I was on a plane to Los Angeles to record the single to be taken from the soundtrack, 'Suddenly'.

Our old friend John Farrar had written the song and also produced the backing track. I recorded my vocal in an odd setting – a small studio John had set up in his engineer's garage. This was fine except for when noisy lorries went thundering by. Every time we did a take, we had to look up the road first to see if a big vehicle was heading our way.

Despite the intrusive trucks, 'Suddenly' was great. It was like an old-fashioned duet: the guy sounds like a guy, and the girl sounds like a girl. On release, it went Top 20 in Britain and America, which was a major boost for both me and Olivia, and for the movie.

I was simultaneously working on my own new album. After we had done so well with 'We Don't Talk Anymore', EMI naturally wanted me to work with Alan Tarney again. We decided that he would also be the producer on *I'm No Hero*. It made sense to me. I trusted Alan and liked working with him.

On our first day in Riverside Recordings in London, Alan looked at me. 'Well, have you got any songs?' he asked.

'No!' I laughed. 'Have you?'

'Well, I've got *this*, but it's only a demo,' he said. He played me an instrumental backing track, which I loved immediately. It sounded like a hit and I *always* like that!

'That's good,' I said at the end.

'It's got no words and I can't think of any,' he admitted. 'But I know a man who can!' He phoned the well-known singer-songwriter Leo Sayer and asked him to come down.

Leo turned up the next day and wrote the lyrics to 'Dreamin'' literally as I recorded it. He wrote the words for the first verse and as I sang them, he wrote the words for the second. *Talk about winging it!* But it came out fine and ended up being a Top 10 hit.

As well as going Top 5 in Britain, *I'm No Hero* also followed *Rock 'n' Roll Juvenile* into the lower reaches of the *Billboard* chart. It gave us the confidence to have another stab at breaking America – almost twenty years since my last one.

In spring 1981, I flew in to play a few small theatre dates. As with all of my attempts on the States, the trip was jinxed. The weekend before the tour began, the truck with all our equipment was stolen from outside our hotel in Los Angeles. We had no instruments, no lights, no sound gear . . . nothing. My tour manager, David Bryce, had to run around buying and hiring gear.

Back in London, I got to meet an original idol of mine. For a television documentary, I played a one-off show at Hammersmith Odeon with Phil Everly. Standing on stage, singing Everly Brothers' harmonies with a true hero – *a real Everly Brother*! – made for a very special night.

Recording and touring an album a year, I was now a full-on working musician again, with no time to host BBC TV series or Saturday night variety shows. However, I still enjoyed appearing on them to do my promo. Well, apart from when they asked me to do the impossible!

At the end of 1980, I went on the Saturday night chat show *Parkinson*. My fellow interviewees were Placido Domingo and US songwriter Sammy Cahn, who wrote great songs such as 'High Hopes' and 'My Kind of Town' for Frank Sinatra.

The producers asked if I would sing another of Sammy's songs for Sinatra, 'All the Way', and then it would segue into Placido singing 'Time after Time'. *What?!* I mean, I have a decent singing voice, but it's another thing to try to compete with one of the greatest opera singers in history!

I took a deep breath and said I'd give it a go. We lined up in front of the studio audience and they put the boom mic rather nearer to me than to Placido. I gave the song plenty of welly, but when it came to Placido's turn, he was something else: I think his stupendous voice parted my hair! *Wow!* I was almost too nervous to watch the show back, but when I did, I was somehow as loud as Placido. Those BBC sound engineers earned their money that night!

On my media rounds, I also re-encountered that then heavily pregnant young Irish broadcaster who had interviewed me in the manse in Lisburn a decade earlier. Gloria Hunniford was by now a rising star, and the first woman to have her own daily show on BBC Radio 2.

Gloria is wonderful. People have asked me so many times over the years if I enjoy being interviewed by her, and I always say, 'I've never been interviewed by Gloria.' 'What . . . ?' they reply. 'But I've seen . . .' And I say: 'Gloria doesn't *interview* me. We have a *conversation*.'

There is a huge difference. Interviewers like Michael Parkinson, and even broadcasters such as the late, great Terry Wogan, always had their list of questions. They would ask me something and, as I answered, they would be looking down deciding what to ask me next, and it's hard to talk to the top of somebody's head.

Gloria never does that. She sits, listens, holds eye contact and you have a proper chat. When you talk naturally like that, it's far more relaxing than a rigid interview, and you normally end up saying more interesting things. It's why Gloria and I get on so well and one of the many reasons why she is still one of my best friends in the world.

A very different kind of broadcaster, but just as talented, was Kenny Everett. Kenny was an anarchic genius. I went on his TV shows a few times and never had any idea what was going to happen. Once, I was singing 'Living Doll' and he ran on and put a gag over my mouth!

Another time, Kenny told me, 'At the end of the show, I'm going to tie your wrists together and swing you in the air behind me.'

'Um, OK,' I nodded, forever game. 'But *why*?'

'It will help me say goodbye to the viewers,' he said, mysteriously.

So, I was dangling in the air behind Kenny as he chuckled into a camera and said, 'As ever, we leave you with a Cliff-hanger!'

As I swung behind him, crying in pretend pain, he began whipping me. Or *was* it pretend pain? I had welts on my wrists for days after that sketch!

Kenny was an extremely funny man, and not many people know this but he was also a good singer. I had heard him doing harmonies on his radio show and so I invited him to sing backing vocals on one of my early-eighties B-sides, 'Under the Influence'. At first, Kenny thought I was winding *him* up, for a change (I must admit, it would have been nice to get some revenge!). But when he realised that I was serious, he came into the studio and got all of the harmonies spot on. And he did it *all in the best possible taste*!

With my recording career firmly back on track, it was great to have a string of hit singles at this stage of my career – and I was about to enjoy another belter. I was having a good time working with Alan Tarney and so was very happy for him to produce my follow-up album to *I'm No Hero*. I was even happier on the first day in the studio when he played me a song that he and B.A. Robertson had come up with.

It was an upbeat, cheery pop-rock nugget that sounded perfect for Radio 1 and the Top 40, and it snagged you right from the start:

I like small speakers, I like tall speakers . . .

I loved 'Wired For Sound' from the get-go – although I knew we'd have to take it down a tone. It was a bit out of my range. I knew we could make it sound good in the studio, but hitting every note on tour, night after night, would be pretty impossible.

We had fun recording it and even more making the video. The script looked great as soon as I saw it: with a Sony Walkman (they were all the rage at the time!) on my hip, and headphones glued to my ears, I was to roller-skate around a sleek modern shopping centre.

Now, I was quite good at skating as a lad but I hadn't done it in years, so I was quite wary. Luckily, it turned out that it had got easier since my childhood! As a boy, I had to clip wheels to the soles of my shoes and they would often fall off. Now, I wore big wheeled boots, which felt much sturdier.

We shot the video in the new town of Milton Keynes and I spent a few hours skating around a plaza and, when it started raining, an indoor car park. We had a fabulous time – it was so enjoyable. I had no way of knowing this day would come back to haunt me, in a terrible way, more than thirty years later . . .

The single was a big hit and we named the album *Wired For Sound* after it. It was to be my third Top-5 LP in a row . . . and it also came tantalisingly close to giving me another Number 1 single. I covered an old doo-wop tune on the album, 'Daddy's Home' – a big US hit for Shep & The Limelites in 1961. Yet again, I learned you can never second-guess what the public will love, as this unlikely song raced up the chart to Number 2.

It was there for four weeks. *Four weeks!* The Number 1 was the same each week: 'Don't You Want Me' by The Human League. It's a fantastic song, but I would like it even more if it hadn't stayed at Number 1 for quite so long!

* * *

235

My career was going from strength to strength in 1981, and I was getting joy and satisfaction from my Christian work too. I was very happy. I was also about to make an incredibly close friend – and pick up a great new sporting hobby.

I had always liked tennis and one afternoon, I was idly watching the final of a tournament in Brighton between the British player Sue Barker and the American Tracy Austin on TV. Sue won and at the end of the match, the camera followed her as she ran to the side of the court and hugged . . . Hank Marvin!

Huh? What was all that about?

It turned out The Shadows were playing in Brighton, had met Sue at her hotel and so had popped along to see her. It was a coincidence . . . and an even bigger coincidence was that I had been talking about Sue recently.

I had never met her, but a mutual friend – a Liverpool vicar named Alan Godson – called me about her. Alan said Sue was on a spiritual journey and eager to develop her faith. He suggested that, as a Christian who had done the same thing in the public eye, I might like to talk to her.

Out of the blue, I called Sue up in London – to her surprise! – and we arranged to go and see The Shadows at the Dominion Theatre a day or so later. We went with Bill Latham and a friend of Sue's, her fellow tennis player Sue Mappin, and then had dinner.

I invited Sue to come with me to All Souls, Langham Place, just off Oxford Street, where I knew the minister. She loved it because it had a very down-to-earth congregation, with a lot of students, and we had a lot of easy, relaxed conversations there about what faith means.

If I gave Sue a little help in easing into the Christian world, she gave me something very important in return – tennis. I had played the sport now and again, with friends, not terribly well. It was no big deal and I could take it or leave it. Even so, it was nice when Sue invited me to have a game with her at her club. *Now I'll get to see how the pros do it*, I thought.

It was another world completely – another *galaxy* from the hit-and-hope-style parks tennis that I was used to. Sue and I knocked the ball around for a bit, although I got the distinct impression that she was kindly hitting it to places that were easy for me to reach. Then she asked me, 'Do you mind if I play flat out for a while?'

'Sure,' I said.

WHAM! The first ball she served to me smacked against the fence behind me before I had even seen it. *WHACK!* The next one did the same. *POW!* When I served to Sue, a yellow blur rocketed back past me at the speed of light.

It was unbelievable! I was so helpless in the face of my new friend's athletic genius that I could only laugh in admiration. Then, as I was getting dressed in the changing room afterwards, a guy struck up a conversation with me.

'I saw that you were playing against Sue Barker,' he said. 'What was the score?'

I stared at him. *'Are you kidding?!'* I asked. 'If we had played a match, it would have been six-love, six-love, and I'd have been lucky to get love! The only time I hit the ball was when I served!'

Playing the international tennis circuit, Sue was away on the road as much as me, and soon afterwards we both vanished to different parts of the globe. I went to play dates in the Far East, but I thought about her a lot and we kept in touch via letters and phone calls.

One day, at the start of 1982, I phoned Sue in the US to ask what she was doing that weekend. She told me she was going to play an exhibition match in Denmark.

'Oh, I'm at a loose end,' I said. 'Do you mind if I come with you?' She said she would like that, and we flew to Copenhagen. Sue also came down to Abbey Road to see me recording some of my next album: *Now You See Me . . . Now You Don't*.

It is well known that Sue and I went on to have a close relationship for a year or more and I have only fond memories of that time. She and I never had a cross word, and forty years on, if I ever see her, our friendship is as deep and natural as it ever was. And that's the way I know it will always be.

* * *

Now You See Me . . . Now You Don't was a bit of a mission for me. I was tired of pigeonholing my albums as either mainstream or gospel, and of the latter being seen as somehow less important than my pop records. I wanted to see if it was possible to combine the two.

Craig Pruess, an American musician and former religious student, produced the album, and while none of the songs were overtly Christian, they all had a spiritual leaning. 'The Only Way Out' was about finding a purpose in life. 'Little Town' was a modern update of 'O Little Town of Bethlehem'.

EMI didn't even notice what I was doing. They marketed *Now You See Me . . . Now You Don't* as a regular Cliff Richard pop album, which was exactly what I wanted. It went Top 5 and I got to sing 'O Little Town of Bethlehem' on *Top of the Pops*. *Result!*

Sadly, my mum was not having such a good time. Her second marriage, to Derek Bodkin, had ended in divorce after he met another woman. To cheer her up, I took her on a holiday to Bermuda with Bill Latham, his mum Mamie and some Christian friends. I think it lifted her spirits a little – I hope so, anyway.

* * *

In the mid-eighties, my ex-guitarist Terry Britten, who had written so many great hits for me, sent a song he had co-written to my office. He wanted to know if I might be interested in recording it.

I never even got to hear it! We were sent so much stuff that I couldn't possibly listen to it all, and so, without telling me, somebody in my office casually sent it back to Terry with a thanks-but-no-thanks note: 'We don't think this is quite right for Cliff.'

And what was the song?

It was a tune called 'What's Love Got to Do with It'. Terry consoled himself by giving it to Tina Turner, and watched it both hit Number 1 in America and win three Grammys, including for Best Song, as Tina sang her heart out and relaunched her career with it.

Well, what can you do? Every artist has them: the classic song that they missed out on. *The one that got away.* I simply had too much going on in the mid-eighties to mope and brood about it – and Tina's version was truly sensational.

Then an exciting new project came my way. Dave Clark, former drummer in the sixties band The Dave Clark Five, phoned me up.

He wanted me to play the lead in an ambitious sci-fi West End musical that he was writing. It was to be called *Time*, and it was about a rock musician who is sent into space to defend Planet Earth in a galactic high court.

I had only met Dave once before, when he had come to a party that I had thrown at Rookswood. I remember that my sister, Jacqui, was very excited, because she and her friends used to run his fan club! But I was flattered by his offer – and extremely tempted.

Ever since I had played Ratty in *Toad of Toad Hall* for Jay Norris in Cheshunt, I had harboured a secret desire to star in a West End play. What was more, the plot's Good versus Evil morality-play aspect appealed to me. I made a snap decision – *OK, I'm in!*

Big West End productions take forever to prepare and it would be two years before *Time – The Musical* hit the stage. In the meantime, I got on with my career. *Silver*, an album celebrating my twenty-fifth anniversary in music, gave me a Top 10 single in 'Please Don't Fall in Love', written and produced by Mike Batt.

The following year's *The Rock Connection* was less successful. Who knows, maybe if it'd had 'What's Love Got to Do with It' on it, it might have been a different story! But I particularly liked a song on it called 'La Gonave', which I wrote on a Tearfund mission to Haiti.

There was poverty and despair in Haiti, yet it also yielded a tune I'm very proud of. On a journey to a tiny island called La Gonâve, the scenery and the chug-chug-chug of the engine of the little boat I was arriving on merged in my mind and I composed a song on the spot. I named it after the island.

My charity work also took me to Norway, in the summer of 1985 – when I found myself in the news for all the wrong reasons. Shirley Bassey and I flew out to appear on a Norwegian telly show to raise funds for the Red Cross. It was to be the main Saturday night TV programme and there would be no avoiding it – at the time, Norway only had one channel!

However, when Shirley and I arrived at our hotel in Oslo, there were a handful of protesters outside. We were puzzled, especially when we got to the TV studio to find more people with placards there. It transpired that we had been added to a United Nations apartheid blacklist for playing in South Africa. Compiled by Jamaican-American calypso singer and activist Harry Belafonte, it urged people to boycott artists who had visited the country.

Shirley shares my 'the-show-must-go-on' mentality, so we set out to do the broadcast as planned. However, when a handful of protesters infiltrated the outdoor audience and began shouting, the producers panicked and pulled the programme.

Shirley and I were given a police escort back to our hotel, where those same police told us there had been death threats against us. Following this, we were given the entire top floor to ourselves, under armed guard. I didn't get much sleep and we flew out again the next morning.

I was outraged by these events and at being on the blacklist in the first place. I thought back to my hours in Johannesburg airport, refusing to enter the country until I was given written permission that I could play to both white *and* black people. *This stigmatisation was totally unfair!* As soon as I was back in England, I wrote a letter to Harry Belafonte, putting him straight.

Yes, I go to South Africa, I explained. But I *don't* get paid for it. I go to play gospel shows, raise money for local churches and charities, and to speak out about apartheid, which I find disgusting. I go there to try to help people and, hopefully, to spark change.

Shirley had a more basic response to the accusations: 'What the hell are they doing calling me a racist? I'm a black woman!' She has always done a lot of charity work and I'm sure she was doing the same as me in South Africa.

Harry Belafonte wrote a very nice reply to my letter. He apologised and removed me from the blacklist. I was grateful – but at the same time, if they had done their research, I should not have been put on it in the first place!

Well, you live and learn. The important thing is that, thanks to heroes like Nelson Mandela, South Africa's abhorrent apartheid system was finally dismantled a few years later, in the early nineties. And I'd like to think that in going to the country, playing for free and speaking out against the bigotry, I helped a tiny bit.

* * *

Back in the UK, production work and rehearsals were going on for *Time – The Musical*. The special effects were so spectacular that the inside of the Dominion Theatre on London's Tottenham Court Road, where it was to run, had to be gutted and refitted. And as I waited, a fun project came along.

Like anybody, I've always liked being mentioned on TV shows (well, apart from *Coronation Street*'s Minnie Caldwell telling the world that I was chubby!). I still remember hearing my name in the famous 'The Blood Donor' episode from comedian Tony Hancock's BBC TV series *Hancock* back in the sixties.

'Off you go, love,' Tony Hancock told a rather large lady about to give blood. 'Just think, Cliff Richard might get some of yours.' *Pause*. 'That should slow him down a bit!'

In the early eighties, BBC2 had a cult comedy series called *The Young Ones* by Ben Elton, about four crazy students sharing a house. It wasn't really my sort of thing because the humour was horrific. I once saw one of them nail his leg to a table. *Ouch!*

But I used to watch the show, because a running joke was that one of the students, Rick, played by Rik Mayall, was obsessed with me and often talked about me. They also used to have musical guests and in one episode, Madness were playing in front of their house.

Rick ran up to their singer, Suggs: 'Do you know "Summer Holiday" by Cliff Richard?' he asked him.

'You hum it,' said Suggs, 'and I'll smash you in the face!'

I thought the joking was affectionate, though, so I was pleased when they approached me in 1986 and asked if we could cover 'Living Doll' together to raise money for that year's Comic Relief. I had just a few reservations, which I outlined to them.

'Listen, guys, I've spent thirty years building an image that people respect and I don't want to blow it in one song!' I laughed. 'I'll do it, but can we not be *too* crude or vulgar?'

They agreed and we had a great laugh. The charity single sold one million copies and went to Number 1 for the second time, twenty-seven years after the first! I tried to look cool in the photo shoots, as ever, but they all put their fingers up their noses. They only hit me on the head with a mallet once, so I guess I got off lightly!

And as the media fuss around *The Young Ones* died down, *Time – The Musical* was finally set to roll at the Dominion.

We had had many long months of rehearsals. Dave Clark was not an easy director to work with. He treated the script as if it were the Bible. He wouldn't allow us to make any changes, even if they were common sense. We would be running through a scene and an actor would say to him, 'I have this line here – but my character said exactly the same thing two pages ago! Can we take this one out?'

'No!' Dave would say. 'You can't change anything!'

Yet the script certainly wasn't poetry. It was quite clunky in parts and, early in the rehearsals, Jeff Shankley, who played The Time Lord, said to me, 'Cliff, if you and I throw ourselves into this and believe it, then so will the audience.'

So, we knew the script wasn't Henrik Ibsen, but *Time – The Musical* still had a lot going for it. I liked its basic premise, that my rock-star character, Chris Wilder, was pleading for humanity's fate before the Time Lord and defending what we had done on Earth.

Larry Fuller and Arlene Phillips choreographed some fantastic dance routines and the high-tech effects were amazing. Sir Laurence Olivier lent his voice as Akash, The Ultimate Word in Truth. He pre-recorded his lines and a huge, spectacular hologram of his head declaimed them every night.

The soundtrack was excellent, too. Dave Clark got Stevie Wonder to produce a song from it called 'She's So Beautiful' for me to release as a single. Dave couriered the music over to Stevie in the States, who sent me a message: 'When can you come over to do the vocals?'

'I can come over any time,' I said. 'But I like to record between two and six in the afternoon because of the jet-lag.'

For some reason, Stevie's people didn't like this: 'No, you have to do it whenever Stevie wants you to,' they said. 'It could be at midnight or four in the morning!'

I have never worked like that and I didn't want to start now. 'Sorry, I can't do that. You'll have to send the tapes to me,' I said. They did and I added my voice to the music in a studio in London. Stevie said I had 'given it more than he expected', whatever that meant, but he finished the track off and even added backing vocals himself. It went Top 20, so I have worked with Stevie Wonder, and had a hit with him, while never actually meeting him!

Conceptually and visually, I thought *Time – The Musical* was superb, a real tour de force. However, when we opened at the Dominion on 9 April 1986, the critics didn't agree. They gave us negative reviews, some of which were totally scathing.

I thought this was hardly fair. We knew the show wasn't perfect but it *was* groundbreaking. Andrew Lloyd Webber was rehearsing *The Phantom of the Opera* down the road with Michael Crawford, but we came out before them and our special effects were breathtaking.

I don't doubt that the fact that I was starring in *Time – The Musical* was what had led to the bad reviews. I had ceased being any kind of critical darling when I became a Christian and, in any case, snooty theatre critics generally don't take well to pop singers trying to do something different. They like you to stay in your box.

The reviews hurt us, but they were soon forgotten because the main thing was that the audiences for *Time – The Musical* loved it. We sold out every show for a year and we got standing ovations every single night. For us, they were the reviews that *really* counted.

Even when the show became a runaway success, my relationship with Dave Clark remained prickly. There was one pivotal scene where I was playing a rock show on Earth with my band and, suddenly, a ray shot from the sky and we were beamed into space to the galactic high court.

At that point, all hell broke loose in the theatre. The stage shook, a side-wall came apart and revolved, lights flashed and even the seats in the auditorium vibrated. It was so spectacular that we had signs up in the Dominion, pre-warning people with epilepsy that it could trigger them.

In Dave Clark's staging, when I was then supposedly drifting in space, the orchestra carried on playing. This didn't make sense to me: surely the sound of space is silence? I knew an eerie silence would make the next lines I said all the more dramatic, and suggested doing this instead.

As usual, Dave wasn't having it: 'No! We don't change anything!' It frustrated me more and more and eventually, a couple of months into the show, I made a stand. I like to think I've never been a prima donna: my faith, and my humble beginnings, have made sure of that. However, one afternoon, at a cast meeting, I confronted our stubborn director.

'Dave, I'm sorry to say this, but I'm the star of the show,' I said. 'If that music keeps playing, I am *not* going on.' By that evening's show, the orchestral accompaniment had vanished.

In truth, I *would* still have gone on if Dave hadn't backed down. There was the entire cast, and a theatre full of people who had paid good money for tickets, to think of. But I was determined to fight my corner and, luckily, he bought my bluff.

Yet even after I had won, Dave was like a dog with a bone. He sought me out every day to argue for the music being put back in to that bit. Eventually, I had to ban him from my dressing room. 'Dave, I like you, and I'll see you *after* the show, but I can't have this row before every performance!' I told him. 'It's too upsetting.'

* * *

While I was in *Time*, Derek Jacobi was down the road at the Theatre Royal, Haymarket, starring in *Breaking the Code*, a play about the mathematician Alan Turing. One day that we didn't have a matinee performance, I went with a lot of our cast members to see it.

We met Derek briefly afterwards but we had to get back to the Dominion to get ready for our evening show. 'Where do you go to have dinner after your performances?' Derek asked me. I told him Le Caprice and he and I arranged to meet there the following week.

I was quite nervous beforehand: *He is a proper Shakespearean actor! Will he be a luvvie? Will we have anything to talk about?* My fears were misplaced. As we sat at the table, I asked him whether he had a philosophy behind his acting.

'How do you mean?' Derek asked me.

'Well, you know, like method acting?' I said.

'Oh, you mean *tricks*!' he smiled. 'Yes, I have a few tricks, if I need to make myself cry, for example!' *Tricks!* I loved that. It was so utterly non-precious and unpretentious. Derek might as well have told me, 'Look, we're all only *pretending*, you know!'

* * *

I was in *Time – The Musical* for twelve months and it was a blissfully happy year. What's not to like about an ecstatic ovation every night? We played to close on a quarter of a million people – a new record for the West End. Not bad for a show with such rotten reviews, eh?

Bound together as we were by the ambitious nature of the show, and the hostility of the critics, the cast also became a close-knit gang. I grew particularly close to the production manager, Roger Bruce. Eventually, he was to leave the theatre to work for me for more than thirty years, and became a very close friend.

For the first half of my *Time* run, I was doing two shows per day on a lot of days. For the last six months, I just did the evenings and let my understudy take the matinees. There was only one exception: the afternoon when Sir Laurence Olivier came to see the show.

When I learned that Sir Laurence would be dropping in to see the musical that his giant hologram head was gracing, I let my understudy know that he wouldn't be required that day. I simply wasn't going to miss the opportunity to play to the greatest British actor of all time!

After the performance, we all met with Sir Laurence. Dave Clark had a backstage room decorated with satin drapes for us to entertain any VIP guests and Sir Laurence sat on a throne-like chair as we all gathered around him and talked to him.

'How has the show been received?' the great man asked us.

'The public have loved us, sir, but the press seems to hate us,' I explained.

Now, I am not usually a big fan of using the F-word, but I'm going to have to do so here to communicate the *gravity* of what Sir Laurence told us.

'Don't worry about the newspapers, dear boy,' he declaimed. 'They send people who can't f***ing act, who can't f***ing sing, and who can't f***ing dance, to criticise the people who *can*!'

At which point, we all fell about. Mainly because he was right.

* * *

While *Time* was ongoing, I managed to do a couple of side-projects when I was no longer doing the matinees. When *The Phantom of the Opera* opened, I got together with Sarah Brightman, who played the lead in that show, to sing a song from it called 'All I Ask of You'. It went Top 3, which I thought was terrific.

Elton John also re-entered my life. He was making an album called *Leather Jackets* and asked me to duet on a song called 'Slow Rivers'. I liked it, so I did, and he put it out as a single. When I went on a TV show to sing it with him and it happened to be my birthday, Elton, who is absurdly generous, gave me a present.

I opened it to find it was an engraved gold Cartier watch.

'Elton!' I said, astonished. 'You don't need to give me this!'

'Well, I wanted to thank you *properly*!' he said.

I love showing that watch off to people, even today.

The other major thing that I did while I was in *Time* was to buy the grandest house I had ever owned. Bill Latham's mother, Mamie, died while I was in the show, which felt like losing my own mum. We had lived together for so long and now she was gone, I felt it was maybe time to move on.

I looked at a house called Charters on a private gated estate, not far from where Bill and I lived in Weybridge. It had a half-acre garden and its own woodland. It was beautiful, but it would cost me £1.5m! Could I possibly justify such extravagance?

I phoned the one person that I always turned to for advice in moments of doubt in both my professional and personal life – Peter Gormley.

'Can you afford it?' he asked me.

'Yes, I suppose so.'

'Well, bloody do it, then!'

If Peter had a speciality, it was straightforward, no-nonsense advice! Bill and I moved into Charters, where I was to live happily for a very long time.

Time – The Musical dominated my life for a year until I left in April 1987. Just before my spell there ended, I was driving to the theatre one day when I saw a headline on a newspaper seller's board:

GOD TELLS POP STAR TO LEAVE SHOW!

My heart sank. *That has to be me*, I thought warily – and it was. When I got hold of it, the newspaper's 'story' said that God had spoken to me with the message that it was time to move on from the production.

I despaired. *Where do they get this drivel?* God has never spoken to me directly, nor have I ever claimed that He has! The article implied I had heard His voice in my head, which, frankly, made me sound like somebody in extreme need of immediate psychiatric treatment.

I felt angry, and foolish. I phoned my office to see if maybe someone there had said something that could be misconstrued, but nobody had said anything at all. So, there was my answer to where the journalists had got this rubbish: *they had just made it up*. It wasn't the first time nor the last – and certainly not the worst – that I would be badly hurt by press lies.

After I left *Time*, the American singer and actor David Cassidy took over my lead role. I went back to see it, to support the cast and to enjoy the production without being in it. I couldn't help but notice that when David and his rock band got zapped into space . . . the orchestral backing had returned.

Ha! I bet Dave Clark was 'Glad All Over' about that!

FIFTEEN
HITTING THE SWEET SPOT

Peter Gormley had by now managed me for a quarter of a century. He had guided my life and career since just before Dad had died and I had come to rely fully on his unerring judgement and support. He had been my rock: he never once let me down.

Yet, nearing his seventies, Peter naturally wanted to slow down and step away from the grind, and he told me in 1986 that he was to retire the following year. He would stay on as a consultant, meaning I could still ask him for advice, but he wouldn't be managing me day-to-day anymore.

I didn't want the upheaval of finding a replacement, so we divided up Peter's role between people I knew and trusted. David Bryce carried on as my tour manager and dealt with the record company; Bill Latham, who had moved from Tearfund, looked after my Christian and charity work and the press; and Malcolm Smith, my accountant, left his partnership at Touche Ross to become my business manager.

Bill brought Gill Snow with him to be our office secretary. Gill did a terrific job for many years, then handed the reins over to Tania Hogan, who has been equally brilliant. You need a great back-up team in our industry and I've been fortunate enough to always have one.

It was David Bryce who suggested that I should reunite with Alan Tarney on my next album, *Always Guaranteed*, and it was great to work with him again. I had recorded it during my last few months on *Time* but we put it out at the end of '87. After *The Rock Connection* had fallen slightly short, this LP – which is now my favourite album of mine – was exactly what I needed. Alan wrote me two cool Top 10 singles in 'My Pretty One' and 'Some People' and the album was to go on to sell well over a million copies. I was really happy with it.

As 1988 dawned, I spent January and February touring Australia and New Zealand – and I developed a recurring habit of visiting those countries at that time of year. I have always loved that particular part of the world, and got on well with Aussies and Kiwis . . . and I can't deny that the weather is also part of the appeal.

I like to chase the sun. I was born in India, I've spent many happy years in Portugal and the Caribbean, and while I have always seen Britain as my home, I'd simply rather wake up in February baked in sunshine. Horses for courses, as they say, and I just don't think I am made for long British winters.

I played a load of spring dates in Europe and then turned my mind to home. I knew 1988 was another big anniversary year for me, marking thirty years since 'Move It', and we celebrated it with a huge British tour. We lined up nearly fifty shows and the two hundred thousand tickets sold out within seventy-two hours! *Wow!*

While I waited for the UK dates to begin, I hit on a very special single. Peter Gormley had lived nearby me in Weybridge for some years by now, and one summer morning, he phoned and asked me to drop around his place.

'I've got this song that you should hear,' my Aussie manager-turned-consultant told me. 'It's right up your street.'

Well, it was and it wasn't. We had a coffee and Peter played me a song called 'Mistletoe and Wine'. I loved the melody and the tune straight away. It had a beautiful festive feel and it was very easy to imagine it being a Christmas hit. I was less keen on a few of the words. It was a pub song, really, with some lyrics about having a drink and a smoke, and a laugh and a joke (in fact, Twiggy had sung it while playing a good-time girl in a TV adaptation of Hans Christian Andersen's *The Little Match Girl* just the year before). I wanted to give it a different slant.

'Do you think they'd mind if I changed a few words?' I asked Peter.

He made some calls and, once I had permission, I added a couple of Christian references to the song. I put in the line *'Love and laughter and joy ever after/Ours for the taking, just follow the master'* and dropped in *'Silent night/Holy night'*. I hung a piece of mistletoe in a studio in Wimbledon on a sunny July day and recorded it.

* * *

My autumn tour was tremendous. We played four nights in every major British city, finishing with four more at the NEC in Birmingham and a triumphant final night at the Hammersmith Odeon. At the beginning of December, 'Mistletoe and Wine' hit Number 1 and was still there on Christmas Day.

It felt very special. The Shadows and I had had a Christmas Number 1 back in the mists of time with 'I Love You', in 1960, but that was just a pop song. This one had an avowedly Christian message and that mattered to me.

'Mistletoe and Wine' became the biggest-selling single of 1988 and rounded off a remarkable twelve months for me. At the end of the year, my single, album, video and CD (that exciting new invention!) were all at Number 1 in their respective charts. I felt gratified . . . and humbled. To survive in show business as long as I have, you need to keep proving yourself year after year. You can never rest on your laurels. I guess this success was proof that at least I was doing something right!

One way to keep going in pop is to keep looking forward, not back, and I have always tried to do that. Yet some milestones just can't be ignored. I began 1989 with a few more weeks of sun Down Under . . . then, in March, I released the hundredth single of my career.

One hundred singles! Had I *really* managed a century of 45rpm (well, 78rpm when I started out!) 7" slices of vinyl since Ian Samwell had written 'Move It' on that Green Line bus? I had, somehow, and the single I chose to mark it with was 'The Best of Me'.

That single, which went to Number 2, was taken from an album that I recorded at the start of the year, *Stronger*, with Alan Tarney producing again. But he hadn't produced the whole album – and one of the tracks that he didn't work on raised quite a few eyebrows.

I met Stock Aitken Waterman (SAW) at a music industry awards lunch early in '89. They were sitting at the next table to me and getting an award for Rick Astley's 'Never Gonna Give You Up'. I leaned over to them and said: 'If you get another song like that, you know where I am!'

Mike Stock, Matt Aitken and Pete Waterman were dominating the British singles charts at the time, producing huge hits for Kylie Minogue, Jason Donovan, Sonia and Big Fun, among others. Serious music critics sniffed at their fun disco-pop – but so what? Serious music critics weren't so keen on *me* either, these days!

I have never been a music snob and I thought I had a lot in common with SAW. Like me, they love pop music – and they love having hits! They called me up, we got together and they wrote and produced an upbeat track for me called 'I Just Don't Have the Heart'. I shelved it to release later that year.

Although I love to look forward, I had to admit my thirtieth anniversary the previous year had triggered nostalgic thoughts – and in '89, I celebrated my career with my most ambitious live event ever. In fact, that was what I called it – The Event – and it dominated 1989 for me.

My idea was to stage a huge one-off show at Wembley Stadium that would serve as a look-back at my life in music, from 'Move It' right through to the current day. I wanted it to reflect all periods of my career, so I decided to open with a re-enactment of the *Oh Boy!* TV show. The Dallas Boys, from whom The Shadows and I had purloined our dance moves, agreed to take part, as did The Vernons Girls and my special guests The Kalin Twins.

The Vernons Girls used to be great on *Oh Boy!* They were a sixteen-piece vocal group of women who had all worked at the Vernons Pools Company in Liverpool and on Jack Good's TV show, they used to wear very short shorts. So, I asked if they would do it again. Like me, these ladies were by now in or nearing their fifties, and fifteen of them reacted with horror: 'No way, Cliff!' Only one brave Vernons Girl dared to dig out her old short shorts (or maybe it was a new pair), and well done, her! Her pins looked as shapely as ever.

The Event would then segue into The Kalin Twins' set. I had always felt a little guilty about what I'd done to them on our first tour, but the two guys were as sweet as ever. I invited Gerry and the Pacemakers and The Searchers as two major Merseybeat competitors from back in the day. I would also duet with a reggae band, Aswad, then sing with The Shadows. The evening would end with me playing a solo set with my current band.

It was to be a five-hour show, spread across three stages, and the rehearsals lasted six weeks. It was a very high-pressure process – especially as I was gambling on the promoter, Mel Bush, selling out 72,000 tickets in order to pay for it all!

The Event was scheduled for 16 June 1989 and I was nervous when the tickets went on sale. Had I overreached myself? Overestimated my appeal? Well, I got my answer when Mel called my office.

'The tickets have sold out in three hours!' he told Malcolm Smith, my new manager. 'Can we add another night?'

Really? I couldn't believe my ears when Malcolm gave me the news. But Mel was confident about a second night, so I gave a tentative go-ahead. In a few days, those sold out, too. So I was to play to one hundred and forty-four thousand people. *Wow!*

The Event was a no-holds-barred extravaganza. I knew if it fell flat on its face, I would look ridiculous – but it didn't. It was a wonderful experience from start to finish, and I could not have been more pleased, or proud, that I had had the idea and seen it through.

My one minor niggle concerned The Shadows. A band is like a family, and I was looking forward so much to playing with those guys again. But . . . there is a caveat. The Shadows and I *have* always been a family, through thick and thin, and I wouldn't have it any other way. However, everybody knows that while you love your family unconditionally, they can also upset and annoy you more than can anybody else.

I wanted The Shadows to play with me right at the start of The Event, in the *Oh Boy!* section. They had still been The Drifters in those days, but Hank and Bruce had been with me on Jack Good's TV show and I wanted us to relive that experience together.

However, they told me that they wouldn't appear before their own set, later in the show. It was *so* frustrating. They didn't want to upstage their own performance – but why would it have done so? I tried to persuade them, but their minds were made up and they just wouldn't budge.

So, for 'Move It', I invited Jet Harris and Tony Meehan to play with me again. I hadn't seen them in years and they both seemed really touched to be asked. It also meant a lot to me that Ian Samwell, Terry Smart and Norman Mitham were watching from the crowd. I still missed 'my boys' – Hank, Bruce and Brian – as we were playing, though.

Those two nights emphasised to me just how far I had come since the days of Elvis sideburns, Transit vans, and being managed by a bloke who drove a lorry around a sewage works. When I walked out in front of seventy-two thousand people, I had a lump in my throat. It was *so* emotional.

At the end of The Event, I sang 'From A Distance' on a pedestal, with the other performers gathered beneath me. A wind machine blew my hair, drapes billowed around me, and when I later saw the video of The Event, it looked fantastic. At one point, I was close to tears on stage. In fact, I admit that I did shed a few.

The Event had been physically and emotionally draining but it was so, so worth it – although I didn't even make any money on it! I had paid for all of the performers and for the staging myself. Luckily, I made money from the DVD sales, which bailed me out.

On the Sunday, the day after the second sold-out show, I felt utterly exhausted. I was so drained. I couldn't speak to anybody. 'It's nothing personal, but *please* don't talk to me!' I told anybody who tried. I went for a swim, then sat on my own and let the enormity of what I had just done sink in.

Sometimes you have to work hard at your dream, and The Event had worn me out – but I was so pleased that I'd done it.

* * *

I had sung my Stock Aitken Waterman single, 'I Just Don't Have the Heart', at Wembley and we released it straight afterwards. It went to Number 3, which made me so happy again that I had dropped into their hit factory. It had been a win-win for all of us.

When we finally put out the album that it came from, *Stronger*, two months later, it went Top 10 in Britain, which was good enough for me. Excitingly, I also got another hint of success in America. The album itself didn't chart there, but the title track went into the US dance chart, and 'Some People' entered the adult contemporary Top 30. My hopes suddenly rose again. After thirty years, could it finally be time for me to happen in the States?

I went to see Rupert Perry, a senior executive at EMI. He had been there for years (although not as many as me!). 'Rupert, these songs are happening out there and I'm not there!' I said to him. 'Can we go over, play shows and have one more go?'

I'll never forget what Rupert told me in response.

'Calm down, Cliff!' he said. 'I'm sorry to tell you this, but I think I have to. EMI America is simply not excited by Cliff Richard material.'

And there it was. I just wasn't my record label's priority. I was grateful for Rupert's honesty, but it was saddening and, in a way, it broke my heart. I just didn't understand it.

I had had hits in America before. Every time I had played there, I scored some chart action. It was the holy grail for all artists and record labels, I was having a tickle of success there yet again – and they didn't want to follow it up?

I didn't understand, and neither did other artists. I can remember once being at the Sebel Townhouse hotel in Sydney when Elton John and Eric Clapton were staying at the same time.

We were up on the pool deck, talking, and Eric asked me: 'What happened, Cliff?'

'What do you mean?' I asked him.

'In America,' he said. 'How come you've never made it?'

'Yeah, you were there way before us,' said Elton. 'What's the story? You should have been big there!'

'Tell me about it!' I sighed. 'I just don't know.'

I still don't – but the strange thing is, now that I'm older, I'm kind of pleased that I never did break America. It means it is the one place I'm still able to go and have something approaching a normal life. I love meeting my fans, and always will, but it can be hard for me to walk around and go about my business in Britain and Europe. In the US, I never get a second glance – and if a Brit ex-pat happens to clock me, we take a selfie and I walk on.

Today, on the whole, I'm grateful for this anonymity.

* * *

You meet the strangest bedfellows in rock and pop. Towards the end of 1989, my management got a message. Van Morrison was making a new album and wanted to sing a duet with me.

Hmm. We weren't an obvious match. Van is nothing like me as a performer. He doesn't like people looking at him and I have heard that he will sometimes walk offstage to do a saxophone solo because he doesn't like the attention. It baffles me: *How can you be an entertainer and not like people looking at you?*

However, I'd never met Van and my response to his request to work together was the same as it always is, whoever it comes from. I sent a message back: 'Send me the song, and if I like it, I'd love to do it.' The song was called 'Whenever God Shines His Light' and I *did* like it, so I was up for it. Van has a reputation for being irascible and difficult, so I didn't know what to expect when I turned up at the studio at the agreed time. What I *didn't* expect was for him to not even be there!

I hung around for an hour or so, waiting, then started to get a bit fed up. 'Look, I have other things to do,' I told the engineer. 'I know the song, so why don't I put my vocal down now? Van can tell me later if he doesn't like it.'

I was just wrapping up when Van turned up, two hours late. Although he was happy with what I'd done, he wanted me to sing one line in unison with him. He has quite idiosyncratic phrasing so it took us a while, but we got there in the end and he seemed happy.

I was about to clear off home when Van produced a couple of bottles of red wine, so I stayed to have a drink. I think he was engaged on a spiritual quest at the time, because we started talking about religion, faith and what life is all about.

Van said something that I didn't properly understand: he said that he thought he belonged to a purple-blood group, which seemed to be some sort of rarefied spiritual royalty. I really wasn't quite sure what to say to that.

'Well, I don't know if my blood is purple or red,' I admitted. 'I just know that I believe in a being that is greater than all of us. There has to be something like that. This planet is so phenomenal that it can't be an accident!'

Van and I didn't exactly agree on the meaning of life, but we didn't argue either and, apart from turning up late, he was extremely polite to me. I went home after an hour or so, leaving the purple-blooded Van in the studio finishing off his red wine.

That Christmas, I got a very special present. My office had its annual Christmas party and a songwriter that we knew, Chris Eaton, came along. While we were having a drink, he told me he had something he wanted to play to me.

We went outside to my Rolls-Royce (I had recently treated myself!) and he put a cassette into the tape deck. Striking chords and pan pipes rang out, followed by a gentle vocal about harvest marking the beginning of winter. The song was 'Saviour's Day' and, just like 'Mistletoe and Wine' before it, I instantly recognised it could be a huge Christmas hit. However, one major obstacle presented itself.

'It's Christmas *now*, Chris!' I laughed. 'I don't think that we'll be able to record and release this in a week!'

'That's fine,' he said. 'I'll keep it for you and you can release it next Christmas.'

And that was it. We had a deal.

* * *

I started 1990 back where I like to begin a new year: in Australia and New Zealand, playing an extensive tour. Then I moved on to Europe, where I managed to double my complement of professional female tennis players who had made mincemeat of me on the court.

Steffi Graf was the biggest superstar in tennis at the time and was close to invincible. After I played a concert near her family home in Germany, she came backstage to say hello and I went out for dinner with her and her parents.

Well, I say dinner, but Steffi didn't eat anything because she was in the middle of a training regime. She left early, and as she went, she asked me a surprising question: 'Cliff, would you like to play tennis tomorrow morning?'

Would I? Yes, please!

I showed up on court next morning expecting a drubbing. Playing Steffi was like playing Sue. Everywhere I hit the ball, she was there, waiting for it already. She ran around the court so quickly that she was a blur in my peripheral vision. Then her coach arrived – and told Steffi that he wanted to hit with me, not her!

I can't hope to compete with tennis professionals, but every dog has his day, so please allow me to digress for a moment just to have a little boast. I was once playing in a charity tennis tournament in Australia against Amélie Mauresmo, the French player who has won both the Australian Open and Wimbledon. And the weirdest thing happened, a once-in-a-lifetime fluke: when I came to serve, I aced her.

I aced Amélie Mauresmo! I have no idea how it happened, but there she was, waving a racquet at thin air. It was so preposterous that I felt I had to apologise. As we changed ends at the end of the game, I spoke to her at the net: 'Sorry about that, Amélie!'

She fixed me with a steely smile, before saying: 'You will be. I'll make you pay!'

And she certainly did!

* * *

After my European dates were over, it was back to Britain, and time for a huge open-air spectacular. The Silver Clef Award Winners

Show 1990 was a charity concert held at Knebworth Park in Hertfordshire to raise funds for Nordoff Robbins, the UK's largest music therapy charity.

The line-up chose itself: it was entirely made up of artists who had been given a Silver Clef award for services to the British music industry. So, it was a stellar bill: Paul McCartney, Pink Floyd, Elton John, Eric Clapton, Phil Collins, Genesis, Dire Straits, Robert Plant . . . and me and The Shadows. It was a thrill to play Little Richard's 'Good Golly, Miss Molly' to a quarter of a million people. I couldn't help thinking that it was a song I'd first played in a Cheshunt youth club, all those years ago.

Major live events were a theme of that year for me, as I also played my largest-to-date UK and Irish tour. It was really a bit of an attempt to take The Event spectacular out on the road, although I knew I couldn't possibly reproduce all of the extravagance of the Wembley shows.

Even so, we kept the *Oh Boy!* tribute at the start of the show and our ticket sales were extraordinary. We did fourteen nights at the Birmingham NEC and eighteen at Wembley Arena, playing to more than four hundred and twenty thousand people overall. What an experience that tour was! Looking back now, and seeing audience figures like that, I sometimes pinch myself that it even happened.

The songwriter Chris Eaton had kept his promise to me so, that December, I put out 'Saviour's Day' as a single. I had fun making a video for it. We filmed on top of cliffs and on the beach near Bournemouth on a sunny day in July, which did make feeling festive a bit tricky!

We advertised for people to be in the video, giving us a major crowd scene at the end. As they surrounded me, in my long white coat, on the top of a huge rock, it looked like a clip from a movie. The single came out and climbed the chart, but a week pre-Christmas, it stalled at Number 2: could it take the last step to the top?

It could. On the day before Christmas Eve, 'Saviour's Day' jumped to Number 1 – the second successive year that I had topped the Christmas chart with a Christian song. And to think that I used to worry about whether it was possible to be a Christian *and* a pop star!

In fact, in the early nineties, I felt as if I had really hit the sweet spot in balancing out show business and my faith. In spring 1991, I played a charity gospel tour around the UK, finishing up at the Royal Albert Hall on Easter Saturday. When it sold out, I added a matinee show the same day.

Sue Barker also had a fantastic idea. She and I still met up to play tennis occasionally, I was keener than ever on the sport and she suggested that I should launch a pro-celebrity tennis tourna-ment, with all proceeds raised going to charity.

Bill Latham helped me to set up the Cliff Richard Tennis Development Trust and we held the first pro-celeb tournament in Brighton at Christmas '91. Tennis and showbiz stars brought their racquets along, and at the end of the evening, I led the crowd in singing carols. It sold out, and raised a lot of cash.

It became an annual event that was to run for the next twenty years, moving from Brighton to Birmingham. Participants included Sue, Virginia Wade, Annabel Croft, Jo Durie, Elton John, Terry Wogan, Jason Donovan, Ronnie Corbett, Bradley Walsh and

Barbara Windsor. It was so much fun and a great fund-raiser – I loved doing it.

At the end of that year, I released a Christmas album, *Together with Cliff Richard*. It gathered all of my festive hits together, plus allowed me to cover hymns such as 'Silent Night' and 'O Come All Ye Faithful'. Singing 'White Christmas' was a joy, too.

I spent the first half of 1992 mainly engaged in Christian projects. A week in Uganda, with Bill Latham and a camera team, making a Tearfund promotional film was both heart-rending and a valuable reminder of how vital that charity's work remained. Seeing how much some countries lack emphasises how much we in the West have.

The second half of the year was spent recording a new album, to be released in 1993, and playing yet another huge UK tour. Records just kept being broken: this time it was fifteen nights each at the NEC and at Wembley. It was Britain's biggest tour of the year.

Everybody has sunny spells during their life when they feel blessed and everything seems to be working out for them. Looking back, I think the early nineties were mine. When I released my next LP, simply titled *The Album*, in 1993, it went to Number 1.

I was shocked to be told that it was my first chart-topping LP, not including compilations and soundtracks, since I had released *21 Today* on my twenty-first birthday! Well, some things are sweeter if you wait a while for them, and it made me very content.

Later in 1993, I also made one of the most important purchases of my life. I had been going to Portugal for thirty years now, yet the charm and the beauty of this picturesque little country had never dimmed for me.

I hadn't always been going to the same location, though. In the early seventies, I had sold my first Albufeira house, then rented a series of holiday homes before buying a lovely cliff-top house in the early eighties. I was happy there and I had never thought of selling it . . . until I went for dinner in a local restaurant one night in '93.

I was friendly with the restaurateur, who came over and told me he knew of a beautiful place for sale. 'Oh, really?' I said. He pulled out a photograph of a sprawling yet quaint property – it looked utterly amazing. The next day, he drove me to look at the place.

Extraordinarily, it looked even better in real life. It was a 350-year-old former farmhouse called the Quinta do Moinho – Windmill Farm – and was all whitewashed stone and painted shutters, in thirty acres of land. I fell in love, I had to have it.

The Quinta was in a state of disrepair so I bought it for less than a million pounds, but I had to spend nearly as much again to repair it and make it habitable. I tried to restore it so that it would look how it used to, and converted a large car port into rooms for guests.

I talked to the farmer who had looked after the land for years and asked him what was the best thing to grow on the land. 'Figs,' he said. 'You can sell them to the north of Portugal, and to Spain.'

OK, so I would become a fig farmer. It's always good to learn a new skill!

My life was going along just great as 1994 dawned . . . and yet, I was on the verge of being gripped by a strange new obsession. I was about to be consumed by the fervent desire to become a legendarily dark, brooding, borderline-psychotic Yorkshireman.

SIXTEEN

'ROUGH AS A SAW-EDGE, AND HARD AS WHINSTONE!'

While I was at school, Jay Norris had opened my eyes to many great works of literature. Her enthusiasm had instilled in me a love for copious classic books and dramas that would doubtless otherwise have passed me by.

Emily Brontë's *Wuthering Heights* was a wonderful example. I had found the first few pages of this powerful 1847 novel a little hard going, and been tempted to give up, but she had encouraged me to persevere and I had become totally immersed in its tempestuous yet seductive world.

The character of Heathcliff fascinated me: this brutal, savage man, so consumed by love and raw passion that he utterly disregarded the conventions of civilised life. In many ways, he was a repulsive figure, but as I read the book, I began to understand *how* and *why* he had become so repulsive. His words and deeds leapt off the page for me.

Jay Norris also inculcated my love of acting, and in the early nineties I began hankering for a return to the theatre stage. Starring in *Time – The Musical* had ticked one box for me, but I had started to realise that there was one dream role that I longed to play above all others.

I wanted to be Heathcliff.

Being realistic, I knew that even if a theatre company were staging a production of *Wuthering Heights*, there was no way that a director would offer the lead role to a fifty-something-year-old Cliff Richard! No, I understood that if I were to make *this* particular personal dream come true, I would have to make it happen myself.

So, that was exactly what I did.

I knew the story of wild Heathcliff could make a fantastic stage musical and I began by assembling a dream team. I was thrilled when John Farrar said he would be involved, as I am a big fan of his ability to write great melodies. Frank Dunlop, who had founded the Young Vic theatre in London, agreed to direct it.

For the song lyrics, I turned to a man who had actually been Norrie Paramor's assistant at EMI in the late sixties. His name was Tim Rice and he has done rather well for himself since then! Tim had always told me off for never recording any of his songs, so I phoned him up.

'OK, Tim,' I said. 'How about if I sing a whole musical's worth of your songs?'

He loved the idea!

I also thought I'd like to take the show on the road, rather than be just stuck in London as *Time – The Musical* had been. I booked twenty-seven nights at venues in Birmingham, Edinburgh,

Manchester and London to open in November 1994. Then I announced the project to the press.

They went to town. They had an absolute field day ridiculing the idea of me playing Heathcliff. The initial coverage that we attracted could not have been more negative or contemptuous. Their main objection was that the 'prim-and-proper, squeaky-clean Christian Cliff Richard', as they routinely portrayed me, was totally wrong for the role of the dark, brooding Heathcliff. They mocked the very idea of me as a crazed, animalistic wild man roaming the Yorkshire moors.

They also said that I was too old for the part, in my mid-fifties, to which I retorted that I looked twenty years younger than my age and still had plenty of energy, thank you very much! I had seen a picture of Emily Brontë's father, Patrick, who at sixty looked one hundred and sixty. I was sure I could play a man in his forties, as Heathcliff was.

The main objection, though, was the same as ever: I was a pop singer. I should stick to what I knew. *Who did I think I was, trying to do something different?*

Tim Rice got stick just for agreeing to be involved. He didn't begin to understand it and wrote a fabulous letter to *The Times*: 'I'd just like to point out to the people criticising my work on *Heathcliff*,' he said, 'that I haven't actually written a word yet.'

I've always been a positive person, but it can be difficult not to be ground down by such relentless media criticism. It's really a form of bullying. I went away to Portugal for a few days' holiday and woke up at the Quinta one night, panicking about just what I was getting into.

Maybe I am the wrong person for the part? I wondered. *Perhaps I should just call the whole thing off?* But then my steely determination – the quality that people always underestimate in me – kicked in. *NO*, I thought. *I WILL show them! I WILL make this work!* I returned to London refreshed, revitalised and ready for battle.

I read and reread *Wuthering Heights* and Jay Norris was there with me in spirit when I visited Emily Brontë's cottage and strode the bleak, windswept Yorkshire moors. It was so inspiring, and I made use of that inspiration when we began rehearsals in London.

Frank Dunlop was initially keen to make the production a pure musical with no dialogue at all, but that wasn't what I wanted: 'No, I want to speak lines as well,' I told him. 'I already know that I can sing. Now, I want to show that I can *act*.'

'Well, if you want to speak words from the book, I'll leave *you* to choose them!' Frank said. So, I did.

The rehearsals were fantastic and I threw myself into the part with a passion. The critics may have felt that Heathcliff's character was too different from mine for it to work, but that was the whole excitement and challenge for me. And isn't that what acting is all about?

As Brontë had said, Heathcliff was 'rough as a saw-edge, and hard as whinstone!' He was a nasty piece of work and utterly amoral and selfish, but I loved becoming him. I did things I'd never do in my normal life – I beat my pregnant wife, after telling her on our wedding day that I didn't love her and I never would. I kicked my foster-brother, Hindley, to pieces – and I didn't pull my punches.*

---

* Of course, I took the actor who played him, Jimmy Johnston, out to dinner after the rehearsal to say sorry!

And the dialogue! Coarse and profane words left Heathcliff's lips that would never usually have passed mine, but I spat them out viciously and made them believable. The strange thing that I found out is that it's far easier to play a baddy than a goody on stage – not to mention a lot more fun!

I found that I *became* Heathcliff as soon as I put my wig on. I had two wigs made. In the second half of the play, when Heathcliff has been away and grown more sophisticated – though no kinder – I had a slick hairpiece with a ponytail. But my first-half wig was raw, ragged and unkempt: just like him.

Once I had that wig on, I felt myself transform. I *was* that evil, troubled soul. My normal conscience fell away and I could do all of the vicious, violent acts that he meted out. I felt my nature change as I slipped it on and it was bizarrely liberating.

The rehearsals were going great but *Heathcliff* was an enormous production to stage and we soon realised that our schedule was hopelessly optimistic. There was no way that we'd be ready for that autumn and we had to announce that the production would be postponed. It was disappointing and it could have given me a major financial headache. There would be no refunds on the four major venues, in four cities, I had hired out for nearly a month, and I stood to lose close on £5m. Luckily, I had an ingenious solution.

While I was out of action musically, EMI had put out a compilation album that summer, *The Hit List*. It was half songs with The Shadows and half my solo stuff. I decided to parlay the record into an autumn tour, using the already booked venues to play the gigs.

The tour sold out – and was also a success on another level. As well as my old hits, I sang three songs from *Heathcliff*, which obviously fans had never heard before. They must have liked them, because the ticket sales for the musical got a real boost while the tour was on.

Rehearsals and production work on *Heathcliff* were to dominate the next eighteen months of my life, yet my career continued apace. At the start of 1995, I took my Hit List tour to the Far East, Australia and New Zealand (*hello, more winter sun!*) – and some other, very special dates.

With Nelson Mandela out of jail, and the evil of apartheid finally condemned to history, I played my first commercial, non-gospel shows in South Africa for almost twenty years. It was great to sing in Pretoria and Cape Town to a sea of happy faces in front of me – white *and* black!

Other momentous occasions for me that year included performing at the fiftieth anniversary of D-Day celebrations, both in Hyde Park and in front of Buckingham Palace ... and getting knighted.

This was *such* a shock to me. Being awarded my OBE fifteen years earlier had been a big deal and a privilege, but people like me, who stick around the entertainment world for decades, do tend to get given them. But a knighthood? I had never even *imagined* that!

It's the ultimate honour and that was *exactly* what it felt like. The best thing was that I learned that, although they are awarded at the Queen's discretion, knighthoods are initially nominated by members of the public. It meant there were people out there rooting for me, and this made it even more special.

Having taken Mum when I got my OBE, this time my three sisters – Donna, Jacqui and Joan – accompanied me to Buck House.

As ever, one thought was in my mind: *I wish Dad could have seen this.* My sisters waited excitedly in an anteroom as a courtier ran me through my paces.

The guy showed me a small kneeling stool with a handle, which was to be set in front of the tiny raised dais where HM The Queen would stand to knight me. 'I'd advise you to make use of the handle, sir,' he advised me. I was a little affronted. *How old did he think I was?*

'Oh, I don't think I'll need *that*!' I said, briskly.

'I have seen people who are so nervous that they fall onto the stage, sir,' he said. 'I would use it.'

When Her Majesty came out, I put my right, slightly trembling, knee onto the cushioned stool and, yes, I found that I was gripping the handle. *Tightly.* The Queen was handed a ceremonial sword and tapped me lightly on both shoulders.

She didn't say, 'Arise, Sir Cliff!' but when I stood back up, she put the chain around my neck and said, '*This* has been a long time coming!' And I said . . . well, Lord knows what I said! My brain had frozen and I mumbled some utter gibberish. She just smiled, sympathetically – *I think!*

I felt so foolish. Back in the anteroom with my sisters, I told them what had happened: 'The Queen must be wondering why she didn't give it to somebody who can speak English!' I said.

Apparently, this happens to many people who meet the Queen. They become so overwhelmed that they can't speak. On a far lesser level, I see the same thing sometimes when fans meet me and freeze. And I would certainly have been the same had I ever met Elvis!

Getting my knighthood was one of the greatest days of my life, but back at the *Heathcliff* rehearsals, it was clear that we were still many months off being able to announce an opening date for the show. So, we released some music in advance of the production.

I put out two singles from the soundtrack: 'Misunderstood Man' and 'Had to Be'. The latter was a duet and, returning the favour from 'Suddenly' from *Xanadu*, Olivia Newton-John sang Cathy's part. I love singing with Olivia – she's always pitch-perfect, every single time.

One of the singles scraped into the Top 20 while the other just missed out. They didn't do as well as I had hoped, but I knew exactly why: because radio wasn't playing them. BBC Radio 1 and 2 had both had revamps and started focussing on playing exclusively younger artists.

I couldn't understand this . . . and I still don't. You don't lose the ability to make music as you get older. I had sold millions of records, I still sold out big tours so, clearly, I still had fans who wanted to hear my music. Who were radio station controllers to deny them the opportunity?

It was hugely frustrating, but there was nothing I could do about it. And it was a problem that was to get worse for me, and other established artists, in years to come.

* * *

Despite all my years as an entertainer, I don't have that many super-close friends in show business. It's rare anyone has gone from being a work colleague to joining my closest inner circle. But one lady that I met late in 1995 certainly did that.

The BBC got in touch with me. They were filming an episode of their travel programme, *Holiday*, in Vienna and they said that one of the presenters, Jill Dando, was a big Cliff fan. Would I be willing to go along, surprise her and film a segment?

Sure, why not? It sounded like fun, so we headed off to Austria. On the plane, the producers explained that they knew Jill was a fan as she had a picture of me on the wall by her desk in their office. But she had no idea what they were lining up for her.

It was Jill's birthday, and the set-up was that she was reporting from a lavish costume ball at the Vienna State Opera and waiting to meet a mysterious Austrian aristocrat, Marco Salvator von Habsburg Lothringen, who was to be her escort for the evening. She was doing a piece to camera when I popped up in front of her instead.

Jill was so amazed to see me that her reaction made great TV and by the end of a night of waltzes, she and I were as thick as thieves. She was such a great girl, so funny, and could easily have been a great actress. She could do any accent – Scottish, Welsh, Indian – perfectly.

I knew as soon as I met Jill that we'd become friends and in no time, I was as close to her as I was to my other huge pal, Gloria Hunniford. The three of us often had dinner with a gang of mutual friends. Jill and I always laughed a lot, which is the sign of a true, relaxed friendship.

One night, Jill, Gloria and I went to a Barry Manilow concert. I wasn't very keen beforehand, because I'd read that he was bland and schmaltzy, but it was a great show and he was a wonderful performer. Then I realised: *Of course! The people writing that about him are the same ones who write that I'm a boring Goody Two-Shoes!*

The moral of the tale? Don't believe everything that you read in the newspapers (part 437)!

When Jill got murdered in 1999, I could not believe it. I was on tour in Denmark when it happened. My friend Roger Bruce, who was my PA on the show, came into my dressing room, ashen-faced.

'Cliff, you need to sit down,' he said. 'I have to tell you something.'

When he did, I was devastated, distraught . . . and outraged. It was the first time I ever got angry with God. How could He let this happen? In my head, I told Him, *Jill was so fantastic, she was near to perfection – why let her die?* It took me a long time to accept her death and come to terms with it.

When somebody is murdered, the police trawl through their address books after clues. Following the shooting, they found my name in Jill's and spoke to me. I couldn't shed any light on it. *Nobody could.* But I never thought the guy they locked up for it, Barry George, had done it – it didn't seem likely at the time, his conviction was overturned on appeal and he was later cleared at a retrial.

Jill was the sweetest, loveliest girl and I guess her senseless murder will forever remain a mystery. God does, indeed, move in mysterious ways and some of them are infinitely more difficult to comprehend than others.

* * *

After I played a couple of live shows in Europe at the start of '96, we finally had *Heathcliff* ready to go. At a London press launch in March, I was delighted – and very relieved – to announce that it would open at the National Indoor Arena in Birmingham on 16 October. This gave us the summer to finish honing the production and knocking it into perfect shape. It was an intense, high-pressure process, so in June, I took a few days off for my favourite English summer activity – the Wimbledon tennis championships.

Ever since Sue Barker had got me heavily into tennis at the start of the eighties, I had been a regular at Wimbledon. I loved – and I still do – sitting on Centre Court and soaking up the athletic brilliance and precision of the world's greatest players from close up.

Of course, the biggest occupational hazard for any activity that takes place in the British summertime is rain. Any sports fan's least favourite words are 'Rain stops play' and, at Wimbledon '96, it had been happening quite a lot.

One afternoon was particularly wet, and, with no end to the downpour in sight, I was asked for an interview by Radio Wimbledon. While I was in their mobile studio, chatting to the DJ, someone came in and passed me a note. I opened it, and read it.

THE WIMBLEDON CHIEF EXECUTIVE WOULD
LIKE TO SEE YOU IN HIS OFFICE

Huh? I had only recently become a member of the All England Club, and was not entirely sure of all the etiquette of club behaviour. My first reaction was that I must have done something wrong. Did he not like my cream jacket? I went along to his office with a degree of trepidation.

'Cliff, it has been raining for nearly three hours now,' the chief executive, Chris Gorringe, said to me. 'The crowd are getting very bored. We were wondering if you might be able to do something to entertain them?'

Goodness me! 'Like what?' I asked him.

Chris suggested that I might do a live courtside interview. I agreed, so one of the BBC sports journalists got a couple of microphones, we sat in the stand and he talked to me about my love of tennis. The crowd listened . . . as did the many millions of viewers watching at home on TV.

At the end of the interview, the journalist had a further idea: 'Before you go, this crowd would never forgive me if I didn't ask you to sing something.'

Goodness me again! Well, I was firmly on the spot and I could hardly say 'No'! I obviously didn't have a guitar with me, so I just got up and, almost as a joke on the rotten weather, sang an a cappella version of 'Summer Holiday'. I even led the rain-sodden crowd in a mini sing-song.

They seemed to like it and it was still pouring down, so I continued my impromptu set with a croon through 'The Young Ones'. By now, the crowd were clapping along. I became aware of people pointing, and some kind of activity behind me, so I glanced around.

Huh? I seemed to have acquired a backing group! Behind me, in a line, top female tennis stars such as Pam Shriver, Conchita Martínez, Gigi Fernández and Hana Mandlíková were swaying, dancing and waving along. Now this was getting *really* weird!

It got even weirder when Virginia Wade and Martina Navratilova joined them. *This was the strangest dream of all!* I threw in 'Bachelor Boy', Elvis's 'All Shook Up' and 'Living Doll' for good measure . . . after which, happily for the world of sport, the sun came out and play could resume.

It was such an extraordinary day. I will never forget it. Even today, journalists occasionally make snarky remarks such as, 'The best thing about Wimbledon now having a roof is that we will never have to listen to Cliff Richard sing there again!' I have a good answer to this: 'Look, pal, I'm the only pop star who's ever played Centre Court. I didn't need tennis balls, and I made my own racket!'

It was such fun and it also did me a lot of good. Malcolm Smith had been saying that I needed to do a few interviews to get my profile up and sell more tickets for *Heathcliff*. Well, suddenly, I'd done a live, open-air gig, watched by millions on the BBC, and my profile was sky-high.

Game, set and match!

* * *

Heathcliff tickets had already been selling well, but by the time we got to the opening night, in Birmingham in October, we had broken box-office records for first-week sales. The performance was spot on: we could not have hoped for better. We got a standing ovation at the end – and the critics tore the show to pieces.

This was interesting, because all of my sisters came to the opening night and happened to have tickets sitting with the press reviewers. Jacqui told me that they seemed to be enjoying it and, during the interval, she heard one of them say to another, 'It's a lot better than we were expecting, isn't it?'

They didn't write that, though. Of course they were never going to. It was *Time – the Musical* all over again. The journalists looked down their noses at the show and the audiences – the *real* people – flocked to it in their hundreds of thousands and loved it. *Heathcliff* was to play to nearly half a million people.

Half a million people! And all because Jay Norris had taught me to love a classic novel called *Wuthering Heights*, nearly fifty years earlier!

The great thing was, by now, I didn't even care what the critics wrote. I had the time of my life playing Heathcliff and I think that I got better and better at it. There was one scene that involved me running to the top of a rock to speak some of my most passionate lines. In rehearsals, Frank Dunlop had told me, 'You'd better get good at running up that rock, because you're going to do it a lot of times.' The first time I tried, I was almost crawling up. As the weeks went by, I was sprinting to the top before triumphantly delivering my best lines in the play.

Becoming Heathcliff was freeing, empowering and liberating for me. I'm as proud of it as I am of anything in my career. On the last night, at Hammersmith Apollo on 17 May 1997, I ran offstage after the final audience ovation, exhausted but exhilarated.

'I've absolutely loved doing this!' I told Roger Bruce. 'I feel like I've had amnesia for months. I have been Cliff Richard all my life, smiling at people, reaching out to them, but being an actor, *being Heathcliff*, has been a totally different experience. It's been wonderful!'

Heathcliff had been so fulfilling, yet also draining, that I didn't do a lot more in '97 except for decompressing and playing my first gospel tour for a few years. I also spent some time on my farm in Portugal, where my farm manager had been overseeing the new fig-growing project. It had gone OK without being a raging success.

One day, the farm manager introduced me to an Australian winemaker named David Baverstock who was now based in Portugal. He had an intriguing alternative suggestion for what I should do with my land.

'You know, this farm is really a great site,' he told me, as we stood on my kitchen balcony. 'Why don't you grow grapes and make wine?'

I told him that I had always read that Algarve wine was pretty low class. In fact, *The World Book of Wine* had stated that all it was good for was 'giving headaches to tourists'.

'Ah, but you could be the first person to grow a *great* wine here!' said David.

As soon as he said that, I loved the idea. Because if there's one thing I have always loved, it's being Number 1!

'OK,' I said, thoughtfully. 'Maybe I could give it a go . . .'

David explained that it wasn't possible to inter-plant grapes and figs. If I wanted to become a winemaker, I'd have to give up the fig side of the business. 'You have a choice – you can either have syrup of figs or a nice bottle of red wine,' he told me.

Now, I've always liked a nice bottle of red – it was no contest.

'OK,' I said. 'Let's do it!'

I thought ripping out figs and planting grapes would give new life to my farm so I decided to make a wine called *Vida Nova*, which is Portuguese for 'New Life'. It was a long, complex process and many years before I made any money out of it, but it was an area I loved moving into.

* * *

By the start of 1998, I was feeling revitalised and ready to go again. I kicked off the year in my favourite style, with a tour of Australasia, which I enjoyed even more than usual as my special guest on the dates was Olivia Newton-John, making a return trip to the land where she had grown up.

Olivia and I also had a date in London that year. There was to be a big premiere for a twentieth anniversary reissue of *Grease*, her huge hit 1978 film musical with John Travolta, and she asked me to be her escort for the event.

I was delighted . . . and yet I was hiding a guilty secret. I could not have been more excited for Olivia when the original movie rocketed her to global superstardom back in the late seventies, but for one reason or another, I had never got around to seeing it!

I didn't want to tell her this, and I went along to the big glitzy premiere at the Empire Leicester Square with her anyway. The movie blew me away – I had no idea that *Grease* was so completely fantastic. After it had finished, I was so complimentary about it that I dropped a boo-boo.

'Wow, Olivia!' I said, as we left the cinema. 'That was just way, way beyond my expectations . . .'

Oops!

Olivia stared at me, through comically narrowed eyes.

'*Beyond your expectations? What?!* You *had* seen it before, hadn't you, Cliff?'

'No,' I confessed, before we both collapsed into giggles. But at least I absolutely loved it when I finally *did* get to see it!

* * *

The demands of *Heathcliff* had meant that I hadn't released a studio album in five years. It was time to rectify that. My management team recommended a successful producer called Peter Wolf, so I flew to Austria to make *Real as I Wanna Be*.

I enjoyed working with Peter and thought the album had three or four potential Top 10 hits on it, but the problem, again, was nobody was playing them. I was officially too old for Radio 1 and even Radio 2 were now loath to put me on their playlist.

It really is so frustrating. *What's the point of making a record that nobody gets to hear?* My loyal, diehard fans always buy my albums, and I'm eternally grateful to them, but any recording artist worth his salt also wants to attract new listeners. It's what it's all about!

To use a tennis metaphor, it's great for the sport when talented new challengers come up and win Wimbledon, or the US Open, but they have to get past the old guys first. They have got to defeat Federer, and Nadal, and Djokovic – and nine times out of ten, they can't do it.

Those veteran players have too much guile for them. After all these years, I'd like to think I'm a veteran performer with plenty of guile – but I'm not even allowed to enter the tournaments! If you're not on the court, i.e. getting radio play, you simply can't ever win!

I began to think: *Should I just shelve making albums and do another big West End musical instead?* I knew people would come to see that, and it wouldn't need media support. But then I thought: *Why should I give up making records? It's what I do. It's what I am.*

The whole conundrum seemed so unfair to me . . . and so, I set a little trap. The first single from *Real as I Wanna Be* was 'Can't

Keep This Feeling In', a rhythm-and-blues ballad. We sent it to a black soul-music radio station as a pre-release white label, telling them it was by a hip new artist called Blacknight 001.

The station *loved* it! It got into their chart and their DJs called the song 'sick' and said, 'I don't know who the singer is, but he's wicked!' (I was relieved to learn that these were actually compliments and not criticisms!)

On the track, I used a lot of falsetto, so nobody knew it was me, but then my secret got rumbled. A DJ from the station phoned me up: 'We've heard a rumour that it's you singing on the Blacknight 001 track,' he told me. 'Is it?'

'Yes,' I told him. 'Yes, it is.'

At which point, I believe the station stopped playing it. But it proved an important point. So many broadcasters don't select what to play according to the quality of the music, or what their listeners want to hear – it's down to their perceptions of the performer. And I think that's wrong.

Rock and roll used to fit radio like a hand in a glove. They were made for each other. We'd make records imagining how they would sound on the radio, and we knew that if they were good, they would get played. It was a great system. I don't know if those days will ever come back again, but I wish they would.

Real as I Wanna Be did respectably well and got into the Top 10, but EMI under-supported it. My record label of forty years promised me TV ads and posters on the Tube in London, but they ended up not doing any of those things. It was the last album of my current contract . . . and I decided not to re-sign with them.

Even if the music industry seemed to be turning its back on me, I knew I still had the love of my fans. At the end of '98, I booked in for four weeks of celebratory shows at the Royal Albert Hall to mark my fortieth anniversary in music. Well, that was my plan, anyway.

They sold out in two days, so we added more dates. And more. And more. The run ended up stretching into 1999 and we ended up doing a total of thirty-two sold-out Albert Hall shows. I'm proud to say that it's a record for the venue.

Workwise, 1999 was a successful year for me. I played big European shows and three open-air summer gigs in Hyde Park. I also filmed *An Audience with Cliff Richard*, a TV special where I entertained other showbiz veterans like Elaine Paige, John Mills, Una Stubbs and Les Dennis.

In my personal life, though, I had challenges. Bill Latham had had some major changes in his life in recent times and in '99, moved out of Charters to live with his girlfriend. It meant that I was living on my own for the first time since I had moved in with Bill and Mamie back in 1965. I didn't like it. Nothing had changed from more than thirty years earlier: I was still a sociable soul, I still liked to chat and hang out, and I simply didn't enjoy living alone. Rattling around that big Charters pile on my own, I felt quite lonely.

Mum had also been deteriorating. We didn't see the signs at first. She was living on her own, and had been forgetting a lot of things, but my sisters and I all just thought she had a bad memory – it seemed part of getting older.

I'd had a little house built for Mum, laid out exactly the same way as the one she used to live in. It was attached to my sister

Joan's house, so Joan could keep an eye on her. Mum seemed happy there, but then she began going out in her car and getting lost, or doing odd things like flushing money down the toilet, and we realised she had a problem.

We spoke to doctors and they told us Mum had textbook signs of dementia. After a while, we had no choice but to move her into a care home. Anybody with ailing parents will know how helpless doing that makes you feel, and how distressing it is for everybody. It was a sad time.

* * *

The millennium was nearing its end and it felt like a time of change. And, at least, I was able to go out with a bang.

I had recorded a song called 'The Millennium Prayer'. It had featured in a Christian musical called *Hopes and Dreams* written for Church audiences, but I couldn't help but feel that the song deserved wider exposure. Its songwriters, Paul Field and Stephen Deal, had merged 'The Lord's Prayer' and 'Auld Lang Syne' to create the song. As we neared the close of the twentieth century, I liked the way that it linked that momentous occasion to Christianity. I decided to release it as a Christmas single.

I had left EMI by now but through courtesy, or simply habit, I offered it to them first. They didn't want it. 'We don't think this is a hit,' they told me. Well, at least their verdict had the merit of straight-talking, if nothing else!

We looked at other options and my management took it to Papillon Records, an offshoot of Chrysalis. They liked the single and I think they couldn't believe their ears: 'This is Cliff Richard's

Christmas single? And *we* can release it? *Now?*' They jumped at the chance.

Without being immodest, I think they were proved right. Papillon put 'The Millennium Prayer' out at the end of November and it went straight into the chart at Number 2. It jumped to Number 1 and spent three weeks there before being knocked off in Christmas week by Westlife.

Even though the song inevitably got hardly any radio play, more than a million people loved it enough to buy it, with all proceeds going to charity. I was so grateful to Papillon. My sole, minor gripe was the timing of the release . . . which robbed me of a very special record.

I had suggested 'The Millennium Prayer' should come out in mid-December. With its three weeks at the top, it would then have been Christmas Number 1 and still at the top for the first chart of the new millennium.

Ever since I had started out, I had had Number 1 singles in each decade. I was the only artist ever to do that. But, having been released so early, it was asking too much to expect 'The Millennium Prayer' to hang on at the top and extend that winning run for me.

What can I say? I got cheated out of my noughties Number 1!

Ah, well. In the grand scheme of things, it hardly matters. I rounded off the twentieth century with ten 'Countdown' shows at the Birmingham NIA, culminating in a grand charity gala on New Year's Eve. They were spectacular shows. I even flew above the audience!

The future began the next day, and the start of mine was going to look very different. I had been on a treadmill – a fantastic, exciting treadmill, but still a treadmill – ever since I had seen my first single become a huge hit back in 1958. Then, I had been just seventeen years old. Now, I was on the verge of turning sixty.

I reckoned it was time for a break: for some 'me' time. I was planning to do something, in the year 2000, that I had never remotely considered doing at any previous point in my career.

I was going to take a year off.

SEVENTEEN
DRIVING MISS CILLA

When I first told my manager, Malcolm Smith, that I wanted to take a year off in 2000, he, not unreasonably, asked me, 'Why do you want to do that?'

I had a few reasons. It wasn't *just* to jump off the treadmill. I wanted to have a good old rethink about my career; my work routine; *my life*. Did I want to keep going at the workaholic pace that I always had set? Or did I want to slow down a bit?

Increasingly, I suspected it might be the latter. But surely a year away from work would be the perfect opportunity to find out.

I couldn't start my sabbatical on New Year's Day as I had promised to appear on *Songs of Praise* from Cardiff Arena on 2 January. But the following morning, I awoke to twelve months of a completely blank calendar stretching ahead of me. *Fantastic! Now, what should I do with it?*

My initial plan was to go to Australia. I had never really done a road trip – my many years in a van with The Shadows didn't count! – and I'd been told the drive across the outback from Perth to Sydney is wonderful. Should I hire a Winnebago and go for it?

It was a great idea . . . but I never did it. Australia is just so far away, and the twenty-hour flight put me off. My 2000 was supposed to be all about rest and relaxation, and that whole day and night in the air felt like too much hard work to me. I decided to go to America instead – with an important stop-off en route.

Previously, I had had a couple of holidays in Barbados and a good friend and tennis partner, Charles Haswell, asked if I might be interested in buying a house there. I told him I wasn't. Barbados has a lot of tourists and I had horror visions of spending all day signing autographs on the beach. But Charles told me that David Lloyd, who runs the tennis centres, had bought land on the island and was building secluded properties.

Coincidentally, shortly afterwards I went on a cruise that stopped in Barbados, so I checked out David's project. I saw a gorgeous plot of land, surrounded by trees that ensured maximum privacy. I loved it! OK, my mind was made up: I was going to build a house in Barbados. It was to be built on coral stone and facing west, so I decided I would call it Coral Sundown.

So, that January of 2000, I flew to the island, met an architect and planned a six-bedroom house with a huge garden, a pool and – *of course!* – a tennis court. It would take eighteen months to build, but what a great thing to have to look forward to!

From there, I went to California. I visited Olivia Newton-John and stayed with John Farrar and his wife, Pat. It was a fantastic trip and I loved catching up with old friends and getting used to relaxing and the luxury of having nothing to do.

Before I left the UK, I had met up with an old friend, Pamela Devis, a choreographer who had worked on my very early London Palladium shows. I mentioned to her that I would also be going to New York.

'Will you have your tennis racquets with you?' she asked.

'Of course! I take them everywhere!'

'Oh, good!'

Pamela told me that she had a friend in New York called John McElynn. He was a Catholic priest who was also a keen tennis player and she thought we would get on. She gave me his number and suggested I give him a call.

Hmm . . . OK, why not?

I called John from Los Angeles to introduce myself. He was friendly and even picked me up from the airport in New York in his dog collar. I had a hotel booked in Manhattan, but John took me first to his sister for dinner – they were both delightful.

The next day John and his sister and brother-in-law took me to their tennis club for a game. We all played at about the same level, so it was great. They invited me to have dinner with them at the tennis club the following evening.

I was having such a good time with them that I went along, and the evening was a hoot. As I say, I'm so anonymous in America that I can normally move about freely without being recognised, but after we had had dinner, the manager of the club came and spoke to me.

'I know who you are!' he told me, triumphantly. 'I know about all of the English rock and rollers – Adam Faith, Marty Wilde and you! Will you sing something for us?'

Well, OK then . . .

The band, who had been playing quietly in a corner of the restaurant, were all Irish, so they were gobsmacked to have Cliff Richard suddenly materialise in their midst! We belted out 'Devil Woman', I sat down again . . . and the night got even stranger.

Three female friends of John's sister came over to our table and said that their book club was currently reading a novel called *The Mammy* by Brendan O'Carroll. This book later spawned the hit TV comedy series *Mrs Brown's Boys*, in which Brendan played Mrs Brown. The women said that I got a few mentions in the book.

'We didn't know that you really existed!' they said, excitedly. 'We thought you were a fantasy character.'

Well, I'd never been called *that* before!

* * *

John and I got on great from the start. Like me, he was also having a life rethink. He had worked for his religious order for nearly twenty years in Panama, Alabama and, currently, New York, but was starting to reconsider his role in the priesthood.

One evening, he invited me for dinner at the priests' residence where he lived. We sat in a large dining hall. 'Take a look around,' he said. 'I've loved my work and what I've done, and there are some great men here. But I'm not sure this is my vocation for the rest of my life.'

His comment stayed with me and I mulled it over. Bill Latham was not around so much anymore, as he and his girlfriend had moved into their own home, and I would need help with my home and to pursue my wider charitable interests. I wondered to myself: *was that something that John might be interested in?*

I mentioned the idea to him a day or two later. He listened, looked interested and said he would think it over. When I left New York to return home, John and I agreed to keep in close touch.

* * *

In October, I turned sixty. *Sixty!* It's an august occasion and so I marked it by taking eighty or so friends and family members on a Mediterranean cruise. Olivia and Gloria came, as did Pat and John Farrar, John McElynn flew over from New York and Shirley Bassey sang 'Happy Birthday' to me.

I also gave a short speech. 'Sixty is no different to any other number,' I said. 'Inside, I'm still a bubbling eighteen-year-old Society seems to think if you're over forty, you can't have fun. Well, they're wrong!'

I had worried beforehand that my year off might possibly drag. I could not have been more wrong. It had flown by, and I returned to work at the start of 2001 ready to go again but also determined to take things that bit easier than I had in the past.

It was time to record a new album and I decided to indulge myself. I asked Alan Tarney to produce me again, for the first time since we'd made *Stronger* in 1989, and on *Wanted*, I embraced the luxury of singing a host of classic songs that I had always longed to record.

This meant Elvis's 'All Shook Up' and 'Love Me Tender', The Beatles' 'And I Love Her' and Carole King's 'You've Got A Friend' among many others. It was a joy to croon 'Moon River' . . . and I finally got to sing 'What's Love Got to Do with It'! The lead-off single was a medley of 'Somewhere over the Rainbow' and Louis Armstrong's 'What a Wonderful World'. Before the album came out, I promoted it with twelve shows at my London second home, aka the Royal Albert Hall.

The other thing that happened in 2001 was that John McElynn took his own sabbatical from the Church, did a load of travelling and eventually told me that he'd like to take me up on my offer of informally helping me out with my charitable activities.

This was great for me. When he moved over, John instantly gave me good company, companionship and the invaluable help I needed. It banished the loneliness that I felt living on my own and gave John the reboot and kickstart he thought his own life needed. It was good for both of us – and long may it last.

The big excitement at the end of 2001 was the construction work on my home in Barbados being completed (this project also ended up occupying a lot of John's time). The house was all that I had hoped for, and I knew already how contented I would be there. I moved in in time for my very first Caribbean Christmas.

Having decided to scale back my work commitments, my life now fell into a very comfortable cyclical routine. Each year, if I was not on tour, I'd spend winters in Barbados and summers in Portugal. I'd also try to take in Wimbledon and the US Open. It was, in many ways, a dream life, but after forty years of near non-stop work, I kind of felt like I had earned it.

It left me plenty of time to fit in other things. Early in 2002, my old acquaintance Des O'Connor came to Portugal to talk to me for a TV special – and to film the uncorking of my first homemade Vida Nova red wine. It was delicious, if I say so myself. The first glass tasted special, as I sipped it and looked down at the vines that had produced it.

In June, I was back at Buckingham Palace to appear in the Queen's Golden Jubilee party. Everybody was there, from Paul McCartney, Elton, Tom Jones and Queen (the band!) to Shirley Bassey and Ozzy Osbourne. Now that's what you *call* a party!

It was a joy to be asked along, and to play a couple of songs as Her Majesty looked on. I sang 'Living Doll' then performed 'Move It' with Brian May and S Club 7. It was funny to reflect that none of that pop band were even *born* until twenty years after that song was a hit!

While I was in London, I met up with Gloria Hunniford. She had just interviewed Neil Diamond on her radio show, and we went to see him play Earls Court. *What a voice!* And I had no idea he'd written so many great songs that had been made hits by other artists, from UB40's 'Red Red Wine' to 'I'm a Believer' by The Monkees.

Gloria said she was meeting Neil for dinner afterwards and he'd specifically said that he'd like me to be there. *Me?* I had no idea why, but I happily went along. Neil and I sat together and chatted like mad and then, out of the blue, he said, 'Well, you sure saved my life back in the sixties!'

'Pardon?' I said, puzzled.

'I was on my uppers in New York,' Neil explained. 'I had no work and no money, was at the end of my tether and suddenly I got a cheque for a few thousand dollars for some of my songs being performed by Cliff Richard.'

Wow!

My mind flew all the way back to the sixties and recording 'Solitary Man', 'Girl, You'll Be a Woman Soon' and 'I'll Come Running', plus doing 'Just Another Guy' as a B-side.

'*Really?*' I said.

'Yeah!' Neil grinned. 'I'd never heard of you and I didn't know who you were, but you pulled me out of the doldrums!'

It was a lovely story to hear. *I had kept the young Neil Diamond afloat!* I went home with a real spring in my step.

* * *

I took the *Wanted* album on a world tour then spent much of 2003 in Barbados, enjoying the sunshine. That summer, I went to Nashville to begin work on my next LP, *Something's Goin' On*. I love going there to record – they live and breathe music.

A guy called Tommy Sims, who used to play bass in a Christian rock band and had toured with Bruce Springsteen and written 'Change the World' for Eric Clapton, produced four songs on the album. As we were packing up for the day one teatime, he mentioned that he was playing a gig that night.

'Oh, can I come to see you?' I asked.

'Sure!'

'Which theatre is it in?'

'It's not in a theatre. It's in a pub!'

So, I went along to see this hugely successful musician playing with his mates in a band in a noisy, crowded bar, not for his career, or for attention, or probably even for any money, but just because he wanted to play. *He needed to play.* And that's what it should all be about – and, in Nashville, what it *is* about.

* * *

My life was going great in the early 2000s but a large part of the wider world was not faring so well. The second Gulf War had kicked off in Iraq and American and British forces had invaded the country to search for Weapons of Mass Destruction (WMDs) and depose the dictator Saddam Hussein. Every night, I watched bombs and missiles raining down on Baghdad on the TV news. I also saw the British Prime Minister, Tony Blair, making his case, and coming under increasing criticism and pressure to explain his actions.

I'm not very political, but I suppose I've never been a natural Labour Party supporter. I always thought the Conservative Party's emphasis on hard work and self-reliance chimed more with the values I inherited from my father, and I used to admire Margaret Thatcher.

However, Tony Blair seemed a very decent man, and as I watched him on TV each night, he seemed to be ageing before my eyes. I could see him growing more and more gaunt and haggard. I had never met Tony but I did know his wife, Cherie, a little after meeting her at one of my shows, so I phoned her up.

'I'm going to be away from Barbados in August,' I told her. 'If you and Tony would like to stay in my house, you're very welcome.'

I think they were grateful for the offer and they accepted. Tony later told me he'd never known such privacy. He said he was able to sit on the balcony off my master bedroom, pull a curtain closed behind him, read and relax.

He certainly hadn't found going into Iraq an easy decision. 'George [W. Bush] and I were in a terrible dilemma,' he told me. 'We were acting on military intelligence and we had no reason not to believe what they told us. We knew if we didn't go in, and Saddam had the WMDs, we lose. If we did go in, and he *didn't* have them, we lose. We didn't sit there saying, "Shall we? Shan't we?" It was an intelligence-led decision.'

'Yes, but Iraq is bigger than California,' I said. 'If I had a few days, *I* could hide something in California and you'd never find it!'

I don't know whether Tony was right or wrong. I just knew that it sounded like an impossible decision, and I wouldn't have liked to have had to make it.

* * *

The next year, 2004, brought a holiday to Australia and a Tearfund trip to Cambodia. I played fourteen more nights at the Albert Hall – I should have been getting my post delivered there! – and also did a 'Summer Nights' tour of British stately homes and castles.

One of the shows was at Leeds Castle, in Kent, and Cilla Black sang with me. I'd known Cilla forever, of course, going right back to the early sixties, but it was only after I got my place in Barbados that she and I became really close.

Cilla was in Barbados before me, because she and her husband, Bobby, had bought an apartment, not long before he died of cancer. When I moved out there, we found that we got invited to a lot of the same parties and events and so we started going together. In fact, I kind of became Cilla's chauffeur!

I'd phone her up: 'Are you going to Eddie's bash?'

'Yes!'

'OK, I'll pick you up at seven!' I drove her around the island to all the great parties.

I didn't mind, because I loved Cilla's company. I was in awe of her music career and her great Number 1s like 'Anyone Who Had a Heart' and 'You're My World', and I also admired the way she had moved on to become such a huge TV star. I used to love watching her on *Blind Date*. She was so funny and smart and could always put everybody at their ease. I told her that I thought she always seemed able to guide the girls towards the best guy.

'I'll let you into a little secret,' she said. 'I used to look through the curtains and watch the boys rehearsing and plotting their answers to the questions. I could spot the wrong 'uns a mile off!'

Cilla had certainly been the music world's loss and TV's gain, but she had been hosting shows for so long now that she'd stopped thinking of herself as a singer. When I asked her to sing a duet with me at my Leeds Castle show, she was horrified.

'Oh no, chuck, I couldn't do *that*!' she said.

I had to sweet-talk her for days before she reluctantly agreed to do it. Then, on the night, we duetted on 'It Takes Two' and she was incredible. When you've got a voice as good as hers, you don't just lose it.

* * *

My new album, *Something's Goin' On*, went Top 10 and I was proud of a single from it called 'I Cannot Give You My Love'. Barry Gibb co-wrote it for me and produced it at his studio in Miami. *Working with Barry from the Bee Gees, my all-time favourite band bar none?* My dream just kept finding more and more ways to come true.

The single charted despite – yet again! – getting hardly any radio play. However, by now another iniquity in the music industry had become even more of a bugbear. The copyright that artists hold on songs they record – which allows them to get paid when those songs are played or sold – used to last for fifty years and then expire. That didn't bother me when I was eighteen! I just thought, *I won't even be ALIVE in fifty years, who cares?*

Well, nearly fifty years later, I was still very much alive, I was about to lose all of my copyrights on my old hits and I *did* care! I started giving interviews and lobbying anybody that I could about what I believed was a very discriminatory law.

I upped my campaign as the deadline neared and in May 2005, I got invited to a lunch with European Union politicians in Brussels. The purpose of the meeting was to discuss a possible Copyright Extension Law to protect veteran performers like me.

At the lunch, I stood up and gave a little speech. 'This is very unfair,' I told the assembled politicians. 'You wouldn't take away somebody's house just because they have lived in it for fifty years so why take artists' copyrights away?' I hoped I had given them food for thought.

The following year brought personal change for me. After twenty years, I sold Charters. I wasn't spending enough time in the UK each year to justify keeping such a big house. Instead, I bought myself a smaller place on the edge of the Wentworth Golf Estate.

I've always enjoyed collaborating with other artists and so I loved doing 2006's *Two's Company*, an album of duets. It got called a covers album, but I don't really like that description. I prefer *revivals*, because I was reviving some fabulous old songs with equally fabulous singers.

It was great to see Brian Bennett from The Shadows again when he drummed on 'Move It' with me and Brian May. We put it out as a double A-side single, with '21st Century Christmas', and it went to Number 2 – just as it had in 1958!

I also did my first posthumous duet, with Matt Monro on 'Let There Be Love'. I called Matt's widow, Mickie, for permission and working on the song showed me just how great his voice was. Frank Sinatra once called Matt the greatest crooner of all time. Now *that* is truly high praise!*

The album had its prickly moments. Dionne Warwick had first sung 'Anyone Who Had a Heart' in 1963, having a big hit with it in America and elsewhere. However, she missed out in Britain because Cilla had nipped in and released her version first.

I sang the song with Dionne on *Two's Company* because I heard she was around and I wanted to sing it with the original performer. I'm not sure she'd ever forgiven Cilla: she passed a comment to me about Cilla 'stealing her song'. At least she was smiling when she said it.

Then, of course, the next time I saw Cilla, she was upset that I'd sung it with Dionne: 'But why didn't you ask *me*, Cliff?' *Gulp!* I did the only (cowardly) thing I could . . . and blamed the record label!

---

* Mickie also told me that Matt had heard my live version of the song and joked that it was the second-best version he'd ever heard – after his own! I was well chuffed with that.

I also got a further insight – as if I needed one! – into the narrow minds of radio programmers. I did a remake of The Carpenters' 'Yesterday Once More' with Daniel O'Donnell and EMI, who were releasing the album, were quite taken with it.

'We don't think that song's been covered before,' they told me. 'Can we release it as a single?' I asked Daniel, who was fine with it, and so EMI played it to Radio 2. Their response? 'We don't play Daniel O'Donnell' – *an artist with a successful 25-year career behind him.* I ask you! What chance did the single have?

And why not Daniel? He's the only artist I know of who has had a Top 30 album every year for almost twenty-five years on the trot! Many of them in the Top 10!

* * *

At the end of 2006 and the start of 2007, I roamed the world, from Southeast Asia to Iceland, on a Here and Now tour of hits from all throughout my career. I also got to record in Barbados for the first time, at Eddy Grant's studio, for 2007's *Love . . . The Album.*

On a sadder, much more personal note, on 18 October 2007, my mother died. She had been in the care home for many years and had stayed lively. The nurses twigged that, despite her dementia, she was somebody who liked to keep active, so they had a little routine going.

If they were working in a storeroom, Mum would always ask to help, so they'd give her some towels to fold. Mum would do it, they'd say 'Thank you!' and she would go away. They'd scruff the towels up again and, ten minutes later, Mum would come back and do it all again. It was harmless and kept her busy.

Mum was eighty-seven when she passed and by then her dementia had truly taken hold and she often wouldn't recognise us. She just slept a lot of the time and eventually died of pneumonia. It was a merciful release but it still hit me, hard – harder than I'd expected it to.

Right from the start, in India, into the time I was Brylcreeming my hair, curling my lip and changing my name from Harry, through all the years of my success, she had never been anything other than caring, supportive ... and loving. I couldn't have wished for a better mum.

I miss her today, and I always will.

* * *

By 2009, I'd been a pop-rock star for more than half a century, but I'd never forgotten that it all started with Cliff Richard & The Shadows (or, if I'm being pedantic, The Drifters!). I was delighted to hook up with them again to record a fiftieth anniversary album, *Reunited*.

Except that the album was rather misleadingly named – when we made it, we never even met! Hank recorded his guitars in Australia, where he's lived for years, Bruce and Brian worked in London, and I did my vocals in Barry Gibb's studio in Miami.

It didn't matter. We know each other so well that the music comes together even when we're apart. Plus, of course, we knew we were to see a lot of each other at the end of the year when we went out on the road together.

The Reunited tour was fantastic. We got on well and laughed together, on and off the stage, just as we had back in 1959. And yet, if I am honest, one specific aspect of the tour niggled and rankled with me.

The Shadows didn't want to play any songs that they hadn't played on the first time around. It limited our repertoire to the six years or so that we'd recorded together, ruling out any of my solo hits since then. So, no 'Devil Woman', no 'We Don't Talk Anymore', no 'Miss You Nights', no 'Some People', no 'Saviour's Day' . . . I could go on!

Although I enjoyed the tour, it was frustrating because that policy made it a bit of a period piece. I'd have loved to play more recent songs as well, and I think most of the fans would have liked to hear them. *Oh well! That's showbiz!*

After the Reunited tour, I moved my British base again. I got an apartment in Sunningdale in a development called Charters – the same name as the house where I'd lived contentedly for twenty years. Sadly, *this* Charters was not to hold such happy memories.

It was all-change for my homes in the UK around now, as I gave my sister Jacqui the Bryn Moel Welsh holiday cottage that I had bought in 1972. With my places in Barbados and Portugal, I just wasn't spending enough time there to justify holding on to it. But it was a wrench to see it go – I'd had so many lovely times there.

When you reach my great age, landmarks come around alarmingly quickly! The end of 2010 saw my seventieth birthday. I always like to do something special for these occasions, so we put out a new album and staged celebratory Albert Hall concerts.

For *Bold as Brass*, I tackled songs from the Great American Songbook by classic songwriters like George Gershwin, Hoagy Carmichael, Cole Porter and Richard Rodgers. It hit Number 3 in the album chart, my highest placing for seventeen years – a *very* cool birthday present!

It was America that inspired my love for music and, over my career, I have returned to that source so many times. Elvis gave me my love of rock and roll – and, in 2011, I went back to the US to drink from another creative and fertile musical well.

I travelled to Memphis to begin work on *Soulicious*, an album that saw me duet with some of the biggest names in American soul music. The project was the brainchild of David Gest, who first told Gloria Hunniford that he felt I should do a soul duets album.

I told Gloria to ask David to give me a call, and when he did, it was clear he had the great contacts to make it happen. He reeled off star name after star name, and the producer was one of the biggest stars of all: Lamont Dozier, one of the greatest songwriters and producers in the history of Tamla Motown, and of music as a whole.

Lamont was part of the classic Holland-Dozier-Holland team, who wrote countless huge US hits for artists such as The Supremes, The Four Tops and Martha & The Vandellas, and he has to date penned fifty-four global Number 1s. People praise Lennon and McCartney, but even *they* never had a success rate like that.

A jaw-dropping succession of legends passed through his Memphis studio while I was there. I sang with Freda Payne, Candi Staton, Dennis Edwards & the Temptations, Peabo Bryson and Percy Sledge. *Percy Sledge!* It was pinch-myself time. I felt very, very lucky.

Naturally, I also took advantage of being in Memphis to pay a return visit to Graceland, nearly fifty years after my first, when Elvis's dad, Vernon, had shown me around. Unsurprisingly, there had been a few changes to the place since I'd last dropped in.

They had built a museum in the backyard (as Americans say) full of Elvis's guitars, clothes and artefacts. They had also buried Elvis, his mother and father and his stillborn twin brother, Jesse, together in that same yard.

Standing next to his tomb, I was overcome: *I can't believe I'm so close to Elvis!* Now in my seventies, I was just as awestruck by him as I had been as a teenager. I had tears in my eyes – and then I saw a guy next to me, who was also having a bit of a moment.

'I'm having a double attack of feelings!' he said, smiling at me.

'Why?' I asked him.

'Because I'm standing next to Elvis's body – and I'm standing next to Cliff Richard!'

It turned out he was a Dutch guy, who knew of me because The Shadows and I had always been big in the Netherlands. We talked for a few minutes, then he wandered off, shaking his head: 'You sure never know *who* you are going to meet in Graceland!'

* * *

After working with Lamont Dozier, I transferred to New York to finish off *Soulicious* with two more soul greats: the husband-and-wife singing, songwriting and production team of Nickolas Ashford and Valerie Simpson. Valerie sang a duet with me, which was a thrill in itself.

Ashford and Simpson also drafted in more stars. Peabo Bryson sang 'Birds of a Feather' with me and the great Roberta Flack wafted by to duet on 'When I Was Your Baby'. In fact, Roberta arrived to do her bit – and kicked me out of the studio!

Valerie told me in advance that Roberta had said she was just going to wing her vocal and she didn't want me there just in case I heard her singing badly! It sounded pretty unlikely to me, but I absented myself from the studio for a couple of hours when she arrived.

I went down the road, found a Starbucks and sat on their stoop outside, drinking a mocha. Watching people going about their daily business, I thought to myself, *None of you realise it, but I'm doing a duet with Roberta Flack RIGHT NOW!* It was a strange moment.

When I got back to the studio, I called ahead to see if I was OK to go up and was told, yes, Roberta had finished. She sounded fantastic, of course, as she was always going to . . . and then she paid me a compliment I will never forget.

'When I Was Your Baby' had a line that went *'Seeing you this way/Just takes my breath away.'* While singing it, I had exhaled softly as I did so. Roberta was very impressed by this: 'Cliff, that's the dollars!' she told me.

Getting praise from Roberta Flack? I don't know if my dream ever dared to extend this far! It was one of the many highlights of the *Soulicious* project, when I felt privileged to get the rare chance to mix with unbelievable singers and soul-music royalty.

There was a sad postscript to making the album. Nick Ashford was very ill with throat cancer and understandably was not able to spend as much time in the studio as he had hoped to. Just a month after we had wrapped up recording, he was dead. I had found him to be a true gentleman.

* * *

Lamont Dozier, Freda Payne, Percy Sledge, Marilyn McCoo and Billy Davis Jr came over to Britain to join me on the road when I took *Soulicious* on a short arena tour at the end of 2011. James Ingram took the part of Peabo Bryson. As we embarked on the road, I got an unfortunate reminder of the ageism I now found myself up against.

The tour kicked off in Nottingham, and on the afternoon before the show, I popped into a local coffee shop. A group of eight or so young people, probably only teenagers, noticed me but they were cool and left me alone. It was only as I was about to leave that they got up, came over and started showering me with compliments:

'Cliff, my mother thinks you're great!'

'My gran says you're fantastic!'

But then came the inevitable kicker: 'Are you still making records?'

I sighed. 'I have an album in the Top 10 right now!' I said. 'But I don't blame you for not knowing – it's not your fault.' At the risk of sounding like a stuck record, how can those kids be expected to know I have new music out if the radio never plays it?

I did at least have some good news from the record industry in 2011. After my assiduous campaigning, and years of deliberation, the EU finally voted to extend the copyright on sound recordings from fifty to seventy years.

It meant that I would continue to receive money whenever my songs were bought and broadcast, yet it was a bittersweet victory. The EU decreed that this new law would only apply to music that was made after 1963 – i.e. five years after I had started recording.

Like many people, the EU seemed to assume that pop music began in 1963, with The Beatles. *Well, let me tell you, it didn't!* The first British rock and rollers like me, Marty Wilde, Billy Fury and Terry Dene were releasing records back in 1958 . . . as were our American heroes.

It means that I'll never again receive royalties on 'Move It', 'Living Doll', 'Travellin' Light', 'The Young Ones', 'Summer Holiday' – so many songs from right at the outset of my career. *How can that make sense?* I think it's wrong and unfair. But there's nothing I can do about it.

I guess the Queen is one of the few figures in British public life who has been around for longer than I have(!), and in 2012, I was back at Buckingham Palace for Her Majesty's Diamond Jubilee concert. I sang a medley of hits, finishing up with 'Congratulations'.

It was a great event, with lots of younger stars: Robbie Williams, JLS, Cheryl Cole and Ed Sheeran. Luckily for me, there were plenty of old-timers as well: Tom Jones, Shirley Bassey, Stevie Wonder, Elton and Paul McCartney. It was a fantastic day.

I had plenty of downtime in 2012, and enjoyed my usual fixes of Barbados, Portugal and tennis. Highlights for me were being invited to carry the Olympic torch in Birmingham and attending Danny Boyle's opening ceremony in London, which was mind-blowing.

After that quiet year, I was ready to gear up again in 2013, which I began with an Australasian and Far East tour. Then, for a very special landmark in my career, it was time to take it all back to right where I had begun.

My next release was to be my hundredth album.* *A hundred albums!* It seemed scarcely believable. So, I decided that, as I brought up my century, I would pay tribute to the pioneering American rock and rollers who had inspired me to begin singing in the first place.

I flew back to Nashville that spring to make *The Fabulous Rock 'n' Roll Songbook*. I worked with a producer, Steve Mandile, who I think would bleed music if you cut him, and I gave myself carte blanche to choose my favourite tracks from the very first wave of US rock and rollers. As usual, the only difficult part was deciding what to leave out.

I felt like a kid on Christmas Day. I covered – no, *revived* – so many great tracks: Little Richard's 'Rip It Up', Chuck Berry's 'School Days' and 'Johnny B. Goode', Ricky Nelson's 'Stood Up' and Buddy Holly's 'Rave On' are to me the very sound of rock and roll being invented.

I loved singing The Everly Brothers' 'Wake Up Little Susie' with Vince Gill, and doing Bobby Darin's 'Dream Lover'. And I was never going to make a record like this without a handful of Elvis songs! I went for 'Such a Night', 'Teddy Bear' and 'Stuck on You'.

While in Nashville, I also got to play an impromptu show at the Grand Ole Opry. All the greats of country music have played there, from Patsy Cline, Hank Williams, Johnny Cash and Dolly Parton right through to Carrie Underwood. Vince Gill was hosting the night I appeared and invited me along.

---

* That includes live albums and compilations – not even I work hard enough to make a hundred original studio albums!

Meeting Princess Diana with tennis players Michael Chang (front) and John McEnroe's doubles partner, Peter Fleming, June 1989.

'Feed the world… again!' Recording Band Aid II in 1989. Who can you recognise?

Receiving my knighthood at Buckingham Palace, 1995. '*This* has been a long time coming!' said the Queen.' Sadly, my reply was tongue-tied gibberish.

Making a racquet (sorry!) at Wimbledon Centre Court, June 1996, with the sportiest backing singers I've ever had.

When I put on the
wig, I transformed…
playing Heathcliff at
the NIA Birmingham,
December 1996.

With Jill Dando: a
wonderful lady and
a terrible loss.

Queens everywhere: performing
'Move It' with Brian May at the
real Queen's Golden Jubilee party,
Buckingham Palace, 3 June 2002.

John with Cilla
(and me), they
became good friends.

I played my favourite sport in the world to raise money for my Tennis Foundation. This is in Birmingham in 2004.

(Left and below) Meeting local children on a Tearfund charity trip to Cambodia, 2004.

With Olivia Newton-John at a Tennis Foundation fundraiser night, Hampton Court, 2004.

One of the greatest light entertainers of all time. And Barry Manilow (OK, OK, I'm joking!)

The very best of interviewers, and a great and loyal friend, Gloria Hunniford, always with me through thick and thin.

Who would ever have thought I'd become a winemaker? Growing the grapes for *Vida Nova* in my vineyard in Portugal, 2006.

Reunited with The Shadows: Bruce, Hank, Brian and me before a June 2004 gig at the London Palladium.

Re-recording 'Move It' with Brian Bennett and Brian May, 2006. It went to Number 2 – just like it had in 1958!

Fifty years on, and still in pink: at the O2 Arena, London, in September 2009 on Cliff Richard and The Shadows' final tour (*well, maybe…*)

The great Lamont Dozier and me in front of Sun Studios, where Elvis first recorded, 2011.

Another soul legend: with Dionne Warwick before a Royal Albert Hall charity show, May 2012.

Old friends – and competitors – reunited: with Sir Paul McCartney at the Queen's Diamond Jubilee concert, 2012.

When you've been around as
long as I have, you get to meet
the most unexpected people!
With Alice Cooper…

… and Rod Stewart.

The London Palladium Wall of
Fame. I'm five bricks up, between
Cilla and Des.

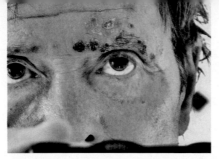

The stress of events in 2014 was so bad that I developed shingles and could have gone blind…

But I cried with gratitude when I saw the yellow ribbons that fans tied on the gates of my Quinta in Portugal when I was at my lowest point.

Without them, I am nothing: my chief songwriters Alan Tarney, Bruce Welch, John Farrar, Brian Bennett and Terry Britten at my 75th birthday concert, Royal Albert Hall, 14 October 2015.

'Seventy-five? But I still feel eighteen!'

On my 58-18=60 tour at Bournemouth BIC, October 2018. Next stop, when this pandemic has cleared: The Great 80…

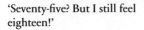

I was transfixed to learn that a teenage Elvis had played the Opry in 1954, but his rock and roll and gyrations were apparently frowned upon, and the unimpressed venue manager had advised him to 'stick to driving a truck'! I was relieved that nobody said that to me after my performance!

After Wimbledon – and watching Andy Murray win the title! – I was happy to see my hundredth album go Top 10 in Britain, just as my first, *Cliff*, had done in 1959. It was a nice end to a very satisfying year . . . then, as 2014 dawned, I got a highly intriguing offer.

Malcolm Smith phoned me and said that the British singer Morrissey had been telling people he wanted me to support him at his show at the 15,000-capacity Barclays Center in New York that summer. I was amazed – *Morrissey? What would he want with me?*

'Is this some sort of bad joke, Malcolm?' I asked.

Malcolm went away and called Morrissey's management, then phoned me back.

'No, it's genuine, Cliff,' he told me. 'Morrissey really likes you. Are you interested?'

Hmm. I Googled Morrissey and read up on him. He certainly seemed an . . . interesting character, but his music was very weird and lyrically downbeat. One of his songs was called 'First of the Gang to Die'! I wasn't sure that we'd have a lot in common.

I spoke to Malcolm again: 'What would I have to do?'

'He wants you to play an hour-long support set.'

An hour! I was used to doing two-hour concerts. If I condensed all of my biggest hits into a one-hour set, I didn't know if

Morrissey would be able to follow me (if I can say so myself!). Although, then again, his fans *are* apparently very loyal to him.

Still, I was flattered to be asked, and playing to fifteen thousand people in New York would be amazing – I certainly couldn't pull that kind of crowd in America myself. And I've always liked trying new things. 'OK!' I told Malcolm. 'Let's do it!'

Sadly, the show never happened because Morrissey cancelled with a health complaint. But he apologised to us – and suggested that I might like to tour with him in Britain.

No, thank you, I said to myself. *I don't do 'support' in Britain!*

My only concern about the New York show being cancelled was that I knew that about two hundred of my fans in Britain and Canada had bought tickets for the show, which they could get refunded – and paid for plane tickets and hotels, which they couldn't. I didn't want them to lose out.

Through Facebook, I sent them all a message: 'Go anyway!' I told them. 'You'll love New York! Just take your tickets for the Morrissey show with you and I'll try to do something for you.'

So, I booked the Gramercy Theater, a small Manhattan gig venue that held maybe five hundred people, for the night I'd been due to support Morrissey. And I played a special, intimate one-off show for all of my fans who'd flown in.

Some of my New York friends came down and told me later that there had been a few Morrissey fans in the audience, and they had spoken to them.

'Oh, really? What did they think of it?' I asked.

'They thought you were *quite* good.'

It was such a cool, great evening – even Morrissey fans thought I was *quite* good!

* * *

After Wimbledon, I headed to Portugal for the summer in high spirits. I was able to completely relax there, as ever, although I did pick up my guitar to play a charity gig for my local winery.

I felt as if the plan I had formulated in 2000 had come together. I had got off the treadmill and wouldn't be getting back on. I was now able to pick and choose my work projects as I saw fit and do whatever I wanted – even if it was tiny, quirky theatre shows!

There was one small downside to my happiness at this point. There are all sorts of nasty things on the internet, and for a few months, I'd been vaguely aware of online rumours and stories linking me to some kind of horrible scandal.

My management had said there were internet conspiracy theories of a paedophile ring based around a place called the Elm Guest House in Barnes, southwest London. Famous people, including politicians, judges and entertainers, had supposedly met there decades ago to abuse young boys.

It sounded so bizarre as to be truly nonsensical. A list of alleged molesters had appeared online, and the names included former prime minister Edward Heath, politicians Leon Brittan and Harvey Proctor, a former head of the British Army – and me!*

---

* Later the accusations were all proved false. In 2016, a report by Sir Richard Henriques dismissed all the allegations and found more than forty irregularities in the police investigation of them. The head of the Metropolitan Police apologised personally to Sir Harvey Proctor.

It was disturbing, and a great example of the bad side of the internet, and yet I wasn't worried about it. I'd never even *heard* of that guest house in Barnes, so what did it have to do with me? It was clearly all a load of spurious rubbish, and I assumed it would just go away.

It was a minor concern. In fact, as I headed into my senior years, I felt as if my musical career and my personal life were both exactly where I wanted them to be. More than at any point in my life, I was living the dream. I felt fulfilled, satisfied, contented . . . and *happy*.

That all came to an end on Thursday, 14 August 2014.

EIGHTEEN
LOTS OF SMOKE. NO FIRE

The phone rang at about ten in the morning. My sister Joan and her partner, Martyn, were with John McElynn and me, and we were pottering around in the kitchen in my place in Portugal. The four of us were about to head off for a short break we were all looking forward to.

Our plan was to have lunch in Alentejo with my friend and wine consultant, David Baverstock, who would show us around his vineyard. Then we would spend a couple of nights in a lovely nearby medieval town called Évora. I'd already thrown my bags in the car.

I picked up the phone, casually: 'Hello?'

It was the manager of the Charters apartment block where I had my place in Sunningdale. 'Sir Cliff, are you alone?' he asked me.

'No,' I said. 'I have friends and family with me.'

'Then you may want to go somewhere private and call me back,' he said. *Huh?* I hung up, went to another room, and rang him straight back on my mobile.

The words he said next were the biggest shock I could imagine – and in that second, my life changed forever. My dream life was about to transform into an utter nightmare. A living nightmare.

'The police are here with a warrant to search your apartment,' he said.

'What is it about?' I asked him.

'I don't know. They just say they have a warrant.'

What?! I couldn't begin to figure what was going on, but I did at least know what I had to do.

'Well, if they have a warrant, you have to let them in,' I replied. 'If you don't, they can just break the door down. Please, let them in – they're not going to find anything!'

'OK,' the manager agreed. We hung up. In a state of absolute panic, I called Malcolm Smith, who happened to be staying in his house in Portugal at the time. He didn't know anything about whatever was going on.

My thoughts were in a whirl as I rejoined the others in the kitchen, told them what had happened, and John, Joan, Martyn and I set off on our trip. All through the ninety-minute drive up the motorway, my mind was in turmoil: *what was this about?* And then our phones began to ring, and the terrible truth unfolded.

My management called back and said that the raid was being conducted by the South Yorkshire Police. It had been prompted by 'allegations of a sexual nature, dating back to the 1980s'. And the police were in my apartment right now.

What the . . . ? Good Lord! How could this be happening? WAS it really happening?

The lunch was horrific. Our phones kept ringing non-stop and we had to keep leaving the table to take the calls. I apologised to David and told him what was going on: 'I'm so sorry, but something horrible is happening to me right now.' And one of the phone calls brought me news so awful, I couldn't begin to process it.

The BBC were reporting on the police raid live. And, as it went on, they were filming the outside of my apartment from a helicopter.

Malcolm and I rushed out a press statement – and I felt we had no choice but to reference the nonsense about the guest house in Barnes:

> *For many months, I have been aware of allegations against me of historic impropriety, which have been circulating online. The allegations are completely false. Up until now, I have chosen not to dignify the false allegations with a response, as it would just give them more oxygen.*
>
> *However, the police attended my apartment in Berkshire today without notice, except, it would appear, to the media. I am not presently in the UK but it goes without saying that I will cooperate fully should the police wish to speak to me.*

We had booked a hotel in Évora and as soon as we got there, I turned on the TV. Rolling news being what it is, it didn't take long for me to see the footage I had been told about – the footage the entire world was currently watching.

'Sir Cliff House Search' screamed the headline at the foot of the screen, as the BBC news theme played. I stared in utter horror as, to a soundtrack of whirring helicopter blades, an airborne cameraman filmed police moving around inside my home. Looking for . . . *what? Why?*

Oh. My. Lord. I stared at the television, deep in catatonic shock. I saw two or three people walking from the front of my building, carrying cardboard boxes and black bin liners. *Why? What could be in them? What was happening?*

I was later told that a detective superintendent had appeared on the screen, outside a South Yorkshire police station. Reading a statement in a flat voice, he said they had 'received an allegation of a sexual nature that involved a boy under the age of sixteen years'.

I didn't sleep a wink in the hotel that night.

We had been due to be away for two nights on that mini-break, but the next morning, we decided to head home. 'Let's get back and sort this out,' said John. On the way home, we phoned the Quinta gardener, Carlos. He said that there were lots of people outside and it was going to be difficult to get back in.

We decided to drive to the house of my business partner in the winery, Nigel Birch, and his wife, Lesley, to work out what we were going to do. I told them what was happening, but they had already seen it on TV. *Of course they had!*

'How on earth am I going to get past the press?' I worried.

'Maybe duck down inside the car?' suggested Nigel.

In the end, I didn't need to. There are three gates leading from the road to the Quinta and as we approached, at sunset, the paparazzi were congregated outside all three of them. Somehow, they didn't see me as we swept through the main gate and up the drive.

We parked the car right in front of the window to my kitchen. It's the only room that you can see into from the road, so the car blocked the photographers' view. It meant that at least I could move around my house without being seen from outside.

My life had changed overnight. I had been accused of a heinous crime, awful beyond belief, by . . . well, I didn't even *know* who by! And the BBC had broadcast that accusation around the world.

That was the worst thing. Before I had a chance to defend myself, or even learn what I was accused of, people all over the globe had seen that news report: *Sir Cliff Richard. Police raid. Historical sexual abuse. A young boy, under sixteen . . .*

My family, my friends, my fans, people in every country I had ever played in my career, would have seen that damning BBC footage. People close to me would know I was innocent, of course. But what of the others? What if most people thought: *There's no smoke without fire?*

My world collapsed. I went into an absolute meltdown. The first day back at the Quinta was the worst. It was the day that John found me sobbing on the kitchen floor, unable to walk, to stand up, to see any way out of the deep, dark hole I'd been suddenly flung into.

John knelt by me and said those careful, consoling words that have stayed with me. They bear repeating:

'Look, did you do this thing they are accusing you of?'

'Of course not!'

'No! And have you ever done anything like that?'

'Of course not!'

'Well, *I* know you haven't! And *you* know you haven't! The truth is on your side. So, what are you doing down there? Get up! Get up – and hold your head up! You have nothing to feel guilty about, or to cry about!'

It gave me strength. I stood up. But I knew that torment lay ahead.

* * *

Elton John was one of the first people to phone me when the storm broke. Elton had had his own previous problems with false sex allegations in the media, of course, so he doubtless had some idea of how I felt. As you would expect, he was empathic and encouraging.

I was also touched to get a call from Tony Blair. Tony said that he and Cherie didn't believe a word of the allegations and listened sympathetically as I told him how helpless I felt as I watched my name being traduced across the globe.

'I can't even look at the internet, Tony,' I said. 'People are saying such awful things about me.'

Tony gave a wry chuckle. 'You want to see people saying even worse things?' he asked. 'Google *my* name!'

I even laughed, for a second.

Four days after the police raid, a legal team flew out to Portugal for a crisis meeting with me and Malcolm Smith. I felt numb and shell-shocked as we sat around my table. The lawyers seemed to understand the allegations were definitely not true – but they told me that the police wanted to talk to me, in Yorkshire, on 23 August.

Five days away.

I cancelled or postponed virtually everything I had lined up. I had agreed to sing in Canterbury Cathedral, to raise money to repair its roof, which – ironically – the BBC had been going to film. But I knew there was no way I could face an audience now.

I have always loved having people come to stay – that was why I'd had the car port at the Quinta converted into rooms – and I had a string of guests lined up in Portugal over the next few weeks. Every single one emailed me when the news broke, offering sympathy and to cancel their visits.

'Don't worry, we won't come,' they all said. 'You will probably want to be on your own.'

I emailed them all back like a shot. 'No, I do *not* want to be on my own!' I replied. '*Please* come!'

I lay low at the Quinta with a few of my friends. They were so kind, and supportive, and we'd even sometimes have a laugh. But the second I stopped laughing, my fear returned. I remembered that I was living a nightmare.

Bonnie Lythgoe, the former dancer and producer, came for a day with her two sons. My tennis court was not visible from the gates, so she and I began a game of tennis. I felt nervous leaving the house, but the game got my blood pumping, as it always does, and I was almost enjoying it until Bonnie stopped dead, as she was about to serve, and pointed behind me.

'I just saw a cameraman take a picture!' she said.

I whirled around, but the photographer who had crept onto my land had already legged it. I phoned the lawyers and they were able to stop the photo being used as it had been taken on my private property. We didn't play any more games of tennis.

The nights were the worst. Each night, I'd fall into a shallow sleep but wake up at 3.15am – *always 3.15am* – and lie awake for the rest of the night. I'd get three hours' sleep, at most. It was the last thing I thought about as I fell asleep; the first when I woke up.

I can never face people again, I thought. *I can never get on a stage again. There is no way out of this hole. No way!*

I'd lie awake at night remembering the dreams of my dad that I used to have after he died, in which he was alive again and we would talk happily. I had always woken after that dream to face the new day feeling comforted.

I prayed to have my Dad dream again, I wanted to talk to him. But it never came.

Even at my lowest point, I never felt suicidal . . . yet I did fear that my terror would kill me. One night, I woke up – at 3.15am, as always – with a start. I was hot, my head was throbbing and my pulse was racing: *BOOM! BOOM! BOOM!* I could hardly breathe.

Was I having a heart attack? A stroke? I was convinced that I was.

If I were not a Christian, and I had never found God, I would not have survived that time. Those first few days of horror would have killed me. But at least when I reluctantly retired to bed, and the long, long night stretched ahead of me . . . I had somebody to talk to.

I spent a lot of time praying, and asking God what the heck this was all about. *Why was it happening?* Sometimes I would fall asleep when I was praying, then wake with a harsh jolt. I'd stare at my bedside clock . . . but I didn't need to.

3.15am.

God didn't reply – that's not how it works – but speaking to Him helped. It helped because He knew I hadn't done those terrible things, just as I knew that I hadn't. And I realised that there was somebody else who knew I hadn't done anything.

My accuser.

In those bleak, pitch-black hours, I thought about him a lot. *Who was he? Why was he saying these things?* I had never molested a soul in my life, so why was he claiming I had done this to him? Did he want money? Was he trying to damage me?

Unless he was a fantasist, or disturbed, he knew he was lying. *But why?* John said to me maybe he had been abused as a child and was transferring the abuse to somebody else. I had heard that sometimes that happened – *but why to me?*

I lay in bed and concocted far-fetched theories as to why he might be doing this. If he had been thirteen in 1985, as he claimed, well, he would be in his early forties now. *Maybe he was married and had a child with a terrible disease? Maybe he needed money, to take the kid to be treated in America?*

These strange thoughts, these crazy speculations, consumed me as I lay wide awake, night after night. Then, one night, I woke up – *yep, 3.15am* – and I talked to God.

'I can't survive like this,' I told Him. 'I'm beginning to hate the person who is doing this to me. I can't live with this hate. I need to forgive him.'

I took a deep breath and addressed my unknown tormenter: 'I forgive you. I don't know who you are, or why you are doing this to me – but you must have a reason. *I forgive you.*'

It was the same as the night I became a Christian. There was no divine reply, no angelic trumpets sounded. Nothing happened. All of my frustrations remained – but at least I had lost the hatred. It gave me a small comfort. It helped . . . *a little.*

* * *

It was time for my first interview with the South Yorkshire Police. I knew the paparazzi would go crazy, trying to get a photo of me leaving the Quinta, so my business partner, Nigel, invited me to stay with him and Lesley the night before.

Nigel drove over in his Range Rover. I lay on his back seat and we drove through the shouting photographers. They rammed their cameras right up to the car windows but they didn't manage to get a shot of me.

It had come to this. I was a 73-year-old man who had to hide like a criminal to leave my own home.

Nigel and Lesley were gracious hosts, as ever, but I didn't get even a minute's sleep that night at their house. Because now my nightmare had a whole new level of terror to it. I had to speak to the police.

Malcolm accompanied me from Portugal to England. I couldn't face loads of curious stares on a plane, so we hired a private jet. We flew from Faro to Doncaster airport and got driven to a South Yorkshire Police training centre.

In an airless room, under a harsh fluorescent light, a senior police officer cautioned me, then informed me of the specific detail of the accusation made against me. *And I could not believe my ears.* A man was claiming that I sexually assaulted him at a Billy Graham religious rally at Sheffield United's football stadium, Bramall Lane, in 1985.

I was flabbergasted. 'How can you think I would *do* something like that?' I asked the policeman. 'You know me. *Your children* know me. You must know I would never, *ever* do that. How can you believe it?'

'If you had met him, you would *know* how,' he replied.

Wow! THAT certainly threw me!

The officer began asking intense questions about my movements at that Billy Graham rally on 28 June 1985. I tried to cast my mind back almost thirty years. I recalled a huge crowd – it had been forty-five thousand people, apparently – and that I had performed a few songs and spoken.

'What time did you arrive?' the policeman asked.

I thought hard. Bill Latham would have driven me there. 'Well, we always tried to get to those events at least half an hour early,' I began. 'So that I could meet Billy Graham, and . . .'

'You must have been there *a lot* earlier than that,' interrupted the officer. He showed me a photograph of myself with a group of people, on the football pitch, in an otherwise empty stadium. It triggered a memory.

'Oh, yes!' I said. 'That's right! The organisers asked if I would meet some volunteer workers before the event. So, I did.'

'And what did you do right *after* the event?'

'Er . . . probably went straight to a hotel?'

The questions kept coming, thick and fast . . . and then the officer became more specific. He explained that the man had said that I molested him in a storeroom within the stadium, full of goalposts and other football equipment, when he was just thirteen years old.

I was floored. I didn't know what to say. It was only that night, on the flight back to Faro, that I thought of some questions I *could* have asked the police:

I was a star guest at that rally – how was I supposed to have found time to discover a storeroom at the stadium? To procure a 13-year-old boy? And, with everybody watching me, to slip away with him and molest him?

The accusations against me were even more nonsensical than I had previously imagined. But I was fast realising that this did not mean it would be easy to disprove them. It was my word against this mystery accuser's. *Me against him.*

I was in despair. *How can I ever prove that I didn't do it?*

* * *

When I got back to the Quinta, the place was still under siege. The paparazzi remained in a pack at my gates. There was no way that I could think of going anywhere – and, in any case, *where could I go?*

My visiting friends told me they had been praying for me while I was being questioned. In a way, it was easier for me to be back inside those four walls because I knew at least they would continue their prayers!

My management office had obviously been besieged with interview requests from TV networks and papers since the police raid, but we said no to everything. I didn't want to talk to anybody – and, in any case, *what could I say?*

I couldn't talk about the charges – and nor did I want to. I said nothing. It was the only strategy. My lawyers sent me an email:

We are very pleased with your dignified silence. Keep it up.

I liked that phrase: *dignified silence*. I couldn't say that I felt terribly dignified, but I was certainly keeping silent.

I was aware that I was still being vilified around the world. Of course, some people decided I must be guilty, *the next Jimmy Savile*, as soon as they heard about the raid. One major supermarket chain stopped stocking my Vida Nova wine. Some stores returned their copies of my annual calendar.*

No smoke without fire. That horrible mantra again.

I found a little hope among the despair. Some people sent me lovely messages. Billy Graham used to have a musical director named Cliff Barrows, and his wife, Ann, sent me a beautiful quote from Corrie ten Boom, who had helped Jews escape the Germans in World War II. Corrie was caught by the Nazis and sent to a concentration camp, so she knew all about the depths of human despair. Yet her wise words simply said, 'There is no pit so deep that God's love is not deeper still.'

Somebody else sent me a quote from Psalm 40: 'Let them be ashamed and brought to confusion, who seek to destroy my

---

* I can understand why, but it was extremely disappointing – they showed no faith in me at all.

life.' *Yes*, I thought to myself. *That's exactly what is happening to me right now!*

But it went on to say, 'He lifted me out of the slimy pit, out of the mud and mire; he set my feet on a rock and gave me a firm place to stand.' And that was what I hoped – I *knew* – that God would do for me.

After two weeks or so of paparazzi-enforced imprisonment in my own home, I had a party of guests staying with me and wanted to take them out to eat. I phoned my lawyers.

'Am I OK to go out to a restaurant?' I asked them.

'Of course!' they said. 'Just do it and behave normally. Try not to get photographed dancing as if you don't care.'

'There's no danger of *that* happening!' I told them, truthfully.

We went to a local restaurant. We had hired the top floor, specifically because I knew there were no higher, overlooking buildings next to it and so no cameramen could get a photograph of us. I was too tense to properly relax and enjoy myself, but the meal was at least a change. It was the birthday of one of the women, so her husband bought Champagne. The waiter filled all of our glasses from a huge bottle of Bollinger.

Literally the next day, I got a call from my management office. One of the tabloids had run a picture of me sipping Champagne, beaming away as if I didn't have a care in the world. The headline ran:

LIVING BOLL!

How the heck had they got that? I went over and over it in my mind. I had been to that restaurant so many times. I *knew* that no buildings overlooked it. The photographer must have used a drone. It was the very last thing I'd wanted to happen.

The paparazzi eventually got bored of hounding me and roamed off to hunt down their next prey. One morning, I looked nervously out of the window and saw that they had all moved on – and, also, that my main gates looked different. They looked . . . *golden*?

For the first time in a month, I dared to walk down my own drive. When I reached the gates, I saw that there were lots of gold ribbons tied to them. Fans and local people had left notes on them:

> 'We love you, Cliff!'
> 'Be strong!'
> 'We're thinking of you!'

It made me think of the old seventies hit by Tony Orlando and Dawn: 'Tie A Yellow Ribbon Round the Ole Oak Tree'. I stood on my own, by the gates, and I cried. Unexpected kindnesses can do that to you.

* * *

Somehow, in the midst of the insane nightmare that my life had turned into overnight . . . I made an album. I had studio time booked in Nashville with Steve Mandile, who had produced *The Fabulous Rock 'n' Roll Songbook*, to record its follow-up.

Could I face doing it?

I had never felt less in my life like making music, yet at the same time I knew that I needed a distraction from panicking and going quietly mad in the Quinta – and at least I would be able to breathe easier away from all the media attention. *OK*, I thought. *Let's try it.*

On the flight to Nashville, I felt as if I was at least slightly leaving the insanity behind. Once I got there, I threw myself into making the record in an attempt to distract myself. Like its predecessor, the album was to be a selection of revivals of classic rock and roll tracks from back in the day.

I wrapped my voice around Chuck Berry's 'Sweet Little Sixteen' and 'Memphis, Tennessee'. I also revisited Chuck's 'Roll Over Beethoven', a song that I have always loved, and that to me sounds like rock and roll incarnate.

I can't say that I *enjoyed* making the album – I was in too much of a dark place for that. However, it was at least a temporary escape to sing Little Richard's 'Keep A-Knockin'' and The Everly Brothers' 'Cathy's Clown'. And Sam Cooke's 'You Send Me' is always a blissful joy.

I recorded a great old blues number, John Lee Hooker's 'Dimples', but I rewrote some of the words because the original lyric was so repetitive: '*You got dimples in your jaw, you got dimples in your jaw!*' After I'd recorded it, Steve Mandile bumped into Peter Frampton, who added guitar to it.

It's sad that I was at such an emotional low point when I finally got to realise my teenage dream of singing with Elvis. *Sort of.* On 'Blue Suede Shoes', we took his vocal from his 1956 single and I duetted with it. It was . . . weird. On my first take, his voice was suddenly in my headphones. I almost turned around, as it felt as if he was right alongside me! I was happy with the result, but it felt . . . yes, *weird*.

It's a sign of how much music can lift you that, even with the weight of the world on my shoulders, I still got a thrill as I stood there singing with the King. *Wow!* I never got to meet the great man, but even as I was consumed with fear and dread, in a way I knew that this was my original, most heartfelt dream of all coming true.

Between making the album and worrying about police developments back in England, I was basically on autopilot. I totally forgot about everyday things; about *normal life*. One morning, I came down to breakfast to find John already in the hotel dining room.

'What time are we going to the studio?' I asked him.

'In thirty minutes,' he said. 'And, by the way, happy birthday!'

'Oh!' I said, glumly. 'Is it my birthday?'

I hadn't even realised.

When we finished the record, I was pleased with it . . . but, so what? Being pleased with an album seemed like a luxury that belonged to my previous, scandal-free life. *My dream life*. In any case, I knew we couldn't release it now, with the furore swirling around me. We shelved it, until a time when it might be possible to do such things again.

If that time ever came.

* * *

From Nashville, I flew to Barbados and started doing a whole lot of waiting. The police investigation into me was 'ongoing' but I had had no further interview requests from them, and the dark cloud still hung over me. I did what anybody would – I kicked my heels and I fretted.

On 10 February 2015, the Chief Constable for South Yorkshire Police wrote an open letter to the Home Affairs Select Committee stating that the investigation had 'increased significantly in size' and that there was 'more than one allegation'. As could have been predicted, the Committee published the letter on its website and those statements were immediately picked up by the news media. This shook me to the core.

Of course, I knew the police had to talk to the people making these allegations. I've never disputed that sexual abuse, and paedophilia, are incredibly serious crimes that must *always* be investigated. Yet it was to transpire that my new accusers were desperate, troubled fantasists.

*Somehow, it seemed, the police just couldn't see that.**

South Yorkshire Police passed the new allegations to my lawyers, who discussed them with me. It took us one minute to realise that these accusers were not remotely credible. One of them was a serial rapist who was already serving a long sentence in jail.

One accusation was so bizarre that I laughed out loud – a hard, bitter laugh. The guy claimed that he had been twenty-one and working in a shop in Milton Keynes in 1981, when I filmed my 'Wired For Sound' video in the town. He said that I had roller-skated alone into his shop . . . and groped him.

What?! Not only had I been surrounded by people all day, but it had been my first time on skates since I was a boy! I might have

---

* I had one small fillip. Towards the end of February 2015, an independent report found that South Yorkshire Police should never have tipped off the BBC and allowed them to film the raid on my property. It remarked that this decision had caused me 'unnecessary distress'. *Well, you could say that again!*

looked OK at skating in the final video, but if I *had* groped this guy, he'd only have had to push me away, and I would have fallen backwards off my skates and flat onto my bottom! To compound the absurdity, the guy also said that I had skated in again two hours later and done it again!

If only the public knew how crazy these allegations were! But they didn't. And I knew only too well what some people would still be thinking: *Yep! No smoke without fire.*

* * *

As I continued to labour under the weight of the accusations, we were also struck by a terrible family tragedy. My sister Joan's daughter, Linzi, the youngest of her three children, died of cancer on 29 June. She was just thirty-five years old.

Normally, parents die before their children, of course, but every now and then, life's regular patterns break down. I saw how difficult it was for Gloria Hunniford when she lost her beloved daughter, Caron Keating, also to cancer. It took Glo a long time to deal with it. I remember when she said, 'I'll get *past* it. But I'll never get *over* it.' When Linzi was diagnosed with cancer, I witnessed what a mother goes through again as I saw Joan's anguish.

Glo, being Glo, called Joan. I don't know what she said, but my sister found her words wise and comforting, and told me that it was wonderful to talk to someone who knew exactly what she was going through and exactly what she was feeling.

Linzi fought for her life, but in the end, even though she was committed to the fight, her body let her down. She was the most happy, loving and organised person, and a great loss to her husband, Mark, and their two daughters, Sofie and Hollie. Joan and I will always be grateful to Glo for helping Joan 'get past' her own loss.

* * *

As 2015 wound on, and the police investigation proceeded at what seemed a snail's pace, I still felt like my reputation was in tatters and my life was in limbo. However, I had a major professional decision to make. Because I was due to go out on tour.

For more than a year, I had had a UK tour of prestigious venues lined up for that autumn to mark my seventy-fifth birthday. It had been intended to be a celebration, yet with these allegations hanging over me, I felt there was no way I could do it.

I sent a message to my promoter: 'I think I'll have to cancel the tour.'

His reply surprised me: 'Well, you really don't have to!'

He reported that virtually all the tickets had sold out as soon as they had gone on sale, and the rest shortly afterwards. There had been no returns when the allegations about me broke. Tens of thousands of people still wanted to see me.

It seemed there were a lot of people out there who had kept their faith in me and who didn't believe a word of the innuendo and the rumours in the media. I've always loved my fans, but I don't think that my love has ever been stronger than in that moment.

Walking from room to room in my Quinta, I reached a decision, took a deep breath and phoned Malcolm Smith.

'OK, Malcolm,' I told him. 'I'll give it a go. Let's do it!'

NINETEEN
RISING UP

I could hardly believe I had agreed to go out on tour. My police scandal was still the first thing I thought about each morning and the last thing every night. I was still always wide awake at 3.15am ... was I really up to going back on the road? To facing audiences?

Well, I'd said I was doing it now! There was no going back.

My band and I decamped to Killarney in County Kerry, southwest Ireland, in the late summer of 2015 for rehearsals. We were also to preview the tour there with an opening date at the INEC Arena, which holds two thousand people. It had sold out many months earlier.

I have always done well, and played to great crowds, in Ireland, but that was before *all of this* . . . and now, I had no idea what reception I would get. *Would people not turn up? Would they boo?* I was still getting very little sleep and I felt horribly, sickeningly nervous.

On that fateful night, I stood in the wings at the theatre. The MC announced, 'Ladies and gentlemen . . . Sir Cliff Richard!' and I walked tentatively onto the stage to face a crowd for the first time in over a year. And the place just exploded.

The crowd leapt out of their seats. They roared a full-throated greeting that nearly took the roof off the place. They clapped, and cheered, and shouted, and yelled, and it must have gone on for five minutes. It seemed like the noise was never going to end.

What a welcome! I was overcome. I couldn't help it . . . I choked up. I just stood there in tears. After all I had been through for a year, it was too much for me to handle. *Wow!* Somehow, I managed to collect myself and signalled with my hands that the audience should sit down.

I nodded to my musical director, Keith, and we eased into the first song of the night, 'Golden'. *It was so good to be back.* I felt as if I was floating on air throughout the whole show. Afterwards, I took Keith to one side and we talked about that amazing welcome at the start of the set.

'It may never happen again, but we should have a plan, just in case it does,' I said. 'I'll step out, I'll take the applause and when I can't take it any longer, I'll look at you and we'll start the first song.'

The same uproar happened at every single show on the tour. It was lucky that 'Golden' has a 25-second piano intro. Each night, I would use those precious seconds to blink back my tears, take a deep breath, and compose myself before I began singing.

In my darkest days, that tour was a beacon; a joy. It ended with five October dates at – *where else?* – the Royal Albert Hall.

The third night was my seventy-fifth birthday and the crowd serenaded me with 'Happy birthday!' and – during the encore – 'Congratulations!'

I could not have been more grateful, humbled – and relieved. The tour had restored my faith in human nature, in music . . . and in *me*. It showed me I hadn't lost my old dream life. It had still been there, all along. Waiting for me to recover and start living it again.

* * *

The police investigation into me had been proceeding at a seemingly glacial pace. By now it had been more than a year since my interview with them in Yorkshire. However, I was then summoned to a second interview at the same police training centre on 1 November 2015.

Malcolm Smith and two lawyers came with me. I spoke to the same officer that I had the first time and he told me that, by law, he now had to tell me the name of my main accuser.

'No – please don't!' I replied. 'There is no need.'

I had thought so much about this guy and what his motivation for dropping me into my living hell might be. Now I was about to learn his identity – and I just didn't want to know. I didn't want to . . . *think of him as an actual person.*

'I'm afraid I have to,' the policeman repeated.

He was determined to tell me, yet I was equally determined not to listen. As he read out the guy's details, I switched off. Instead, I ran a lyric through my mind, from a song that I had been singing in Nashville the previous autumn: the lyric to Chuck Berry's 'Roll Over Beethoven':

'Well, gonna write a little letter, gonna mail it to my local DJ . . .'

I ran through the lyric of Chuck's entire song. By the time I got to the end, the officer had stopped reading me the details and I was none the wiser. Even today, I still don't know my accuser's name. And I still don't want to.

For me, he does not exist.

The encouragement from my second interview was that the police had not arrested me, nor made any move to charge me. And, both from the interviews and conversations with my lawyers, it was becoming clear that there were a lot of holes in my accuser's story.

He had apparently first told the police the abuse had happened in 1983 – only to change his story when it emerged the rally was not until '85. He also hadn't known whether it had happened at Bramall Lane or at Sheffield's other football ground, Hillsborough.

The Sheffield United people had also contradicted some of what he said. They had told the police the room he claimed we had been in did not exist in the mid-eighties. Not only that: the club had *never* kept its goalposts in a storeroom.

These flaws in my accuser's evidence, and the fact that no charges had been brought, meant that I began to dare to hope that my nightmare might soon be over. Surely soon the police would have to admit that it all made no sense? *That I was innocent?*

They did nothing of the sort, for a very long time. But, then . . . *I began to get my life back.*

Six months later, on 10 May 2016, South Yorkshire Police sent their file of evidence to the Crown Prosecution Service, the UK body that decides whether to press criminal charges against people. And in June, the CPS threw it out.

It had taken the police almost two years to piece together their case against me. It took the CPS just over five weeks to see through it and dismiss it as the work of fantasy that it was. Having analysed the so-called 'evidence', they must have realised *there was nothing there. There never was.*

I felt a sense of relief like I had never known before. *At last! It was over!* And yet my delight at the decision was tempered because the wording of the CPS's verdict rankled with me. It felt inappropriate; inadequate.

The CPS merely declared they had decided there was 'insufficient evidence' to proceed with charges against me. *Well, excuse me!* I didn't want to hear 'insufficient evidence', I wanted – I *needed* – to hear 'Not guilty!' 'Or 'Cleared!' Or 'Innocent!'

What I wanted was something that showed the world the lie behind my least favourite phrase: *There's no smoke without fire.* Because anybody who has ever gone to a rock concert knows they may find lots of smoke there and *absolutely no flames at all.*

So, when the CPS made their decision public, I issued a strongly worded statement:

> *I was named before I was even interviewed, and for me, that was like being hung out like live bait.*
>
> *I know the truth, and in some people's eyes the CPS announcement today doesn't go far enough because it doesn't expressly state that I am innocent, which of course I am. There lies the problem.*

My reputation will not be fully vindicated because the CPS's policy is only to say something general about there being 'insufficient evidence'. How can there be evidence for something that never took place!

Immediately after I was cleared, I did a TV interview with my dear friend Gloria Hunniford, in which I expressed my anger in rather more direct terms. Glo did what she always does: sat in front of me with no notes, made eye contact and asked all the right questions.

Did it bother me, she wanted to know, that I'd not been declared *innocent* and the CPS had instead talked of 'insufficient evidence'?

'It bugs me a lot!' I declared, and then, possibly channelling a mildly more polite Jim Royle from *The Royle Family*, I added, *'Insufficient evidence . . . my backside!'*

The South Yorkshire Police apologised for the 'additional anxiety caused' to me by their 'initial handling of the media interest'. Despite the fact that the police had concluded their investigation, the BBC never apologised for what they had done, they simply said that they were 'very sorry' that I had 'suffered distress'.

The police's statement was a welcome expression of semi-contrition. But I thought there probably needed to be a rather greater reckoning than that.

When the CPS reached their decision not to prosecute, my lawyers warned me that the accusers could appeal against that decision. Two of them did. However, it again took only a short time for the CPS to reject those appeals and confirm that the case would not be pursued.

Coincidentally, just as my ordeal was ending, the police investigation into the crazy allegations about the guest house in Barnes was also collapsing. It was also found to have been a complete fabrication by a fantasist.

It had been a period of my life that was ... well, 'nightmare' doesn't begin to describe it. My career, my reputation and my health were all affected – at times, I thought beyond repair. I had developed a persistent cough: at my worst, I had even had shingles.

But I *had* been lifted out of the slimy pit, out of the mud and mire. God *had* set my feet on a rock and given me a firm place to stand, just like I knew He would. I *would* repair everything about me that had been damaged. And, more than anything, I was just desperate to move on.

I wanted to get back to my old life – the life of singing, and of music, and of performing, that had been brutally wrenched away from me for reasons utterly beyond my control. And I also had another, very important date ringed in my diary.

The previous year, feeling unable to appear in public, I had missed Wimbledon for the first time in twenty years. Now, with my name finally cleared, I felt able to return to the Centre Court seat that I had traditionally occupied for so many years in the members' area.

It was such a joyous experience. I was hugged by so many ladies, who all told me, 'Oh, we're so happy to see you back! We missed you last year!' And one woman was particularly vociferous in her delight that I had returned.

There is a raised platform just outside the members' restaurant at Wimbledon and a middle-aged lady stopped me as she was coming out and I was going in. She had such a posh, cut-glass accent that she sounded like landed gentry.

'Oh, Cliff, how simply marvellous to see you!' she announced. 'I have been *so* worried for you! I have cried many tears for you – and I have prayed for you EVERY F***ING NIGHT!'

Good Lord! I had never heard somebody swear like a navvy in such immaculate received pronunciation!

'Well, I think that everything helped,' I said, happily receiving the kiss on the cheek that she gave me.

* * *

At the start of August 2016, my eldest sister, Donna, died. She had a chronic kidney disease and the last time that I saw her, which was not very long at all before her death, she was bed-ridden.

Like all of my family, Donna had been terribly upset by the mistaken police investigation into me, and I was so pleased that she had lived to see the CPS throw the false accusations out. She opened her eyes, smiled, reached up and stroked my cheek.

It is my last memory of her.*

* * *

From the date of the police raid through to the date on which the CPS had announced that there would be no charges brought against me, my lawyers had been readying legal actions. In October

---

* When Donna was horribly ill, I knew her husband, Terry, would always be there for her. Terry recently died, and one of his sons emailed me to say that the last thing Terry had said to him was, 'I dreamed I was riding my horse, and the love of my life, Donna, was on the horse behind me.' Theirs was a true love story.

2016, I started my legal claim against the BBC and the South Yorkshire Police.

I had been advised that I could do this but, initially, I had strong reservations about pursuing both actions. *Would it not be better just to move on?* South Yorkshire Police had made a mess of everything, but should I really *sue* them? 'The police work for the public,' I worried to my lawyers. 'Isn't it like suing Britain?'

They assured me that it wasn't, and conversely, in so many respects, I felt it was important I brought the case to make other police forces wary of ever behaving in that manner again. However, I was even more hesitant about suing the BBC.

I love the BBC. I've been on its TV shows for sixty years; I've hosted variety series for them; I've appeared on *Top of the Pops* more times than any other artist. Even now, I watch the BBC and listen to its World Service, no matter where in the world I am. It's a truly peerless broadcaster.

For me, the BBC is the great presenters and directors and producers and engineers who make its shows. It is talented, terrific people such as Gloria Hunniford, and David Attenborough, and David Dimbleby, and Paul Gambaccini, and Ken Bruce. And I certainly didn't want to sue *them*.

'Do I *have* to sue the BBC?' I asked my lawyers. 'Can't I just sue some named individuals – the journalist who covered my raid, his news bosses and the top dogs who OK'd it?' But they were adamant. Legally, there was no way around it. I had to sue the Corporation.

I couldn't say that I was looking forward to it, but my lawyers issued the claim against the BBC for their gross intrusion of my privacy in naming me. It was to be eighteen months before the case came to court.

In the meantime, I could finally release the second album that I had recorded in Nashville, two years earlier. Originally, I had wanted to call it *The Fabulous Rock 'n' Roll Songbook II*. I figured it might even build into quite a nice little series.

It was to be released by Sony as they owned the rights to the Elvis song 'Blue Suede Shoes', and they begged to differ. Their marketing people said that follow-up albums like that 'don't work' and so we would need to find a different title.

Really? Rod Stewart, who had amazing success with no fewer than *five* albums of *The Great American Songbook*, might have something to say about that! But I let it go. After all, I had been fighting rather larger battles lately.

Instead, we called it *Just . . . Fabulous Rock 'n' Roll*. It came out in November and, to my delight, it did well. The singles didn't chart because – *guess what?* – radio didn't play them, but the album went to Number 4, which was great. I knew I was back in business and back in the game.

In May 2017, I reached a settlement with the South Yorkshire Police out of court. As part of it, they agreed to pay me damages for the harm I had suffered, although that was never the main reason for my legal action. South Yorkshire Police made a public statement in court, and it meant more to me to be given their 'sincere apologies', along with a public admission that their conduct had been unlawful, than any amount of damages would.

It was time to move on and, that summer, I played two dates in Denmark before a short tour of British stately homes and venerable buildings. It was amazing to belt out the great old songs on *Just . . . Fabulous Rock 'n' Roll* in inspiring venues from Lincoln Castle to the Old Royal Naval College in Greenwich.

I played shows in Oman and Tel Aviv that autumn, and then it really felt like time for a holiday. A long cruise from Los Angeles to Hawaii was easily the most relaxed that I had felt in three years, then I stayed with friends in America for Christmas before heading off to Barbados.

During all of this time, I was subconsciously steeling myself for the very last chapter of my legal nightmare: my court case against the BBC.

I was incredibly nervous arriving at the High Court in London on 12 April 2018. The case hinged on whether the BBC had infringed my privacy and breached my rights under the Data Protection Act by identifying me as a suspect and filming and broadcasting the police raid. I was to be the first person to give evidence and be cross-examined.

My leading counsel Justin Rushbrooke, QC, could see how anxious I was beforehand and tried to put me at my ease. As I took the witness stand, Justin smiled at me and asked, 'Are you content for me to address you as "Sir Cliff"?'

'Yes, absolutely!' I said. 'I prefer it to "Mr"!' I was trying to be light-hearted to cover my nerves. Of course, the next day, one of the newspapers reported that I had taken the stand and immediately *insisted* on being referred to as Sir Cliff! It was a lie, and it gave such a bad impression of me . . . but I'm afraid that's tabloid journalism for you. I expect no better from some of them by now.

Giving evidence was hard. I thought some of the questioning was a little intrusive, and I found pouring out everything that had been pent-up inside of me for the last four years emotional and cathartic. I broke down on the witness stand a few times but, thankfully, managed to collect myself very quickly.

Once I had given my evidence, I had no obligation to be in court – but I kept going. I wanted to hear all of the evidence, and I thought it was important for the judge to see me there every day and realise the case meant a lot to me. That it was a very big deal in my life.

The BBC again said sorry for 'my distress' but they didn't apologise for *what they had done*. They said that they had just been doing their job in covering the police raid and claimed their reporting had been 'accurate, in good faith, and a matter of legitimate public interest'.

The hearing was heard in thirteen days, plus it was adjourned for a week as the case overran each day, and the judge had to hear another case that week. Because I had to fly to Florida to begin a new album, I had to miss the last two days of closing statements – which I *really* did not want to do.

Justin Rushbrooke made a point of offering the judge my personal apologies for my absence. The judge said there was no need, but I wanted to make sure that he knew it was down to my recording commitments, and that I would have been there every day if I could.

It would be a month or two before the judge delivered his verdict, and it would have killed me to have been sat twiddling my thumbs and stressing out as I waited. So, while he deliberated, I was hard at work in a studio in Miami.

Despite the successes of *The Fabulous Rock 'n' Roll Songbook* and *Just . . . Fabulous Rock 'n' Roll*, my record label didn't want me to do another backwards-looking album of classic hits. They said that they felt it was time for me to make a record of new, original material.

This pleased me. Much as I will always love harking back to the first golden age of rock and roll that inspired me, I have no wish to be regarded as a vintage or retro artist – not even at the venerable age that I am now! I would always much rather look to the future.

The album had its title as soon as Terry Britten sent me 'Rise Up' (which he wrote with Graham Lyle, of Gallagher and Lyle). Terry said he had written the lyric for me, and about me, and as soon as I heard it, I knew it was the perfect summing-up of what I had been through, what I had survived, and my journey back to normality:

> *Yesterday the clouds were darkest, I could not see the end of it,*
> *But something inside of me never learnt to quit . . .*

Once I had recorded 'Rise Up', I sent my version to Terry for his feedback. I was proud when he got back to me and said, 'It's fantastic! You sing it with such feeling and attitude – Cliff, it's great!'

'Terry,' I told him, 'your song *gave* me attitude!'

We made the album with the band recording in Surrey and me doing my vocals in Miami, but this separation didn't matter. Once I had my headphones on, and their playing was loud in my ears, I could just lock into the music as if they were there. It was a seamless process.

There were a lot of tracks that I loved on *Rise Up*. I sang a duet with Olivia Newton-John, on a song called 'Everybody's Someone' – again, without being in the same studio! I sent Olivia the song. She said she loved it and would love to do it with me, but would it be OK if she changed it a little as it wasn't in her key?

'Olivia, I'll love it however you do it,' I told her, honestly.

One very funny moment – in fact, I'm afraid it was a *senior* moment – came when Alan Tarney sent me a song called '(Let's Go) Where There Are Horses to Ride'. I thought it was tremendous. Soon afterwards, Linda, a friend who runs my Facebook page, dropped in to see me. I played Linda a few of the demos that we were working on, and when I got to '(Let's Go) Where There Are Horses to Ride', she began singing along with it.

'Linda, how do you know this?' I asked, puzzled. 'This is a new song!'

'No, it's not,' she laughed. 'You've recorded it before and I've got it at home!'

Oops! It turned out that I *had* done the song before, as the B-side to 'Somewhere Over the Rainbow', back in 2001 – and Alan Tarney, who produced it back then, and I had both forgotten all about it! Well, I guess when you record more than a thousand songs in your life, that sort of thing is bound to happen . . . and at least I'd liked it enough to record it twice! But we didn't put it on the album.

Another great track didn't make *Rise Up* – not because I didn't like it, but because I wasn't allowed to use it. I got sent a country-style song called 'PS Please'. It was a posthumous song, about a father writing on his deathbed to a 17-year-old daughter he had never met.

It was the work of three songwriters and when we emailed them, saying I wanted to include it on *Rise Up*, one of them refused to let me do it. He was holding out, hoping a big-name US country singer would use it and give him a serious payday.

I didn't blame him for this – *we all have to eat!* – but I was so keen to record it that I wrote him what was virtually a begging letter. 'You all sent me the song, which is how I know it and love it,' I told him, 'and I want to pay tribute to you three great songwriters by recording it.' But the guy wouldn't budge.

I was so taken by 'PS Please' that I went ahead and recorded it anyway, even though I can't release it. Mark Knopfler of Dire Straits played guitar on it. I did my best vocal of the entire *Rise Up* sessions and it would have been perfect for the album. It was *such* a shame.

I hope one day I'll be able to put it out. For the moment, at least I can play it live and I think I might do so on my next tour. I even know how I'm going to introduce it – with a little black humour. I might say:

'You have to be of a certain age to sing this song. Well, I'm probably nearer to my death than anybody else in this room, so I think I have the right to sing it!'

Or, maybe not. I don't want to upset my fans too much!

* * *

I was back in London on 18 July 2018 to hear the judgement being handed down in my legal action against the BBC. I genuinely hadn't known how it would go . . . but, thankfully, we won the case.

The judge found that the BBC had infringed my privacy rights in a 'serious' and 'sensationalist' way and there had not been a genuine public interest case in seeking the cooperation of the police, filming the police raid and publishing to the world the fact that I was subject to a criminal investigation before the police had even had the opportunity to gather any evidence. In fact, he didn't pull any punches. He really gave the Beeb what for!

When he delivered his judgement, I didn't feel like standing up and punching the air. I just sat quietly, took a deep breath and absorbed his verdict. Gloria Hunniford had come to support me in court, and afterwards she told me that she had been surprised by my muted response.

'I thought you'd get up and go "Yeah!" like you do when you win a tennis match!' she told me.

I shook my head. 'Gloria,' I said, 'all that I felt was extreme relief.'

When she and I left the court, arm-in-arm, the reporters thronged around us, wanting a comment. *But I just couldn't.* I was still teary-eyed and I felt as if I had been emotionally cleaned out. I had no words left.

'Look, I'm sorry,' I told them. 'Please talk to me in a couple of weeks, I can hardly speak right now.'

And we climbed into a taxi.

When I later saw press photos of me leaving the court, I was horrified at how gaunt and haggard I looked. People have called me the Peter Pan of pop but, that day, I looked more like Rip Van

Winkle. Nor did I feel remotely triumphant. More than anything, I just wished it had all never happened. Because there had been no need.*

I don't wish to dwell anymore now on this dreadful episode in my life because, thank the Lord, it has passed. But I will say this: like Gloria when she lost Caron, I have got *past* it, but I don't think I will ever get *over* it. *Not fully.* It did too much damage and it left too much of a stain on my life.

It's certainly not the kind of thing you can ever just forget.

* * *

Well, you can't forget, but you can try to move on and that was exactly what I intended to do. After my usual summer break in Portugal, I went straight into rehearsals for a UK, Irish and Danish tour to mark my sixtieth anniversary in show business: sixty years since 'Move It' had shot me to fame as a teenager.

We gave the tour the somewhat cryptic title of 58+18=60, like a bad mathematical calculation! Well, *I* thought it was cryptic, anyway, but the fans soon worked it out: 1958 to 2018 equals sixty years. If only I'd been that good at maths back at Cheshunt Secondary Modern!

The first night of the tour, on 27 September, was particularly poignant. We opened back at the INEC Arena in Killarney, where

---

* A year later, I was finally paid a further contribution towards the legal costs I had incurred in bringing the case. In all, I received £2m from the BBC and South Yorkshire Police towards my costs. It didn't cover them in full – in fact, it wasn't even half of them – but, for me, it felt like closure. And as the Bible shows, sometimes David *can* beat Goliath!

my fans had been so supportive of me when I was deep in my personal hell. It was a wonderful night, again: that venue will always be special to me now.

The tour revisited many venues that are dear to me. We did Sheffield City Hall, and I realised with a start that it was nearly sixty years since Bruce Welch had used our 1959 soundcheck there to arrange 'Living Doll' as a country song. *Sixty years! Where had the time gone?* I looked at the exact spot where The Shadows and I had sat as Bruce had plucked the chords and I smiled to myself.

What a memory.

No venue is more special to me than the Albert Hall, of course. We did two nights there this time around. The first was my seventy-eighth birthday, and Bonnie Tyler emerged from the wings to sing 'Happy Birthday' to me with the crowd. It was fantastic – you can't beat a good birthday surprise!

Rise Up came out as the tour finished and did well. Radio 2 played two singles off it – I don't know if that was due to the BBC feeling guilty, but I was grateful either way! The 'Rise Up' single even hit Number 1 in the vinyl-only chart.

Ah, I've still got it, after all these years!

After Christmas in Barbados, I began 2019 by recording a duet with Bonnie Tyler (it was the least I could do, after she serenaded me on my birthday!). Our voices worked well together on 'Taking Control' (no, it wasn't about Brexit!) for Bonnie's new album, *Between the Earth and the Stars*.

I only played three shows in the UK and two in Denmark in 2019, but it was quality over quantity. After Scarborough Open Air Theatre, we went to Cartmel Racecourse in Cumbria (I recalled working at Atlas Lamps at sixteen and not knowing where Cumbria was!), before finishing off back at the glorious Old Royal Naval College at Greenwich.

And I realised, doing those shows, that I finally felt fitter; stronger; *repaired*, like I was totally myself again. I wasn't the only person who thought this, because Keith, my musical director, had some very welcome words for me.

'You're a different person, Cliff,' he noted. 'You've totally changed from when I toured with you last year.'

'How do you mean?' I asked. 'I was OK last year, wasn't I?'

'Yeah, you were *OK*,' Keith replied. 'But now you're *more than OK*. You're completely back to how you always were. And you're singing as well as you ever have done again.'

It was lovely to hear . . . and he was right. The stresses and the tensions that had bedevilled me had all finally gone. I felt like my true self again, and it showed. Maybe I was even turning back into that lucky dreamer again!

All my life I've been a dreamer, some might say a lucky one . . .

I was putting my nightmare behind me – but I knew I never wanted anybody else to go through it. That summer, with Paul Gambaccini, who had also endured false sexual allegations, I supported a petition organised by Falsely Accused Individuals for Reform (F.A.I.R.) to try to safeguard others from the same fate.

The petition was launched by Daniel Janner, QC, whose late father, Lord Janner, had also been accused of historic sex abuse. It called for people accused of sexual offences not to be named unless charged unless in exceptional circumstances. Paul and I attended the launch outside the Houses of Parliament.

I've always been fond of quoting Gandhi – maybe it's my background in India! – and so I told the media: 'Gandhi said, "The worst thing about Christianity is Christians." I'd like to add: "The worst thing about humanity is humans. In so many ways, we have become inhuman; *inhumane*." '

On a much happier note, I enjoyed a wonderful evening at London's Marriott Hotel when Variety, the children's charity, honoured me for sixty years in show business. I sang five songs to an audience including Bruce Welch, Brian Bennett, Una Stubbs, Elaine Paige and Gloria Hunniford. Jimmy Tarbuck, the compère on one of my earliest tours, made a very funny speech about me.

Yet the night's star turn was Hank Marvin, beaming in by video link from his home in Australia. Hank has always been a very funny man and he excelled himself on this occasion.

'Cliff, I'm so sorry I can't be there tonight,' he began. 'But I'm thrilled they're honouring you, and I want to send you this brief message.' Then the screen went blank – as if that were the end of the message! Everybody laughed.

Hank reappeared a few seconds later. 'Cliff has worked *so* hard throughout his career to get everything right,' he said. 'It's a shame that he's never managed it . . .'

Ha! I'm never buying HIM another Stratocaster!

* * *

One thing that happens as you grow older is that milestones in your life come around with increasing regularity. In October 2020,

I will turn eighty, and in late 2019 we began planning a major UK tour to mark (or should I say mourn?!) it. I went on Lorraine Kelly's TV show to announce The Great 80 tour, then repaired to Barbados for some rest and recuperation.

As a lifelong sun worshipper, one of the many things I love about Barbados is that it's warm enough to have barbecues in January. A friend invited me to one at the start of 2020 . . . and I found myself sitting next to Tom Jones.

It's a funny thing. Tom and I have been public fixtures in music and show business forever, and people probably assume we know each other well. But that's not the case. I'd bumped into Tom at Royal Variety Performances and said 'Hi!' but that was pretty much it.

Tom told me that he had a couple of weeks' break from filming *The Voice* so he had flown out for a holiday, and the two of us sat and chatted for the entire afternoon. He was great company – and, of course, unlike me, he had actually met Elvis!

'Someone called Regine has invited me to a party tonight,' Tom said. 'Do you think I ought to go?'

'Yes, it's Regine Sixt from the family who own the car-hire company,' I told him. 'I'm going, too! I'll pick you up at your hotel!'

So, the two of us ended up hanging out all day. I left the party at eleven, but I heard later that Tom was there enjoying himself until two in the morning! It had only taken us sixty years to get around to getting to know each other, but we had a blast!

I felt chilled and relaxed. Happily ensconced in Barbados, I foresaw myself enjoying a blissful, laid-back winter there, flying to the UK for Wimbledon, and then spending the late summer rehearsing with my band for the big, celebratory eightieth birth-day tour.

Well, it's strange how the world can sometimes turn all of your best-laid plans upside-down . . .

EPILOGUE
IT'S ALWAYS BEEN ELVIS AND CLIFF!

When you have been knocking around this planet for as long as I have, you might flatter yourself that you have seen everything. I certainly had to revise that opinion in the early months of 2020, when the awful Coronavirus pandemic came along and the world closed down.

It's been like living in a very different kind of dream – a bleak and surreal one – hearing about thousands of deaths across the globe on the news bulletins every night. It's been disturbing and bizarre to see scared people in face masks scuttling through deserted streets.

I happened to be in Barbados when the lockdown came in March. Obviously, at my ripe old age, I fall into the at-risk category, so I found myself confined to home. Some people may feel that doesn't sound like a great hardship but, well, *four walls are four walls!*

I know I'm lucky to have a nice home to lock down in – I hate to think what lockdown would have been like when I was a boy, and my family were living six to a room in Waltham Cross! I just count my blessings – and I'm full of admiration for the doctors, nurses, care workers and other brave souls on the frontline fighting this deadly illness. They are true heroes.

When the virus hit, I was beginning to mentally plan The Great 80 tour for the end of the year. Even after all these years, I start to prepare for tours way in advance to make sure I get everything right. I think it all over for months, consumed by thoughts of things that might go wrong, particularly on the first few nights. *Will the mics all work? And the lights? Will I forget any lyrics? Will I fall off the stage?* That's not a bad thing. I've learned in my career that nerves and apprehension help a show. They keep you on your toes.

It's a special tour for me, and I'd like to make it special for the audience. That's why I need all this preparation and planning – it's normally the end of the pre-tour rehearsals before I can get it together to sing and dance at the same time!

Coronavirus has thrown everything up in the air, and just as I am finishing writing this book, that awful pandemic has meant that I have had to postpone my tour for a year. It's frustrating, of course, but we need to wait for the danger to pass, and for the world to get back to something approaching normal – and I promise my fans that it will be worth waiting for! I'm really looking forward to it.

One good thing about modern technology is that you are never truly alone, even in a lockdown. I don't like everything about the internet, and I've read some truly awful things there, but the positive aspect is that it helps me to keep in touch with my family and fans.

Family has always meant a lot to me, and now, in my later years, it means more than ever. I email and talk to my sisters, nephews and nieces regularly. They've all got their own kids, so I can keep in touch with my *grand*-nephews and -nieces. I've got an app that lets me mess with photos, so I send them funny pictures of me, and sometimes of themselves. They love it!

When you're writing your autobiography, and you're locked down with nothing to do, you think a lot about all the things you have done in your life. You marvel at some of them; others are so extraordinary that you find yourself wondering if they ever really happened.

Was it all a dream?

Yet what has pleased me is that, as well as thinking back, I've also been looking forward. It's how I am. I've always found the future so much more interesting than the past, and there are still so many things that I want to do and to achieve.

I'd love to do more duets. I've been talking to Tony Rivers, the king of harmonies, whom I first worked with over forty years ago, about an album of Everly Brothers songs. Tony says he'll help out with the harmonies. Will this happen? I don't know – but I want it to!

I'd like to sing with Shania Twain. She has a tremendous voice. I've asked her twice. The first time, she had a throat infection, and the second time, she was on tour. Well, I'm going to keep trying, and ask her again. I'm persistent like that!

Here's a funny story: a few years ago, I heard an amazing singer on the radio. 'Wow, listen to her!' I said. 'What a voice! I'd love to sing with her!' The friend I was with stared at me, slightly pityingly: 'Cliff, that's not a woman,' he said. 'It's Pharrell Williams.' *Oops!* But my point stands – he has a wonderful voice, and I'd love the opportunity to work with him.

Of course, the person that I would *most* like to perform with, more than anybody else in the history of music, is no longer with us.

Duetting with Elvis's original vocal on 'Blue Suede Shoes' in 2014 whetted my appetite, and I'd love to do the same on a whole album of his songs. The concept is so exciting to me that I have spoken to his widow, Priscilla, about it.

Priscilla said that she likes the idea but, while she has some say in the matter, Sony Music own the rights to all of Elvis's recordings and they will never let me do it. 'If it was down to me, I would say "Yes",' she told me, 'because Elvis knew all about his competition.'

'*Really?* Did he know about *me?*' I asked her, eagerly.

'Oh, yes,' Priscilla said. 'Elvis kept an eye on his main rivals, all over the world. He certainly knew *all* about you!'

Wow! What a thought! And yet I knew exactly what Priscilla meant. For a long time, outside America, that was how it seemed to be. Wherever you went in the world ... it was always Elvis or Cliff.

When I was starting out, in the early days of rock and roll, I used to visit schools. The kids always told me they were split in half: half of them liked Elvis, the other half liked me. I still meet women of my age today, who tell me, 'Oh, my sister loved you, but *I* always used to love Elvis!'

'Ha! Me, too!' I usually say.

So, maybe it is true – *it was always Elvis or Cliff.* And I think there would be a market for us duetting. My fans loved Elvis – after all, I've always given him the credit for my very existence as an artist! Who knows? We might sell a million copies . . . and I even have a sleeve prepared for it.

Years ago, I commissioned a Spanish artist to paint a picture of Elvis and me. He did a great job – we look as if we are on stage together. It's still a treasured possession, and it would make a perfect album cover. I can picture it now, with the title across the top, in Elvis's famous font:

ELVIS AND CLIFF!

Oh, well! It may never happen, but a boy can dream! And even if it never does, knowing that Elvis took note of me, and even viewed me as his competition, makes my day; my month; my year. No: in a funny way, it makes my *life*.

In some respects, I have changed. It bugged me for so many years that I never broke America, and that my record company never really seemed to care if I happened there or not. Well, now that I'm older, I am glad that I never did. I think they were doing me a favour!

Today, I appreciate that I am faceless in the States and I can stroll around New York or Los Angeles and rarely attract a second glance. In fact, I jealously guard my anonymity. I recently turned down doing *Carpool Karaoke* with James Corden – I don't want him blowing my cover!

I fell in love with America via Elvis, and I still love visiting that great nation today. For one thing, I don't have to deal with false media stories there. Unfortunately, I've learned not to trust the British press. They seem to be immune to anything that is nice or good or decent.

For instance, a few years ago, my sister Joan and I were talking about losing our mum to dementia. We were wondering whether it runs in the family.

'I don't know, but if it happens to me, *you'll* have to look after me!' I told her.

'OK,' she laughed back. 'But if it happens to *me*, you'll have to do the same for me!'

It was a funny, jokey conversation and, shortly afterwards, I told a journalist about it in an interview. They changed the story around and ran it under this headline:

CLIFF AND SISTER MAKE SUICIDE PACT!

So, really, why should anybody bother with them, when they behave like that? I talk to them as rarely as I can nowadays. We try to do a lot of our album and tour promotion via Facebook, and that suits me just fine.

I've always loved living in different places around the globe but now that I'm nearing my eighties, I think it's time to simplify things a little. After twenty-seven years, I have decided to sell my Portuguese Quinta and the vineyard that goes with it. I will miss the Algarve, and my home there, a lot. It has been my haven and my refuge, not least when I went through my hard time. And yet . . . everything comes to an end. It just feels like time.

I've also put my house in Barbados on the market. It's been my Caribbean paradise for so long, but I simply don't need anywhere that big any longer. I will stay on the island, but when the pandemic has lifted, I would like to downsize and get somewhere more manageable.

I want to stay as active as I can. Happily, I'm still in rude health. I play tennis with a coach two or three times a week, and on the other days, I try to make myself go to the gym. It's funny how I enjoy the one so much more than the other!

You're never too old to pick up new health tips. A few years ago, I played in Dubai, and had a massage beforehand. The masseur was talking so much that I was about to politely ask her to be quiet, so that I could relax . . . but then, my ears pricked up.

She started talking about healthy diets, and I was so fascinated that she gave me some notes about them. Basically, she said to avoid wheat, dairy (*especially* those two), red meat, crustaceans, mangoes, aubergines, tomatoes, potatoes, papayas and bananas. It's not so much a diet as an eating lifestyle. I started doing so, found it really easy to keep to, and, within a month, I had lost more than an inch from my waist. I'm still basically the same weight that I was in about 1962 – and a lot slimmer than I was when Minnie Caldwell on *Coronation Street* declared her love for 'that chubby Cliff Richard'!

Even so, I suspect I have done my final topless photo for my annual calendar. When I did my last one, Chris Evans said on the radio that it couldn't be my body – they must have superimposed my head onto somebody else! That made me laugh. But now I suspect it's time to gracefully exit the Chippendales market . . .

The most important thing is that staying fit helps me to prolong my career for as long as I can. I'm obviously slowing things down now. I'm in the autumn – no, the *winter* – of my career and not even I can go on forever.

Because the radio never plays my records and young people don't get to hear me, my audience today is nearly all my long-term fans, who have been there since the start and grown old with me. Obviously, each time I come to tour, there are less of them still around.

I used to be able to play to seventy-two thousand people at Wembley Stadium, or do thirty-two nights at the Albert Hall, but those days have long passed. Today, if I can play to five thousand or seven thousand people a night, that's great. I would be very happy to carry on doing that for as long as I can.

I'm scaling things down but I don't want to *retire*. That word isn't in my vocabulary. If I retired, and then decided I wanted to play more shows, I would have to 'make a comeback'. So, you see, if I don't retire, I can't make a comeback . . . *because I have never gone away! I have just always been here!*

* * *

When I cast my mind back over my dream life, I came from a pretty humble background and I made something good happen. I've always stayed true to the values that my parents gave me, and I have no doubt at all that's how I have lasted so long – and managed to retain my sanity.

If I had never heard, or seen, Elvis, I would have remained plain old Harry Webb. I wouldn't have got started without being inspired by his music, and his image, and realising, *Ah, THAT'S how it's done!* But, luckily, I managed to find my way quite quickly into being Cliff Richard. Some of it was planned. A lot of it was an accident.

How have I survived for so long? I ask myself that all the time! Why me, and not Frankie Avalon, or Billy Fury, or any of those other stars who were huge back then? I don't know. It's like trying to work out how the 'x' factor works, and I have no more idea than anybody else. I've just made it up as I've gone along.

I know that I looked quite cool when I started out, and that helped, but since then I've been seen as cool at some times, then very *uncool* at others. And, when it comes down to it, I don't think it really means anything. *What is cool?* I think the only true measure of coolness is success. So, I haven't done too badly.

It's more important to me, this late in my life, that I feel contented and I feel *happy. And I do.* I feel happy with where I am, what I am, who I am and what I do. And, if you can feel that way, I think you are doing well.

I had an amazing dream, and it came true. Looking back on it now, it all seems extraordinary to me. *What a story it's been!* Well, just as every story needs to start somewhere, it also needs to have an ending. Even I won't be here forever (!) and, when I go, I would like to leave a nice, classy little tombstone epitaph to remember me by.

Occasionally, I wonder what that should be. Well, I remember after I played a gospel concert in Belfast, back in the years of the Troubles, there was a headline about me in the *Melody Maker* that I particularly loved:

ROCK 'N' ROLL AND GOD WORK WELL TOGETHER IN THE HANDS OF SOMEONE WHO LOVES THEM BOTH

Yeah. That will do.

ACKNOWLEDGEMENTS

My thanks to Penguin Random House for giving me the
opportunity to write this book.
AND
My grateful thanks to Ian Gittins,
an author who was an enormous help in putting my words
and feelings into cohesive order.
Many thanks, Ian.
AND
Also to Bob Stanley, whose knowledge of our
pop/rock world is second to none:
record release dates, who sang what when and even where.
Many thanks, Bob.
AND
Of course, Malcolm Smith and Tania Hogan.
Thank you both for your continuous
support over these many years.
Thank you, Malcolm.
Thank you, Tania.

PERMISSIONS AND PICTURE CREDITS

With special thanks to:

Victor Rust for providing a comprehensive discography

Jay Norris for the use of the picture of Ratty

Picture sections:

Section 1: p. 1 all private collection except bottom © Moviestore Collection/Shutterstock; p. 2 top © Jay Norris; p. 4 middle Beverley Lebarrow/Redferns © GettyImages, bottom right V&A Images/ Hulton Archive © GettyImages; p. 5 middle and bottom right Mirrorpix © GettyImages, bottom left Beverley Lebarrow/Redferns © GettyImages; p. 6 top left and right Paul Popper/Popperfoto © GettyImages, middle left © ITV/Shutterstock; p. 7 middle Daily Herald Archive/SSPL © GettyImages, bottom Mirrorpix © GettyImages; p. 8 top David Redfern/Redferns © GettyImages, middle Central Press/Hulton Archive © GettyImages, bottom Daily Herald Archive/SSPL © GettyImages.

Section 2: p. 1 top and bottom Mirrorpix © Getty Images, middle Paul Popper/Popperfoto © GettyImages; p. 2 top Sydney O'Meara/ Hulton Archive © GettyImages, bottom left Rolls Press/Popperfoto © GettyImages, bottom right Photoshot/Hulton Archive © GettyImages; p. 3 bottom left GAB Archive/Redferns © GettyImages, bottom right Chris Walter/WireImage © GettyImages; p. 4 top and middle Radio Times © GettyImages, bottom Mirrorpix © GettyImages; p. 5 top left Mirrorpix © GettyImages, middle Evening Standard/Hulton Archive © GettyImages, p. 6 top Photoshot/Hulton Archive © GettyImages, middle Mirrorpix © GettyImages, bottom right Tim Graham © GettyImages; p. 7 top Mirrorpix © GettyImages, bottom © Ted Blackbrow/Associated Newspapers/Shutterstock; p. 8 top left and right Dave Hogan/ Hulton Archive © GettyImages, bottom Pete Still/Redferns © GettyImages.

Section 3: p. 1 top © David Levenson/Shutterstock, middle left Dave Hogan/Hulton Archive © GettyImages, middle right Photoshot/ Hulton Archive © GettyImages, bottom © Andy Hooper/Daily Mail/Shutterstock; p. 2 top Pete Still/Redferns © GettyImages, bottom left Dave Benett/Hulton Archive © GettyImages, bottom right Tim Graham © GettyImages; p. 3 top MJ Kim/Getty Images Entertainment © GettyImages; p. 5 top Eamonn McCabe/ Popperfoto © GettyImages, middle left Jo Hale/Getty Images Entertainment © GettyImages, bottom Neil Lupin/Redferns © GettyImages; p. 6 middle © Alamy; p. 8 middle left Chiaki Nozu/ WireImages © Getty, bottom right Harry Herd/Redferns © Getty Images.

DISCOGRAPHY

Compiled by Victor Rust (author of *The Cliff Richard Recording Catalogue*)
💿 denotes certification (silver, gold, platinum)
⭐ indicates Top Ten chart ranking

STUDIO ALBUMS

2010s

2018   Rise Up
        #4 ⭐   💿💿 Gold

2016   Just . . . Fabulous Rock 'n' Roll
        #4 ⭐   💿💿 Gold

2013   The Fabulous Rock 'n' Roll Songbook
        #7 ⭐   💿💿 Gold

2011   Soulicious
        #10 ⭐   💿 Silver

2010   Bold as Brass
        #3 ⭐   💿 Silver

2000s

◇◇

2009   **Reunited**
        #4 ⭐   💿💿 Gold

2007   **Love – The Album**
        #13   💿💿 Gold

2006   **Two's Company: The Duets**
        #8 ⭐   💿💿 Gold

2004   **Something's Goin' On**
        #7 ⭐   💿💿 Gold

2003   **Cliff at Christmas**
        #9 ⭐   💿💿💿 Platinum

2001   **Wanted**
        #11   💿💿 Gold

1990s

◇◇

1998   **Real as I Wanna Be**
        #10 ⭐   💿 Silver

1995   **Songs from Heathcliff**
        #15   💿💿 Gold

1993   **The Album**
        #1 ⭐   💿💿 Gold

1991   **Together with Cliff Richard**
        #10 ⭐   💿💿💿 Platinum

1980s

〰〰〰〰〰〰〰〰〰〰〰〰〰〰〰〰〰〰〰〰〰〰〰〰〰〰〰〰

| 1989 | **Stronger** |
| | #7 ✪   ◉◉◉ Platinum |

| 1987 | **Always Guaranteed** |
| | #5 ✪   ◉◉◉ Platinum |

| 1984 | **The Rock Connection** |
| | #43   ◉ Silver |

| 1983 | **Silver/Rock 'n' Roll Silver** |
| | #7 ✪   ◉◉ Gold |

| 1981 | **Wired for Sound** |
| | #4 ✪   ◉◉◉ Platinum |

| 1980 | **I'm No Hero** |
| | #4 ✪   ◉◉ Gold |

1970s

〰〰〰〰〰〰〰〰〰〰〰〰〰〰〰〰〰〰〰〰〰〰〰〰〰〰〰〰

| 1979 | **Rock 'n' Roll Juvenile** |
| | #3 ✪   ◉◉ Gold |

| 1978 | **Green Light** |
| | #25 |

| 1977 | **Every Face Tells a Story** |
| | #8 ✪ |

| 1976 | **I'm Nearly Famous** |
| | #5 ✪   ◉◉ Gold |

| 1974 | **The 31st of February Street** |

1973	Take Me High
	#41
1970	His Land
	Tracks 'n' Grooves
	#37

1960s

~~~~~~

1969	Sincerely
	#24
1968	Established 1958
	#30
	Two a Penny
1967	Don't Stop Me Now!
	#23
	Cinderella
	#30
1966	Finders Keepers
	#6 ★
	Kinda Latin
	#9 ★
1965	Love Is Forever
	#19
	When in Rome . . .
	Cliff Richard
	#9 ★

1964   Aladdin and His Wonderful Lamp
        #13

        Wonderful Life
        #2 ⭐

1963   When in Spain . . .
        #8 ⭐

        Summer Holiday
        #1 ⭐

1962   32 Minutes and 17 Seconds with Cliff Richard
        #3 ⭐

1961   The Young Ones
        #1 ⭐

        21 Today
        #1 ⭐

        Listen to Cliff!
        #2 ⭐

1960   Me and My Shadows
        #2 ⭐

1950s

1959   Cliff Sings
        #2 ⭐

        Cliff
        #4 ⭐

GOSPEL ALBUMS

2000s

2002   Rockspel

1980s

1988   Carols

1986   Hymns and Inspirational Songs

1985   It's a Small World

1984   Walking in the Light

1982   Now You See Me . . . Now You Don't
    #4 ✪   ◉◉ Gold

1970s

1978   Small Corners
    #33

1974   Help It Along

1970   . . . About That Man

1960s

1967   Good News
    #37

COMPILATION ALBUMS

2010s

2019   The Best of the Rock 'n' Roll Pioneers
#11   💿 Silver

2017   Stronger Thru the Years
#14   💿 Silver

2015   75 at 75 – 75 Career-Spanning Hits
#4 ⭐   💿💿 Gold

2010   Rare EP Tracks: 1961–1991

        The Early Years

2000s

2009   Rare B-sides: 1963–1989

        Lost & Found (from the Archives)

2008   50th Anniversary Album
#11   💿💿 Gold

        . . . And They Said It Wouldn't Last!
(My 50 Years in Music) *(boxed set)*

2005   The Platinum Collection
#51   💿💿 Gold

2003   My Songs

2002   1990s

The Singles Collection *(boxed set)*

1950s

2000   The Whole Story – His Greatest Hits
#6 ⭐   💿💿💿 Platinum

1990s

∞∞∞

1998   1960s 1970s 1980s

1980s

1970s

1960s

The Hits in Between

Yesterday, Today, Forever

1997   The Rock 'n' Roll Years 1958–1963 *(boxed set)*
#32

1996   Cliff Richard at the Movies 1959–1974
#17

1995   The Winner

1994   The Hit List
#3 ⭐   💿💿💿 Platinum

1980s

∞∞∞

1988   Private Collection 1979–1988
#1 ⭐   💿💿💿 Platinum

1984   **20 Original Greats**
#43

1981   **Love Songs**
#1 ⭐   💿💿💿 Platinum

1970s

1977   **40 Golden Greats**
#1 ⭐   💿💿💿 Platinum

1972   **The Best of Cliff Vol. 2**
#49

1960s

1969   **The Best of Cliff**
#5 ⭐

1965   **More Hits by Cliff**
#20

1963   **Cliff's Hit Album**
#2 ⭐

SINGLES

2010s

2019	Mistletoe and Wine/Saviour's Day *(limited edition double A-side)*
2018	The Miracle of Love/Everything That I Am *(double A-side)*
	Reborn
	Rise Up
2017	(It's Gonna Be) Okay *(with The Piano Guys)*
	Blue Suede Shoes *(with Elvis Presley)*
2016	It's Better to Dream (Christmas Mix)
	Roll Over Beethoven
2015	Golden
2013	Rip It Up

2000s

2009	Singing the Blues *(with The Shadows)* #40
2008	Thank You for a Lifetime #3 ★
2007	When I Need You #38

2006   21st Century Christmas/Move It!
(with Brian Bennett and Brian May) (double A-side)
#2 ★

Yesterday Once More *(with Daniel O'Donnell)*

2005   What Car?
#12

The Day That I Stopped Loving You
(download only)

Grief Never Grows Old *(as One World Project)*
#4 ★

2004   I Cannot Give You My Love
#13

Somethin' Is Goin' On
#9 ★

2003   Santa's List
#5 ★

2002   Let Me Be the One
#29

2001   Somewhere over the Rainbow-What a Wonderful
World
#11

1990s

1999   The Millennium Prayer
#1 ⭐   💿💿💿 Platinum

The Miracle
#23

1998   Can't Keep This Feeling In
#10 ⭐

1997   Be with Me Always
#52

1996   The Wedding *(with Helen Hobson)*
#40

1995   Had to Be *(with Olivia Newton-John)*
#22

A Misunderstood Man
#19

1994   All I Have to Do Is Dream *(with Phil Everly)/*
Miss You Nights *(double A-side)*
#14

1993   Healing Love
#19

Never Let Go
#32

Human Work of Art
#24

Peace in Our Time
#8 ★

1992   I Still Believe in You
#7 ★ *(re-entered charts in 2014 – #57)*

1991   This New Year
#30

We Should Be Together
#10 ★

More to Life
#23

1990   Saviour's Day
#1 ★   ● Silver

From a Distance
#11

Silhouettes
#10 ★

Stronger Than That
#14

1980s

1989   Do They Know It's Christmas? *(as Band Aid II)*
#1 ★   ● ● ● Platinum

Whenever God Shines His Light *(with Van Morrison)*
#20

Lean on You
#17

I Just Don't Have the Heart
#3 ⭐   💿 Silver

The Best of Me
#2 ⭐   💿 Silver

1988   Mistletoe and Wine
        #1 ⭐   💿💿 Gold

        Two Hearts
        #34

1987   Remember Me
        #35

        Some People
        #3 ⭐   💿 Silver

        My Pretty One
        #6 ⭐

1986   Slow Rivers (with Elton John)
        #44

        Live-In World (as The Anti-Heroin Project)

        All I Ask of You (with Sarah Brightman)
        #3 ⭐   💿 Silver

        Born to Rock 'n' Roll
        #78

        Living Doll (with The Young Ones and Hank Marvin)
        #1 ⭐   💿💿 Gold

1985   It's in Every One of Us
        #45

She's So Beautiful
#17

Heart User
#46

1984   Shooting from the Heart
#51

Two to the Power of Love *(with Janet Jackson)*
#83

Baby You're Dynamite/Ocean Deep *(double A-side)*
#27

1983   Please Don't Fall in Love
#7 ✪   💿 Silver

Never Say Die (Give a Little Bit More)
#15

Drifting *(with Sheila Walsh)*
#64

True Love Ways
#8 ✪

She Means Nothing to Me *(with Phil Everly)*
#9 ✪

1982   Little Town
#11

Where Do We Go from Here?
#60

The Only Way Out
#10 ✪

1981	**Daddy's Home**
	#2 ⭐ 💿💿 Gold
	Wired for Sound
	#4 ⭐ 💿 Silver
	A Little in Love
	#15
1980	**Suddenly** (*with Olivia Newton-John*)
	#15
	Dreamin'
	#8 ⭐ 💿 Silver
	Carrie
	#4 ⭐ 💿 Silver

1970s

1979	**Hot Shot**
	#46
	We Don't Talk Anymore
	#1 ⭐ 💿💿 Gold
	Green Light
	#57
1978	**Can't Take the Hurt Anymore**
	Please Remember Me
	Yes He Lives
1977	**When Two Worlds Drift Apart**
	#46

My Kinda Life
#15

1976   Hey Mr. Dream Maker
#31

I Can't Ask for Anything More Than You
#17

Devil Woman
#9 ✪   💿 Silver

1975   Miss You Nights
#15

(There's a) Honky Tonk Angel

It's Only Me You've Left Behind

1974   (You Keep Me) Hangin' On
#13

1973   Take Me High
#27

Help It Along
#29

Power to All Our Friends
#4 ✪   💿 Silver

1972   A Brand New Song

Living in Harmony
#12

Jesus
#35

1971   Sing a Song of Freedom
#13

Flying Machine
#37

Silvery Rain
#27

Sunny Honey Girl
#19

1970   I Ain't Got Time Anymore
#21

Goodbye Sam, Hello Samantha
#6 ⭐   💿 Silver

The Joy of Living *(with Hank Marvin)*
#25

1960s

1969   With the Eyes of a Child
#20

Throw Down a Line *(with Hank Marvin)*
#7 ⭐

Big Ship
#8 ⭐

Good Times (Better Times)
#12

1968   **Don't Forget to Catch Me** *(with The Shadows)*
#21

Marianne
#22

I'll Love You Forever Today
#27

Congratulations
#1 ★   💿 💿 Gold

1967   **All My Love (Solo Tu)**
#6 ★

The Day I Met Marie
#10 ★

I'll Come Runnin'
#26

It's All Over
#9 ★

1966   **In the Country** *(with The Shadows)*
#6 ★

Time Drags By *(with The Shadows)*
#10 ★

Visions
#7 ★

Blue Turns to Grey *(with The Shadows)*
#15

1965 Wind Me Up (Let Me Go)
#2 ⭐ 💿 Silver

The Time in Between *(with The Shadows)*
#22

On My Word
#12

The Minute You're Gone
#1 ⭐ 💿 Silver

1964 I Could Easily Fall (in Love with You)
(with The Shadows)
#6 ⭐ 💿 Silver

The Twelfth of Never
#8 ⭐

On the Beach *(with The Shadows)*
#7 ⭐ 💿 Silver

Constantly (L'Edera)
#4 ⭐ 💿 Silver

I'm the Lonely One *(with The Shadows)*
#8 ⭐

1963 Don't Talk to Him *(with The Shadows)*
#2 ⭐ 💿 Silver

It's All in the Game *(with The Shadows)*
#2 ⭐ 💿 Silver

Lucky Lips *(with The Shadows)*
#4 ⭐ 💿 Silver

Summer Holiday *(with The Shadows)*
#1 ⭐   💿 Silver

1962   The Next Time *(with The Shadows)*/
Bachelor Boy *(with The Shadows)* *(double A-side)*
#1 ⭐   💿💿 Gold

It'll Be Me *(with The Shadows)*
#2 ⭐   💿 Silver

I'm Looking out the Window *(with The Shadows)*/
Do You Wanna Dance? *(with The Shadows)*
(double A-side)
#2 ⭐   💿 Silver

The Young Ones *(with The Shadows)*
#1 ⭐   💿💿 Gold

1961   When the Girl in Your Arms (Is the Girl in
Your Heart)
#3 ⭐   💿 Silver

A Girl Like You *(with The Shadows)*
#3 ⭐   💿 Silver

Gee Whiz It's You *(with The Shadows)*
#4 ⭐

Theme for a Dream *(with The Shadows)*
#3 ⭐   💿 Silver

1960   I Love You *(with The Shadows)*
#1 ⭐   💿 Silver

Nine Times Out of Ten *(with The Shadows)*
#3 ⭐   💿 Silver

Please Don't Tease *(with The Shadows)*
#1 ★ 💿 Silver

Fall in Love with You *(with The Shadows)*
#2 ★ 💿 Silver

A Voice in the Wilderness *(with The Shadows)*
#2 ★ 💿 Silver

1950s

1959   Travellin' Light *(with The Shadows)*/
Dynamite *(with The Shadows)*
(unofficial double A-side)
#1 ★ 💿 Silver /#16 *(Dynamite charted separately)*

Living Doll *(with The Drifters)*
#1 ★ 💿💿 Gold

Mean Streak *(with The Drifters)*/
Never Mind *(with The Drifters)*
(unofficial double A-side)
#10 ★/#21 *(Never Mind charted separately)*

Livin' Lovin' Doll *(with The Drifters)*
#20

1958   High Class Baby *(with The Drifters)*
#7 ★

Move It! *(with The Drifters)*/
Schoolboy Crush *(with The Drifters)*
#2 ★ *(initially released with titles reversed)*

EXTENDED PLAYERS (EPS)

1990s

1991   We Should Be Together: Christmas EP

1960s

1968   Congratulations

1967   Carol Singers

            Cinderella

1966   La La La La La

            Thunderbirds Are Go!
            #6 ⭐

            Love Is Forever

            Hits from When in Rome . . .

            Wind Me Up

1965   Take Four
            #4 ⭐

            Angel

            Look in My Eyes Maria
            #15

            Cliff's Hits from Aladdin and His Wonderful Lamp
            #20

            Why Don't They Understand?

1964   Hits from Wonderful Life

Wonderful Life No. 2

A Forever Kind of Love

Wonderful Life No. 1
#3 ⭐

Cliff's Palladium Successes

Cliff Sings Don't Talk to Him
#15

When in France

1963   Love Songs
#4 ⭐

Cliff's Lucky Lips
#17

More Hits from Summer Holiday

Hits from Summer Holiday
#4 ⭐

Holiday Carnival
#1 ⭐

Time for Cliff and the Shadows

1962   Cliff's Hits

Cliff Richard No. 2
#19

Hits from The Young Ones
#1 ⭐

Cliff Richard No. 1

Cliff's Hit Parade
#4 ★

1961   Listen to Cliff! (No. 2)

Dream
#3 ★

Listen to Cliff! (No. 1)
#17

Me and My Shadows No. 3
#6 ★

Me and My Shadows No. 2
#8 ★

Me and My Shadows No. 1
#5 ★

1960   Cliff's Silver Discs
#1 ★

Cliff Sings No. 4

Cliff Sings No. 3
#2 ★

Cliff Sings No. 2
#3 ★

Cliff Sings No. 1
#4 ★

1950s

⌇⌇⌇

1959   Expresso Bongo
#1 ⭐ *(also entered the singles charts, reaching #14)*

Cliff No. 2
#4 ⭐

Cliff No. 1
#4 ⭐

Serious Charge
#9 ⭐

INDEX